The Speech Acts of Irish

The Speech Acts of Irish

Utterance, situation, and meaning

Brian Nolan

UNIVERSITY OF TORONTO PRESS
Toronto Buffalo London

Published by University of Toronto Press in 2024
Toronto Buffalo London
utorontopress.com
Printed in Canada

ISBN 978-1-4875-6633-3 (cloth)
ISBN 978-1-4875-6634-0 (paper)
ISBN 978-1-4875-6636-4 (EPUB)
ISBN 978-1-4875-6635-7 (PDF)

Publication cataloguing information available from Library and Archives Canada.

Cover credit: Mark Lee / hisandhers.design
Cover image: Sliabh gCuillinn/Sliabh Gullion in County Armagh, Ireland, 5000 year old passage tomb © Brian O Nualláin, 2022

We wish to acknowledge the land on which the University of Toronto Press operates. This land is the traditional territory of the Wendat, the Anishnaabeg, the Haudenosaunee, the Métis, and the Mississaugas of the Credit First Nation.

University of Toronto Press acknowledges the financial support of the Government of Canada, the Canada Council for the Arts, and the Ontario Arts Council, an agency of the Government of Ontario, for its publishing activities.

Canada Council for the Arts

Conseil des Arts du Canada

Funded by the Government of Canada

Financé par le gouvernement du Canada

Contents

1 The speech acts of Irish

1.1 What this study is about

This study is about characterising the different types of speech acts as they are expressed in Irish. We apply speech act theory to a wide range of syntactic constructions underpinning Irish speech acts. Importantly, we formalise the situation of an utterance such that those parts of context and common ground important for the resolution of utterance meaning are reflected in the model of the various speech acts. While the theory of speech acts proposed by Searle (1969), Searle & Vanderveken (1985), and Vanderveken & Kubo (2001) motivate the analysis, the model of speech acts proposed here is extended to include context and common ground of the interlocutors, framed within a situation.

The theme of this book is the characterisation of speech acts of Irish, and that the situation, as a cognitive framing mechanism, is at the heart of utterance interpretation. Throughout the study, the situation is shown to provide a systematicity that contributes towards pragmatic utterance interpretation and understanding. Additionally, the situation is demonstrated to have a dynamic structure and to act as a template for understanding, functioning as a templatic schema, to differentiate between speech act utterances in real-time language use, while encapsulating relevant context and common ground.

As people in society, we communicate with other people through our use of language. However, language-in-use and communicative interaction are heavily underspecified. *What is said* is not the same as *what is meant*. While speaking, interlocutors presuppose a large multitude of background assumptions, based on the common ground. Then, utterance meaning is constructed via enrichment with hearer-based inferences, as well as various conversational implicatures which contrast with entailments and presuppositions based on what the speaker uttered. In a discourse, cooperation between the speaker and hearer is normally taken for granted in order to advance a dialogue. Sometimes, though, this sense of cooperation can be disengaged within adversarial or egocentric contexts. There is a relationship between the uttered speech act and the clause used to deliver it which gives a cue to the hearer to guide interpretation.

Clauses represent propositions which encapsulate situations and events. Sometimes within the syntax of a clause, subject and object constituents may be omitted, through elision, as long as their meaning can be recovered from context. We will see examples of elided constituents later in the discussions across the various chapters. In this study, we recognise the prominent role of the hearer H and the speaker S in the construction of meaning, so as to counterpoise any inclination towards speaker-centrism, or views that see communication as the mere exchange of information. Speech acts in dialogue are richer than that. Speaking, as an instance of language-in-use, involves a doing component, since speaker and hearer, by virtue of their mutual intentions, use language to get things done and get their various activities organised and advanced. The relationship between illocutionary force of a speech act and its associated clause form in Irish is an important facet of this book.

Specifically, the topics of this study include the formalisation of direct and indirect speech acts of Modern Irish as a part of the pragmatic structure of language, relating utterances to their illocutionary force, and determining the underlying syntactic constructional schema that acts as an illocutionary force identifier. We follow the Searle (1979) taxonomy of speech acts. As well as pre-conditions to the success of an utterance, the realisation factors for the speech act and post-conditions are considered.

1.2 The purpose, aims and hypothesis of the study

The purpose of the book is to provide an account of the speech acts of modern Irish (assertive, directive, commissive, expressive, declarative, and indirect speech acts), and their various significant clausal/sentential constructions. The study is strongly descriptive in the first instance while delivering an analysis of these diverse speech acts of Irish in a way that is intended to strike a balance between depiction, explanation, and technical characterisation. The choice of topics, the characterisation of speech and illocutionary acts, covered in this study is guided primarily by speech act theory. We relate the speech acts of Irish to each other.

The aims of the study are therefore to:

1. Provide a characterisation of the speech acts of Irish.
2. Develop a schematic representation of a speech act using the notion of a situation as a cognitive framing device. A situation consists of that which the speaker believes, desires, intends, and knows, in order to make a particular speech act, and it also encompasses what

it is that the speech act is intended to achieve, what is communicated to the hearer, and the mechanism of signalling the illocutionary force of the utterance.

3. Provide a model that captures the role that common ground and context play in the speech act situation during the realisation of a successful and felicitous speech act.
4. Identify the clausal form that maps to an illocutionary force in a particular speech act.

The underlying hypothesis of this study on characterising the speech acts of Irish, is that 1) an utterance, as a speech act of a certain type, is underspecified and its meaning is informed with a real-time informational contribution from context and common ground via a situation; 2) the situation, as a dynamic cognitive frame, has a key role in the determination of utterance meaning; and 3) the formalisation of the situation reflects this intricate set of relationships and interfaces from pragmatic meaning over and above semantic meaning, into syntax.

The key questions for us, therefore, in this study are:

1. How might we characterise the speech acts of Irish?
2. As a template, how does the situation of the utterance encapsulate those relevant parts of context and common ground in support of the speech act?
3. In a situation, how can we represent the contents of context and common ground, with the appropriate level of specificity?
4. How might the situation be represented such that it becomes operationally useful in linguistic analysis?

We support our study with an in-depth analysis of the assertive, directive, commissive, expressive, and declarative speech acts of Irish, plus indirect speech acts. We address the occurrence of evidentiality as a type of assertive speech acts that has epistemic connotations. We also provide a comprehensive analysis of question forms as special instances of the directive request for information, as against a directive request for action. A characterisation of indirect speech acts is provided, where the inferencing over the primary speech, via a conceptual graph model of the situation, is shown to yield a secondary but intended speech act.

1.3 Irish – The target language of the study

The target language of this study is Modern Irish. The structure of contemporary Modern Irish is described in Nolan (2012). That account examined Irish from the perspective of a semantically motivated syntax, within Role and Reference Grammar, a theoretical framework that justifiably makes strong claims to be a universally valid theory of grammar. Modern Irish is a VSO language.

To date, as far as I am aware, there has been to-date no study of the pragmatic dimensions of Irish, its *language in use*, or a characterisation of its speech acts. This study is one contribution towards addressing that goal. Irish, or *Gaeilge* as it is known in the Irish language itself, is, together with Scottish Gaelic and Manx, a member of the Q-Celtic grouping of Insular Celtic. Figure 1.1 indicates the position of the Irish language within the Celtic family of languages.

Within Modern Irish, there are three distinctive dialect areas, generally called Munster, Connacht, and Ulster or Donegal Irish, named after the regions in which they are found. For a descriptive account of regional differences of Irish, including morphological and phonological analysis covering all dialects, the reader should consult Ó Siadhail (1991). In this work we

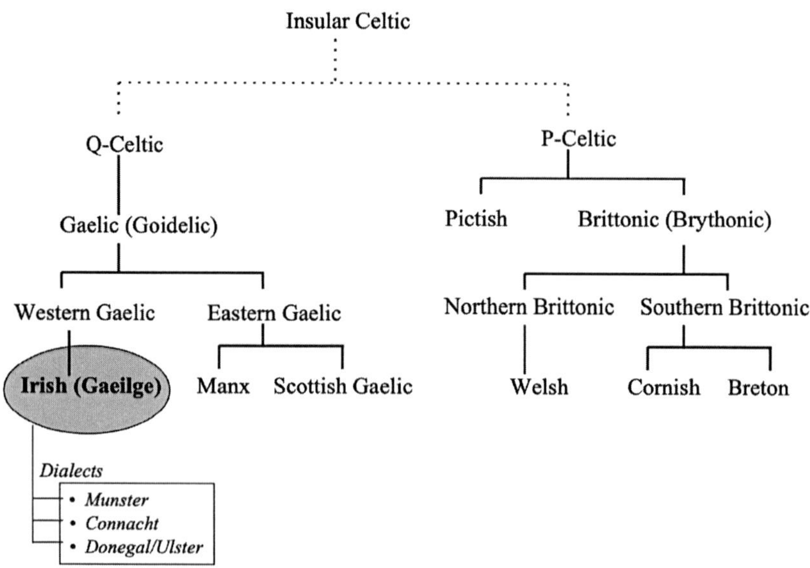

Figure 1.1 The relationship between the Celtic languages (Nolan 2012:2).

have intentionally avoided discussion of regional or dialectical variation to concentrate on more universal structural and constructional considerations of the speech acts of Irish.

1.4 What are speech acts and why are they so interesting?

> It is an undisputed fact that people do things with language. Indeed, Austin (1962) gave a name to the 'things that people do with words' – he called them speech acts (SA).
>
> Verschueren (1980:11)

Within the discipline of linguistics, a speech act is considered to be that something expressed by an individual which presents information but also performs an action of some kind. Speech act theory is an important branch of the theory of language (Searle 1969, 1979; Grice 1975). The modern use of the term speech act is due to Austin (1962) in his book *How to Do Things with Words* which dealt with the development of performative utterances along with his theory of locutionary, illocutionary, and perlocutionary acts. Some definitions[1] would be useful here, and these terms are provided in Table 1.1.

According to Austin's description, the idea of an illocutionary act reflects the idea that by saying something, we do something. Speech acts serve their function once they are communicated. These functions include acts such as apologising, promising, ordering, requesting and answering, complaining, warning, inviting, refusing, and congratulating, amongst others. What then are these locutionary, illocutionary, and perlocutionary acts?

Speech act theory emerged in part from Wittgenstein's (1958, 1961) philosophical theories. Wittgenstein believed in the importance of language in use to accomplish objectives within specific situations. Wittgenstein's idea of 'don't ask for the meaning, ask for the use' delivered new insights into language as a medium for social activity, whereby, through the application of rules to accomplish a goal, communication becomes a (set of) language

---

[1] The definitions are from: https://glossary.sil.org/term/illocutionary-verb
https://glossary.sil.org/term/performative-verb
https://glossary.sil.org/term/illocutionary-act
https://glossary.sil.org/term/speech-act
https://glossary.sil.org/term/perlocutionary-act

Table 1.1 Definition of terms.

Illocutionary verb	This is defined as a verb that, as part of its meaning, expresses at least one illocutionary force, or some component of illocutionary force.
Performative verb	This is a verb that names an illocutionary force, used to perform an illocutionary act having that force.
Locutionary act	A locutionary act is the performance of an utterance. The actual utterance and its meaning correspond to the verbal, syntactic, and semantic aspects of any meaningful utterance.
Illocutionary act	This is a complete speech act, made in a typical utterance, that consists of the delivery of the propositional content of the utterance and a particular illocutionary force. An illocutionary act is the active outcome presented by the locutionary act by the speaker.
Speech act	This is an act that a speaker performs when making an utterance, and includes a general illocutionary act that a speaker performs, with: the uttering of words in an the utterance act, making reference and predicating, and having a particular intention in making the utterance (the illocutionary force), an act involved in the illocutionary act, and the production of a particular effect in the hearer of the utterance, via a perlocutionary act.
Perlocutionary act	This is a speech act that produces an effect, intended or not, achieved in an addressee by a speaker's utterance. A perlocutionary act is concerned with getting the hearer to do or realise something. Perlocutionary acts always have a perlocutionary effect. This is the effect that the speech act has on a hearer, and it could affect the hearer's thoughts, emotions or their physical actions.

games. Austin introduced the notions of locutionary act, illocutionary act, and perlocutionary act to the study of speech acts. All of these three acts are nowadays commonly classified as speech acts. Today, the concept of an illocutionary act is central to the concept of a speech act. Searle (1969) gave an alternative to Austin's explanation of the illocutionary act saying that a speech act often refers to exactly the same thing as the term 'illocutionary act'. Searle's work on speech acts emphasised a psychological interpretation based on beliefs, desire, and intentions. An noteworthy observation is that while illocutionary acts relate to the speaker, perlocutionary acts are centred around the hearer, by virtue of their perlocutionary effect.

A type of illocutionary speech act of considerable interest is that of the performative utterance. In the cases of performative utterances, the action that the sentence describes (nominating, sentencing, promising) is performed by the utterance of the sentence itself. Typical instances of these include 'I nominate Bob Dylan for President', 'I sentence you to five years' imprisonment', or 'I promise that I will pay you back'. Austin, in his terminology, claimed that performative sentences could be either *happy* or *unhappy*. They were only happy if the speaker does the actions talked about but were unhappy if this did not happen.

Another interesting type of illocutionary speech act is indirect speech acts. In the normal course of performing speech acts people communicate with each other. However, one common way of performing speech acts is to use an expression which indicates one speech act, and indeed perform this act, but which at the same time also performs a further speech act which is indirect. The speaker must rely upon the hearer's powers of reasoning over context, and shared knowledge in common ground, to successfully unpack the intended meaning. A speech act is considered more indirect in proportion to the amount of information needed from context and common ground.

The study of speech acts provides a means for us to understand the functions and the functioning of language as we use it. Linguistics can have explanatory power only if language use is connected with the language system. The possibility of making linguistics interesting in that way is provided by, among other theories, speech act theory. A number of compelling reasons as to why we should study speech acts are suggested by Verschueren (1980:28), and one of these reasons is to reflect on the things we continuously do with language.

Though Austin and Searle were primarily interested in speech acts (illocutionary acts, illocutionary forces), it is clear that they could not avoid using speech act verbs in describing speech acts or illocutionary forces. This is especially clear when they present their typologies (Austin 1962; Searle 1976). As Searle's (1969) typology is stronger that Austin's, being based on a more detailed analysis of speech acts (Verschueren 1980:42), we will veer towards Searle's theory of speech acts across our analysis of Irish. Searle (1975b) is not really interested in the analysis and classification of speech act verbs, but in universal speech act types. According to Searle (1975b), the main characteristic of a speech act type is its illocutionary point. For example, Searle argues that the point of an order is that it is an attempt to get the hearer to do something. The point of a description is that it is a representation of how something is. The point of a promise is that it is an undertaking by the speaker of an obligation to do something. In the case of an order the illocutionary point is an intended perlocutionary effect (Verschueren 1980:54). Austin's performatives largely appear to be verb-based. One of the problems with a verb-based taxonomy, indeed with any form of taxonomy, is that the speech act conveyed by some utterance may be heavily dependent upon the interpretation of that utterance, rather than the literal verb meaning. There have been several attempts to describe the variety of speech acts in terms of a taxonomy of speech act verbs, including, for example, those reported on in Wierzbicka (1987), Searle & Vanderveken (1985), and Bach & Harnish (1979).

A reasonable assumption, then, according to Verschueren (1980:12), is that every language has a number of verbs which describe the types of speech acts available in that language, and these are typically called speech act verbs. These differ from language to language, of course, including Irish, and the set of speech act verbs of a particular language does not exhaust the set of speech acts that can be performed in that language. The analysis of speech act verbs (Verschueren 1980:42) has relevance for us as their primary function is to describe speech acts, and the analysis of their meaning yields a description of the speech acts to which they refer. The study of speech act verbs can be related to several domains of knowledge. Therefore, such an analysis gives us some insights into the nature of speech acts. Verschueren believes that studying the semantic content of speech act verbs effectively is the same thing as studying the speech acts to which they refer. An examination of speech act verbs can potentially tell us about the functions of language since every speech act verb describes a type of speech act with a particular function in language.

1.5 The audience for this book on the speech acts of Irish

This book is intended for a broad and diverse scholarly audience. Primarily, it is intended to be of value to linguists interested in the pragmatics of Irish. Linguists studying the interaction of syntax, semantics, and pragmatics are likely to find many of the descriptions and analyses of the speech act language phenomena of Irish both interesting and useful.

To my knowledge, this is the first study of the speech acts of Irish, and the pragmatic dimension of Irish *language in use*. It is intended that this book will also be useful to the many researchers and postgraduate students in universities worldwide who would like a characterisation of important elements of the speech acts of Irish, a minority European language within the Celtic branch of the Indo-European family. Additionally, this study will be of interest to the community of researchers who work in functionalist-cognitive approaches to language-in-use.

1.6 The organisation of the study

This study is organised over 12 chapters. Next, in Chapter 2, *The role of situation, context, and common ground in speech acts*, we discuss context, common ground, and the situation of utterance of the speech act. A speech act within a dialogue is part of a collective behaviour that evolves within the context of a social environment and is grounded in the situation of the utterance. The interlocutors draw on the associated context, and a shared common ground is established. This chapter examines the questions: What are context and common ground? How do context and common ground relate to the situation of the utterance in support of a felicitous speech act?

In Chapter 3, *Understanding speech acts*, we briefly summarise some approaches to speech act theory, including the approaches of Austin (1962), Searle (1969), and Searle & Vanderveken (1985). It is argued that meaning and language are related through use, and it is through the performance of illocutionary acts that speakers, using language, communicate their thoughts in discourse. Searle (1979) proposed a taxonomy of speech acts. Along with this taxonomy, Searle also proposed a typology of possible illocutionary points of performative verbs and a classification of illocutionary forces of utterances. We draw upon these insights in this study.

In Chapter 4, *The assertive speech act*, the assertive speech act of Irish is examined. This includes a review of a number of assertive verbs of Irish. We explore the expression of the assertive speech act and its intended meaning, over and above what is simply said, and in this we will appeal to belief, desire, and intention of the speaker (and hearer, as appropriate) as component parts of the speech act, framed within a situation. The convention of denoting the speaker as S and the hearer as H is adopted and we will employ this throughout the study, on the understanding that these roles will invariable swap during the course of a discourse exchange. We apply the formalism of the model in the representation of the speech act. An assertive commits S to a proposition p being true such that, in uttering the assertive, S asserts that p if S expresses a) the belief that the p holds, and b) the intention that H believes that p.

In Chapter 5, *The evidential utterance as a type of assertive speech act*, we examine the evidential as found in modern Irish as a type of assertive speech act. Irish uses a combination of lexical syntactic, and potentially adverbial, means within an evidentiality strategy to signal information about knowledge source. The language also has a rich repertoire of evidential adverbials that are frequently deployed. The conceptual domain of evidentiality, based on Aikhenvald (2003:1), is understood as stating the existence of a source of evidence for some asserted information; that includes stating that there is some evidence, and also specifying the type of evidence. In the evidential strategy of Irish, the evidential reporting of facts in the world based on a knowledge source is understood as stating the fact plus the existence of a source of evidence for some information, including that i) there is evidence, and ii) specifying the actual type of evidence. A mix of lexical, syntactic, and adverbial means is used in this strategy within Irish to encode this asserted evidential information.

The aim of a directive speech act is to cause the hearer H of the directive utterance to perform some specific action, and this is explored in Chapter 6, *The directive speech acts*. This communicative function of a directive speech act is both central and indispensable to human interaction. Directives express the attitude of a speaker S toward some prospective action by the hearer H. That is, a directive expresses an attitude of S toward some future specific action by H and reflect S's intention that the utterance, or the attitude it expresses, is to be taken as a reason for H to undertake the action. The term 'directive' is due to Searle. Directive speech acts are satisfied, and complied with if the world comes to match its propositional content. They have a world-to-word direction of fit.

Questions are directive speech acts and an attempt by S to get H to provide an answer to the question. In Chapter 7, *The question as a type of directive speech act*, we characterise in substantial detail the pragmatic dimensions of the question forms of Irish and the various functions of these questions. When S asks a question of H, S requests that H perform a speech act of providing an answer-response to S's question. Importantly, the form of the response is determined by the propositional content of the question. Irish has three question forms: alternate questions, polar yes-no interrogatives, and information questions. Questions are best understood as part of a dialogue with a chain of speech acts. The required response to one of these question forms may be constrained in certain ways depending on the nature of the question. Therefore, to gain a more complete insight into the question forms and their functions, we also consider the nature of answers given in response.

In Chapter 8, *The commissive speech act*, we examine a) the form the commissive takes as a speech act and its manifestations in Irish, b) the felicity conditions under which these commissive speech acts can be successful, and c) the range of commissive speech acts of Irish and their distinguishing features. The commissive speech act can take on a range of linguistic manifestations. While a commissive commitment can be made to oneself, typically, it is made to another person. In this instance, the role of H, then, is essential as, if the commitment is made by S to H, and H does not understand, hear or accept the commitment made, then it is taken as invalid. In other words, one needs H as a cooperating discourse partner. We specify a variety of conditions necessary for the success of the commissive speech act. Importantly, these conditions rely on extra-linguistic knowledge, both from context and from common ground. Therefore, context and the shared knowledge in common ground function as an extra-linguistic knowledge source for the success of the commissive speech act.

In Chapter 9, *The expressive speech act*, we examine how expressive speech acts communicate S's feelings about themselves or the world. Searle & Vanderveken (1985:211) find that expressive speech names expressive forces, and they argue that expressive speech acts are typically hearer centred. Therefore, expressive speech acts are public expressions of emotional states by S to H. Our discussion in this chapter includes consideration of how thanking, apologising, congratulating, greeting, amongst other expressions of emotion, are expressed in Irish. The use of expressive speech acts can be found with several types of speaker-hearer interactions.

In Chapter 10, *The declarative speech act*, we examine the declarative speech act of Irish, including declare/pronounce, adjourn, resign, approve, confirm, and name. In their successful performance, declarative speech acts bring about a correspondence between the propositional content and actual reality such that their successful performance guarantees that their propositional content corresponds to the world. The declarative speech acts have a single illocutionary point that has two directions of fit consisting simultaneously of word-to-world and world-to-word. This is because the point of a declarative is to bring about a change in the world. The declarative speech acts are seen to require an appropriate context for their successful realisation. In turn, as an illocutionary act, declaratives are a special kind of action where the expression of the intention to perform the action, in the correct context, is sufficient for the performance of that action. The core function of the declarative speech act is therefore to establish social facts during its performance.

Indirect speech acts as they occur in Irish are considered in Chapter 11, *Indirect speech acts*. An indirect speech act (ISA) is an utterance that contains the illocutionary force indicators for one kind of illocutionary act but which is uttered to perform another type of illocutionary act. A (non-exhaustive) selection of ISAs are considered: a) a question on ability → yielding a request for action X; b) a yes-no question → yielding a directive request for action X; c) an assertion with a proposal → yielding a directive yes-no question; and d) an assertion → yielding a request for information. While ISAs are a puzzle consisting of two speech acts in one, they still arise from general principles of collaborative discourse under the reasonable assumption that the interlocutors are rational and cooperate with each other. A way to treat utterances whose force differs from what their force indicators (IFID) is to assume that they have both a *literal* force, and an *indirect* force that is inferred by virtue of knowledge available to the interlocutor H. Our account makes use of the notion of a mental model, represented as a conceptual graph, over which H traverses in search of a relevant meaning once the initial literal meaning of the utterance has been evaluated and found wanting in context. Along with relevance, the cognitive operations of salience, prominence, attention, and expectation play an important role in guiding the traversal of the conceptual graph of the situation. The situational context plays a decisive role in the interpretation of an ISA utterance.

In Chapter 12, *Concluding comments on the speech acts of Irish*, we provide some final comments of the (direct and indirect) speech acts of Irish, role of the situation of the utterance, common ground, and context.

2 The role of situation, context, and common ground in speech acts

2.1 The situation of a speech act

In this study, as we characterise the speech acts of Irish, we will argue that, in order to compute the utterance meaning, a consideration of the situation, its context, and common ground is necessary. One of the appealing advantages of employing a situation in the analysis of speech acts is that it provides us with the means to relate relevant context and common ground to the resolution of underspecified components of the utterance. We argue that a speech act must be interpreted through the lens of a given situation, taking into account the different speech act types, along with appropriate context, and common ground. A situation can be formalised as a structured entity with important attributes to reflect its functions as a unifying means to link utterance meaning through to semantics and syntax. Amongst other features and attributes, we propose that the structure of a situation needs to include the constructional signature, illocutionary force, initial context at the time of the speech act utterance, and the initial common ground of the speaker S and hearer H, along with the preconditions that exist, the speech act proposition, the belief, desire, and intention (BDI) cognitive states of the speaker, and the post-context '*as it is*' after the utterance of the speech act. The events and arguments of the situation remain represented, of course, as befits the speech act. The situational preconditions, while taking into account the context and common ground of the utterance, constrain the interpretation of the speech act. We can view these preconditions as ranging over the cognitive state of the agent with respect to Belief, Desire, and Intention (BDI). These conditions may additionally have a degree of strength. In determining the meaning of a speech act, all of these situational and contextual factors need to be considered. The syntactic form of the construction, its syntactic pattern, acts as the utterance signature. We refer to this as the constructional schema. The formalisation of the situation also needs to show the realisation factors and the resulting post conditions that will exist following a successful felicitous utterance.

In a dialogue, this formalisation of the situation occurs dynamically and naturally between the human interlocutors. The view argued for here is that speech act theory forms the basis for a model of successful communications, based on the idea that with language you not only make statements, but also perform actions. Speech act theory attempts to characterise this facet of language in use in some level of explanatory formalisation. As part of this formalisation, we characterise the cognitive states for an actor in a dialogue utterance (1) while the proposed model of a situation reflects several dimensions that are essential to speech act characterisation (2).

We propose a model of utterance meaning for the speech acts based on a situation of utterance that accounts for context and common ground along with a variety of other factors important to speech act interpretation. Context, common ground, belief, desire and intention are important dimensions of this. Intentions are a matter of what an agent really wants to achieve and reflect the agent's preferences, based on its beliefs and desires. Utterance meaning is therefore highly context sensitive and is determined following a summation of information arrived at through different routes. We have outlined these in our speech act formalisations to provide a specification of the information needs that feed info the information flows of the meaning summation (Figure 2.1) of the particular utterance speech act.

(1) Cognitive states for an agent in a dialogue
   a. **BEL'** (Actor, P): the actor *believes* that P is true, where P is a proposition.
   b. **KNOW'** (Actor, P): expresses a *knowledge state* of the actor with respect to P.
   c. **WANT'** (Actor, P): the actor *desires* the event or state implied by P to occur.
   d. **INTEND'** (Actor, P): the actor *intends* to do P.

(2) Essential dimensions of speech act characterisation
   a. The set of *beliefs* that the Actor has at any given time;
   b. The *goals* that the Actor will try to achieve;
   c. The *actions* that the Actor performs and
   d. The *knowledge of the effects* of these actions;
   e. The *environment information/knowledge* that the Actor has.

wThe felicitous unpacking of the meaning of a speech act, the '*what is meant*', depends on the situation in which the dialogue utterance occurs and the context of the situation. The situational frame, which is schematically

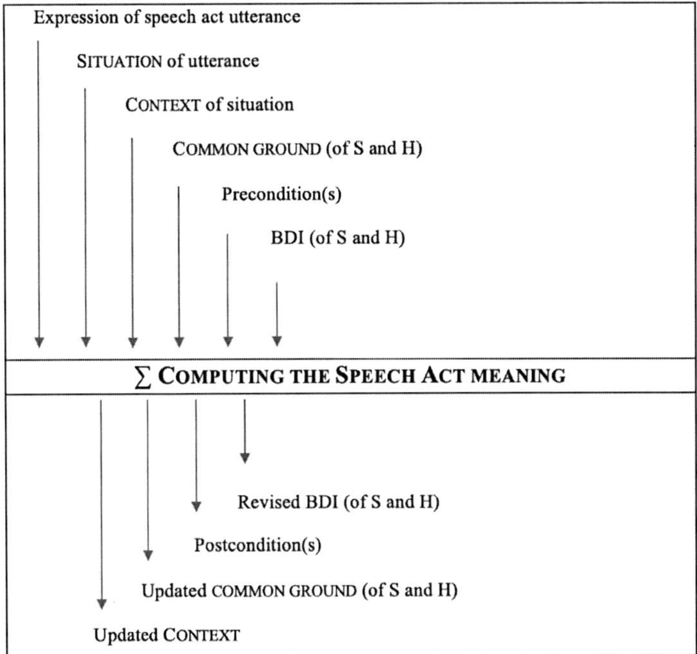

Figure 2.1 Computing speech act meaning from multiple information sources.

represented in (3), includes context, common ground (CG) and other features, and logical structures (LS), all of which contribute to the felicitous speech act (SA).

(3) Modelling the speech act in the situation of the utterance

Situation	*This*.SIT
UTTERANCE SIGNATURE	Utterance syntactic pattern
Pragmatics	
INITIAL CONTEXT	CONTEXT INFORMATION
Common ground	CG.S INFORMATION
	CG.H INFORMATION
Speaker	S
Hearer	H
Speech act	**UTT$_1$: [LS]**
PROP	**[LS]**

Preconditions	
ILLOCFORCE (IF)	
IFID	IFID TYPE
illocutionary point (IP)	
degree of strength of IP	
mode of achievement (MoA)	
position of authority	
position of power	
preparatory conditions (PrepC)	
sincerity conditions (SC)	
BELIEF	**BEL'**(S, [**LS**])
DESIRE	**WANT'**(S, [**LS**])
INTENTION	**INTEND'**(S, **BEL'**(H, [**LS'**]))
Degree of strength of SC	
Direction of fit (DoF)	
Semantics	
Event(s)	**EXPRESSION**$_1$: [**LS**]
Arguments	< ARG$_1$, … (ARG$_{N)}$ >
Semantics of EXPRESSION$_1$	<*this*.SIT$_a$ < CG.S < CG.H <[**do'**(S, **say'**(S, **UTT**$_1$)) & CAUSE (**hear'** (H, SA))] >>>>
Location.time	time
Location.space	location
Realisation	
Postcondition(s)	

In a situation, a successful and felicitous utterance needs to be sensitive to information from a variety of different sources and the dimensions of the situation, as we have discussed. While sentence meaning (the semantic meaning) is determined from the syntactic structure of the expression, a felicitous utterance meaning (the pragmatic meaning) is determined from the situation of use and its actual contextual environment, common ground with its shared cultural knowledge, general knowledge, and local context-specific knowledge.

In our characterisation of the pragmatic and syntactic expression of the speech acts of Irish over the following chapters, we will identify a particular speech act's constructional signature, its syntactic pattern, and that speech act type's formalisation within a situation, such that its meaning as an utterance can be determined and processed.

Formalising the nature of communicative interaction is an ongoing challenge in linguistics, as multiple views of what can be formalised are possible, including what constitutes context, an evolving dynamic common ground over a situation in a discourse.

2.2 The importance of context in speech act meaning

When two or more interlocutors engage in a dialogue, they are engaging in a form of social behaviour that typically unfolds in the context of a well-defined social environment and some situation that frames the utterance. In such situations, the interlocutors draw on the associated context, initially to build a shared common ground and determine its scope and parameters. What, then, is context and common ground, and how do these relate to the situation of the utterance in support of a felicitous speech act?

In the first instance, the interlocutors in a dialogue mutually assess the extent of their knowledge to inform and progress the conversation towards common understanding and a felicitous speech act. A linguistic communication is identified on the basis of *what is said*, together with mutual contextual beliefs in a co-constructed common ground. *What is meant* by an utterance is carried in part by *what is said*, the type of speech act uttered, the utterance context, and the contribution of common ground. Belief, desire, and intention are interrelated in speech acts and communication. The hearer can proceed to the identification of the speaker's illocutionary act through determining the speech act via its syntactic pattern, its constructional signature, and then through determining the belief(s), desire(s) and intention(s) that the speaker is expressing. Therefore, to inform someone of something is not only to express a belief in it but also to express one's intention that the hearer believes it. An act of communication is then successfully achieved if the hearer identifies the belief or desire expressed, in the way that the speaker intends it to be identified. In a dialogue, the role of S and H swap as conversational turns are taken.

The importance of context in the determination of speech act meaning in a dialogue has long been acknowledged (Nolan 2022:123–178). Indeed, the centrality of context in speech act meaning is fundamental, along with the shared common ground. Context is shared by discourse interlocutors in the construction of the discourse common ground. A subset of available contextual knowledge is activated in the ongoing interaction as it becomes relevant, and is eventually shared by discourse interlocutors in the construction of the shared common ground. Context has a central role as a component of cognition in the determination of the conditions of knowledge activation as well as which elements of our knowledge apply in a given situation. It includes various kinds of knowledge, including cultural, general, and shared communal beliefs, and the understanding that arises from the interaction of culture and social community. Our contextual knowledge also includes the worldview, knowledge of the world around us, of our location and environment. Context is richly populated with information on things and events that are constantly unfolding and evolving. According to Monaghan (1979:1), an analysis of the speech act with its context of situation will assist us to 'account for language in its social situation, rather than as merely a collection of structural units to be analysed individually'. In determining the meaning of a speech act utterance, situational and contextual factors need to be assessed.

Language is a vehicle for many kinds of action that may seem uniform, but whose regularity somewhat masks the fact that these actions through utterances are actually quite diverse. Speech act theory allows us to differentiate between different kinds of utterances. We use the term 'speech act' here to refer to illocutionary acts. Without a clear understanding of the different kinds of speech acts, we would have some difficulty understanding how people use language. Central to this understanding is the idea is that speech acts can be understood in terms of their effects on a dialogue's context. To perform or interpret an illocutionary act, a speech act, requires recognising the context in which the utterance was made. One major challenge with this is to account for underspecification, the fact that the speech act one performs is seldom fully determined by the linguistic meanings of the expressions one uses to perform it. This is precisely because dialogue happens in some context. In the sense of context intended here, contexts are shared knowledge and evolving representations of the state of play of knowledge in a dialogue, overlapping with common ground, that both shape the qualities of speech acts and are in turn shaped by them. The situation frames the speech act utterance.

Each major clause type (assertive, directive, commissive, expressive, and declarative) has a syntactic pattern that acts as a construction schema according to which uttering a clause of a given type results in a distinctive kind of context update. The meaning of any clause then is an operation on contexts, and clauses of different kinds manipulate different components within contexts. Speech acts, then, need to take account of context. In considering a speech act, we identify the components of context that we have reason to posit, identify the different ways in which those components can be manipulated by speaking, and characterise the speech act categories in terms of the different ways of manipulating the diverse components of context and common ground. In this view, speech acts are seen to function to change the state of the context.

Examples of speech acts, from English, are provided in (4). We can see immediately that the syntactic realisation of these clauses follow various different patterns that act as a construction schema accordingly. Uttering a clause of a given pattern type results in a distinctive kind of context update and acts as a cue to the hearer as to what type of speech act might be involved. The syntactic pattern (5) acts as a constructional schema. Of course, there will, in reality, be some levels of variation in the patterns across and within the various speech acts. The patterns shown here are illustrative for these examples.

We will now examine in more detail the situation encapsulating the speech act in (6) the example of an assertive speech act given in (4a), followed by an example of an indirect request (4f), where context plays a role in the construction of the emergent common ground. In example (6), the speaker asserts 'Lorcan broke the pencil', but the hearer does not know whether this is true or false. The hearer needs to be guided by context and common ground knowledge as to its appropriate interpretation: *Is the pencil actually broken or not?* A precondition of accepting the utterance as true is the contextual evidence, that knowledge in common ground, which will reveal, say, that the pencil is indeed broken. Once this is accepted from context, the assertion can be accepted as a true fact. Once this happens, emergent common ground is updated with this new information fact. The speech act of the utterance is more fully modelled as a situation according to the situation frame proposed in (3).

(4) English speech acts

a.	Assertive:	Lorcan broke the pencil. N V DET N
b.	Directive:	Close the door! V DET N
c.	Commissive	I promise to help. PN V PREP V
d.	Expressive:	Happy birthday! ADJ N
e.	Declarative:	I hereby name this ship the Lusitania. PN ADV V DET N DET PropN
f.	Indirect speech act:	It's warm in here. PREP+COP ADJ PREP DEICTIC (meaning: I request that you open the window.)

(5) The syntactic pattern as constructional schema (for English examples in (4)).

a.	Assertive:	N V DET N
b.	Directive:	V DET N
c.	Commissive	PN V prep V
d.	Expressive:	ADJ N
e.	Declarative:	PN ADV V DET N DET PropN
f.	Indirect speech act:	PREP+COP ADJ PREP DEICTIC

(6) Speech act: assertion
Speaker utters: 'Lorcan broke the pencil'
From CONTEXT:
a. The pencil is broken or
b. The pencil is not broken
The hearer processes the utterance:

- We assume that a. holds. Therefore, from common ground, we are informed that the proposition is TRUE in a. The hearer accepts the assertion.
- Emergent common ground is updated and now contains as an outcome:

  BEL' [**do'**(Lorcan) CAUSE BECOME **broken'**(the pencil)]
- Consequently, speaker and hearer now believe that 'Lorcan broke the pencil'.

As regards the speech act of indirect request in (7), the speaker utters what looks at first glance like an assertion 'It is warm in here!' However, the speaker can get information from context to guide the interpretation: *Is it actually warm? Is the window open or closed?* In this situation leveraging the available context, the hearer can see that the window is closed (and not open) and therefore the hearer interprets the utterance as an indirect request by the speaker for the window to be opened such that the warmth will be removed. The hearer then reasons that 'It is warm in here' + window closed → The speaker is making a REQUEST to 'open the window'. Emergent common ground is now updated.

(7) Speech act: indirect request
Speaker utters: 'It's warm in here'.
From CONTEXT:
a. The window is closed or
b. The window is open.
Hearer processes the utterance:
- From consulting context, we are informed that proposition a. is TRUE.
- The hearer reasons with the speaker's utterance, while informed by context.
- The hearer infers the speaker's indirect REQUEST to 'open the window'.
- The hearer can decide whether to act on the indirect request from the speaker.
- In any event, emergent common ground now contains the following information:
  It is warm in here + The window is closed
  $\rightarrow_{\textbf{hearer reasoning}}$ = speaker makes REQUEST to 'open the window'
- The speaker acts upon the indirect request and emergent common ground is updated to contain the new information: the window is open.

Language, considered as a representational system, requires a significant degree of cooperation for linguistic communication to occur. In turn, dialogue involves coordination and contributions to a common topic, around a common ground, taking into consideration the context of the utterance and its framing situation. In thinking about linguistic communication, we generally assume that conversation is a cooperative enterprise in which interlocutors, speaker S and hearer H, contribute information to a shared task of figuring out how the world is. However, much of what is communicated is not explicitly articulated. In order to determine these contents, whether triggered by specific expressions or by the overall utterance in context, H must consider what would make the utterance a cooperative contribution to the conversation (Grice 1975). Overall, the goal of communication is to construct and maintain the common ground between S and H in a dialogue, and to update the context for S and H in order to advance a conversation.

While cooperation is indeed usual and normal, in reality, many dialogues do reflect an egocentric or not fully cooperative behaviour which involve only a partial alignment of interlocutors' interests, whether in terms of the goals of S or the information to be shared. In all such situations, reflecting an egocentrism, one interlocutor becomes strategic about their conversational contributions, by minimising their overall commitments and/or by directing the conversation towards (or away from) some contents. Such egocentric conversations are characterised by the same discourse and pragmatic principles as fully cooperative conversations. Interlocutors still undertake speech acts in a joint task of establishing a consistent set of claims and other commitments; and they still take turns and obey basic conversational principles. The fundamental difference from more standard dialogues is one interlocutor considers themselves to be bound to only token or reduced standards of cooperation. That is, rather than aiming to produce utterances that are as informative as possible with the minimum cognitive processing cost to H, an egocentric S may aim to ensure only that there is some particular interpretation of their utterance that is an accessible and relevant contribution to H, possibly to the distinct advantage of S.

2.3 Common ground, shared knowledge, and a speech act

Common ground is argued by Kecskes & Zhang (2009) to be a dynamic construct of shared knowledge that is mutually constructed by interlocutors throughout the communicative process as a dynamic subset of the discourse context. They propose an integrated concept of common ground in which both a core common ground of assumed shared cultural and ontological knowledge and an emergent common ground converge to construct a rich background for communication.

The types of knowledge found in common ground (Nolan 2022:111–122) encompasses declarative, procedural, heuristic, meta, and structural knowledge. While declarative knowledge is to do with concepts, facts, and entities, and describes what is known, it includes simple statements that are asserted to be either true or false. This type of knowledge also includes, for an entity or concept, a matrix of attributes and their values so that they may be fully described. Procedural knowledge is concerned with processes, rules, strategies, and agendas. It depicts how something operates or how a problem is solved, and provides directions on how to do something. Heuristic knowledge is empirical experiential knowledge that informs our reasoning process. Our heuristic knowledge is accumulated through our experience of solving past problems. Meta-knowledge is high-level knowledge about the other knowledge types. It describes knowledge that we use to direct our selection of other types of knowledge for solving a particular problem and it enhances the efficiency of our reasoning processes. Structural knowledge represents our sets of rules, concept relationships, and concept to entity relationships. It describes actual knowledge structures within our mental models of concepts, sub-concepts, and entities with all their attributes, values, and relationships.

Overall, common ground contains activated knowledge of the dialogue as it locally unfolds. Typically, the interlocutors S and H have knowledge of the language of the dialogue and understand each other. They also have a subset of contextual knowledge of their environment, and (some level of) knowledge of recent events perhaps with relevant historical knowledge. Both can safely be assumed to have common sense knowledge, and knowledge of their culture. Knowledge of the local dialogue is rather dynamic in nature while cultural knowledge is less volatile and stable. These sets of knowledge in common ground therefore represent a continuum from dynamic to stable. The purpose of representing knowledge is to capture essential features of a set of things in some domain area and to make that information available to suitably describe some particular entity. This representation of our knowledge must be available to the language facility for use in cognition and dialogue. The representation of knowledge that is found in both context and common ground is an important dimension of a model of the speech act. As a part of the formalisation of the speech act via a situation frame, we will present common ground, for both S and H, as specialised knowledge representations relevant to the communication process.

3 Understanding speech acts

3.1 Meaning and language are related through *use*

Some approaches to speech act theory, including the approaches of Austin (1962), Searle (1969), Searle & Vanderveken (1985), are summarised in this chapter. It is argued that meaning and language are related through use, and it is through the performance of illocutionary acts that speakers, using language, communicate their thoughts in discourse. Searle (1979) proposed a taxonomy of speech acts and a typology of possible illocutionary points of performative verbs with a classification of illocutionary forces of utterances. We draw upon these insights in this study. In the evolution of Speech Act Theory, Austin (1962) recognised that not all statements could be verified as *true* or *false*, and he distinguished three main kinds of speech acts in the use of language that he called locutionary, illocutionary, and perlocutionary acts. Austin concluded that utterances have a felicitous (which he called happy or unhappy) dimension, an illocutionary force, a truth/falsehood dimension and a locutionary meaning. In the terminology of Austin, by uttering sentences, speakers perform *locutionary* acts: they utter words with a certain sense and reference. They perform *illocutionary* acts with a certain force such as assertions, promises, orders, declarations and apologies. Likewise, speakers are considered to perform *perlocutionary* acts when their utterances have effects on the hearers of the utterance. They can, for example, convince, please, influence, amuse, or embarrass the hearer.

Austin happened upon his idea of illocutionary acts when he noticed that successful utterances like ‘I request that you help me’ and ‘I open this session’ are performative, in that they constitute the performance by the speaker of the illocutionary act named by their main verb. He called this kind of sentence a performative sentence and their main verb a performative verb. Austin further developed his thinking on illocutionary acts in order to analyse the meaning of performative sentences, in contrast to what he called constative sentences. According to Austin, utterances of constative sentences are *true* when they represent *things as they are in the world*. On the other hand, an important feature of the utterance of performative sentences is that they are not *true* or *false* but rather *happy* or *unhappy*. They are happy when the speaker does the things represented with his words by virtue of uttering them in the appropriate context. A speaker performs an illocutionary act in a particular context to the utterance, and the performance of an illocutionary act is part of what the speaker intends in order to get a hearer to understand. All kinds of sentences function to perform illocutionary acts. Constative sentences function to make statements, interrogative sentences to ask questions, and imperative sentences to direct the hearer (Vanderveken & Kubo 2001:3). In their discussion of speech acts and illocutionary acts, Vanderveken & Kubo observe that Wittgenstein (1953:PI 43) argued that meaning and language are related through *use*. That is, according to Wittgenstein, we learn about the meaning of words through studying language-games.

> For a large class of cases, … the meaning of a word is its use in language.
>
> Wittgenstein (1953:PI 43)

As language-games, sentences are seen as instruments with a role and function.

> Here the term 'language-game' is meant to bring into prominence the fact that the speaking of language is part of an activity, of a form of life.
>
> Wittgenstein (1953:PI 23)

Searle, being rather sceptical about this locutionary, illocutionary, and perlocutionary acts distinction of Austin, preferred instead to employ a somewhat more rigorous approach to the description of illocutionary acts (Smith 1991:3). The taxonomy of speech acts proposed by Searle (1979) is shown in Table 3.1. According to Vanderveken & Kubo (2001:4), the primary units of speaker meaning in the use and comprehension of natural languages are illocutionary acts with felicity conditions rather than propositions with truth conditions. It is through the performance of illocutionary acts that speakers, using language, communicate their thoughts in discourse. Searle consequently proposed a typology of possible illocutionary points of performative verbs and a classification of illocutionary forces of utterances (Vanderveken & Kubo 2001:5).

Table 3.1 Searle's (1979) taxonomy of speech acts (Smith 1991:8)

Assertive	• An assertive commits the speaker to something's being the case and to the truth of the expressed proposition. • Examples include assert, predict, and insist.
Directive	• These are attempts by the speaker to get the hearer to do something. • Examples include direct, order, and entreat.
Commissive	• These are acts that commit the speaker to some future course of action. • Examples include commit, promise, threaten, and bet.
Expressive	• This kind of act expresses the speaker's feelings, the psychological state specified in the sincerity condition. • Examples include apologise, thank, and praise.
Declarative	• This act brings about a corresponding change in the world, by virtue of the utterance in context. • For example, in the appropriate context and with the assumption that the speaker has the authority to utter the declaration, 'I declare X to be Y, such that X will now be known as Y'.

3.2 The illocutionary acts differ in respect of several dimensions

Searle offers a categorisation of speech acts based on comparatively clear principles of distinction. These emphasise how speech acts may differ in various respects. Searle (1979), in particular, described the differences between the different types of illocutionary acts, and noted several important points (Searle 1975b, Smith 1991:4–7).

The differences between the different types of illocutionary acts occur by virtue of the following:

1. Illocutionary point of the type of act.
2. Direction of fit between words and the world.
3. Expressed psychological/cognitive state.
4. Force or strength of the illocutionary point.
5. Status or position of the speaker and hearer.
6. The manner in which the utterance relates to the speaker and hearer interests.
7. Relationship of the utterance to the flow of the discourse.

8. Propositional content determined by illocutionary force indicating devices (IFID).
9. Acts that require a specific extra-linguistic institution for their performance.

For Searle, the illocutionary acts differ across these dimensions and we examine each of these differences in turn. Differences may exist in the illocutionary point, the purpose of an act of a particular type – one of the important components of Searle's theory. The illocutionary point of an assertive, for example, is to state how certain things are.

Differences may exist in the direction of fit between words and the world. Direction of fit is related to the set of beliefs and desires. A belief has a mind-to-world direction of fit.[2] A belief that p depicts the world as being in a state of affairs such that p is true. Beliefs aim at the truth and so aims to fit the world. Consequently, a belief is satisfied when it fits the world. A person holding the belief that p when confronted with evidence of not-p will revise that belief. A desire expresses a not-yet realised state of affairs and has a world-to-mind direction of fit. A desire that p, doesn't depict the world as being in the state that p. Instead, it expresses a desire that the world be such that p is true. A desire is a state that is satisfied when the world fits it. In turn, a person who desires p may preserve the desire that p despite the evidence that not-p. Searle maintains that there are four directions of fit in language, which he expresses in terms of word (instead of mind), and world. These are:

i. Word-to-World, where the utterance fits an independently existing state of affairs in the world. A statement of fact exhibits this direction of fit.
ii. World-to-Word, where the world is altered to fit the propositional content of the illocution. An example of such an act would be a directive speech act, such as an order.
iii. The double direction of fit is when the world is altered to fit the propositional content of the utterance, by being represented as so altered. For example: I name this ship the *Lusitania*.
iv. The null direction of fit is found where there is no successful of fit between word and world. According to Searle, expressive acts, where the speaker is expressing feelings, provide examples of the null direction of fit.

---

[2] Based on https://en.wikipedia.org/wiki/Direction_of_fit

Differences may exist in the expressed psychological state, such that an illocutionary act may express belief (as in an assertion), intention (as in a promise), or desire or want. Given the assumption that there are indeed a number of psychological states related to illocutionary acts, it follows that we should be able to represent the acts in terms of these (belief, desire, intention (BDI)) states.

Differences may exist in the force or strength of the illocutionary point. An illocutionary point can have a degree of strength associated with it, and we consider, for example, that the act of insist has a stronger degree of strength than the act of suggest. Indeed, it is the case that some assertive acts have a more forceful degree of strength than others.

Differences in the status or position of the speaker and hearer relates to how the status/position of a speaker might shape the illocutionary force of the utterance. While Searle defines this difference, he makes little use of it.

Differences may exist in how the utterance relates to the speaker and hearer's interests. Here, the perspective from the speaker and hearer motivates the difference on the interpretation of the act. By way of example, Searle illustrates this distinction using the pairs of words 'boast' and 'lament'. It is possible for individuals to contradict each other, with one boasting that p and the other lamenting that p. To boast that p is to assert p while expressing *pleasure* that p is the case. To lament that P is to assert that p while expressing *regret* that P is the case. Similarly, a statement construed as harmless by a speaker in one context might be construed as offensive by a hearer in a different context: 'We try to keep *our* garden clean and tidy.'

Differences may exist in relating the utterance to the discourse. Searle notes that certain performative expressions function to relate the utterance to the rest of the discourse. Examples of this include: 'I reply as follows', or 'I deduce that …'. Differences may exist in propositional content determined by illocutionary force indicating devices (IFID). Searle recognised that the syntactic occurrence pattern or form of certain constructs may affect the illocutionary force of the utterance. He called these the illocutionary force indicating devices. For example, the use of adverbs may strengthen or weaken the (modal) force of the utterance. The use of the adverb *i ndáiríre* 'really' adds a greater force to the utterance. This can place an obligation on the hearer (1).

(1) Adverbs may impact the force of the utterance

a.

Ní mór duit imeacht <u>i ndáiríre</u> anois.

You *really* need to leave now / You *really* <u>must</u> leave now.

b.
Ní mór duit imeacht anois.
You need to leave now

c.
Caithfidh tú imeacht anois i ndáiríre.
You *really* have to leave now / You *really* must leave now.

d.
Caithfidh tú imeacht anois.
You have to leave now / You must leave now.

Differences may exist between acts that require a specific extra-linguistic institution. Some acts require a specific formal context or extra-linguistic institution for their successful performance. Speech acts of this category, which require a specific extra-linguistic institution, are called performatives by Austin and declaratives by Searle. In many ways, this type of act involves the greater role of context in the realisation of a successful performative/declarative, with a somewhat reduced role for common ground.

3.3 The illocutionary force and its components

In the formal theory of speech acts described in Searle & Vanderveken (1985), the notion of illocutionary force has a very central place. What, then, is an illocutionary force and its components? Searle & Vanderveken define illocutionary force as having several constituent components (see also Smith 1991:10). In the performance of illocutionary acts (Vanderveken & Kubo 2001:5), speakers express propositions with forces, refer to objects under concepts, make acts of predication and express a propositional content with certain truth conditions. The five illocutionary forces have an illocutionary point, which is one of: the force of assertion (assertive point), the force of a linguistic attempt to get someone to act (directive point), the force of a commitment to a future action (commissive point), the force of expression of an attitude (expressive point), and the force of declaration (declarative point). We summarise these in Table 3.2.

In this view, illocutionary acts are of the form F(p): they are composed of a force F and a proposition p. An assertion can be *true or false*, a promise can be kept or violated, and a request can be granted or refused. Searle & Vanderveken (1985), in their *Foundations of Illocutionary Logic*, analysed

Table 3.2 The five illocutionary points

The assertive point:	• Speakers achieve the assertive point when they represent how things are in the world. • IF the speaker presents a proposition as representing an actual state of affairs of the world THEN a statement has an assertive point.
The directive point:	• Speakers achieve the directive point when they try to get hearers to do something. • IF the speaker is trying to get the hearer to undertake the action specified by the propositional content of the utterance THEN a statement has a directive point.
The commissive point:	• Speakers achieve the commissive point when they commit themselves to doing something. • IF the speaker commits to carrying out the action specified by the propositional content at some future time THEN a statement has a commissive point.
The expressive point:	• Speakers achieve the expressive point is when they express their attitudes about objects and facts of the world. • IF it expresses the psychological feelings and states of the speaker THEN a statement has an expressive point.
The declarative point:	• Speakers achieve the declaratory point is when they do things in the world at the moment of the utterance solely by virtue of saying that they do. • IF the world is changed in a way specified by the propositional content of the utterance THEN a statement has a declarative point.

the logical form of illocutionary acts and formulated basic laws of speech act theory. They have decomposed illocutionary forces into their various components (illocutionary point, mode of achievement, degree of strength and propositional, preparatory and sincerity conditions).

These forces are restricted by the mode of achievement of their illocutionary point, special propositional content, preparatory or sincerity conditions, or a smaller vs. greater degree of strength (Vanderveken & Kubo 2001:6). The illocutionary acts have success and satisfaction conditions. Searle has spoken of the mental states like beliefs, desires, and intentions that speakers express verbally in language use and of their meaning intentions in attempted performances of illocutionary acts (Vanderveken & Kubo 2001:9–11). Intentionality is the fundamental feature of the mind by which our thoughts are directed at objects and facts of the world other than themselves. In Searle's view, our intentional thoughts are satisfied when a success of fit is achieved between the mind and the world from the appropriate direction. In Searle's classification, as we mentioned earlier, there are only three possible directions of fit between mind and the world: one that goes from mind to things (particular to beliefs), one that goes from things to mind (particular to desires and intentions), and the last null or empty direction of fit (particular to regrets and gratitude). Illocutionary acts are successfully performed by uttering words in the contexts of utterance.

The illocutionary point reflects is the point or purpose of a particular type of act. The purpose of an assertive is to make a statement about the world. It is the illocutionary point that essentially distinguishes each broad category of speech act. In Searle's approach, there are five illocutionary points that speakers can achieve on propositions in an utterance, namely: the assertive, commissive, directive, declaratory, and expressive illocutionary points (as we have indicated in Table 3.2). In making assertive, commissive, directive, and declaratory utterances speakers do more than express their attitudes. They want to achieve a success of fit between words and the world. The five illocutionary points correspond to the four different directions of fit that can exist between words and things. Assertive utterances like assertions and predictions have the word-to-world direction of fit. Commissive utterances like promises and threats have the world-to-word direction of fit. To achieve success of fit the world must change to match the propositional content of the utterance. Directive utterances like requests and commands also have the world-to-word direction of fit. Declarative utterances have the double direction of fit. Expressive utterances like thanks and congratulations the empty direction of fit.

The degree of strength of the illocutionary point may be stronger for certain types of speech acts than for others – insist is stronger than suggest. Typically, the degree of strength of the illocutionary point is considered a point on a linear scale.

The mode of achievement is a collection of extra-linguistic additions to a speech act that transform it into a more complex speech act. The mode of achievement helps us distinguish between speech acts, for example, between a request vs. command, or testify vs. assert. A command is issued from a position of authority and it is this leveraging of the position of authority that reflects the mode of achievement of the command. The mode of achievement can be associated with some sort of formal or ceremonial context as is found in swearing an oath (Smith 1991:80–86). We can see that the speech act testify differs from the speech act assert in that testifying takes place under a formal sworn oath, typically in the context of a court of law. Then, in the case of testifying, being under oath is the mode of achievement.

Propositional content conditions are constraints imposed on the speech act type by the nature of the propositional content itself. Propositional content conditions include constraints such as the fact that one cannot *predict* something that has already taken place – we cannot predict that which already happened. We cannot *report* on something that has yet to take place in some future time. Also, it would not make any sense to promise to undertake some action that would have to take place anyway.

Preparatory conditions relate certain presuppositions to an illocutionary force. Also, the notion of a preparatory condition ranges over and includes cognitive states. Preparatory conditions therefore include such things as the fact that promising presupposes that the speaker can fulfil the promise. That is, a presupposition of making a promise is that the speaker has the ability to deliver on the promise made. As regards cognitive states and preparatory condition, we can regard a request as communicating a desire for something, in which the speaker communicates to a hearer the desire for the hearer to (do) something specific. If we then consider this communicated desire within the overall discourse context, then fulfilling the request can be seen as responding to that desire. The request by a speaker might be for some particular information from the hearer, who responds with an answer of some kind. In this way, a relation is set up between the original request, and the response to that request and the two acts are related via the context. A shared common ground is needed and co-constructed.

Sincerity conditions ensure that the speech act performed is in accordance with the speaker's beliefs, desires, and intentions (BDI). When asserting, for example, one should ideally have evidence for that which is asserted. For example, the speaker believes that an assertion just made is true, or the speaker has the intention to carry out a promise made. To derive sincerity conditions, we can appeal to the Gricean (Grice 1957, 1969) maxims of quality and quantity (Smith 1991:80–86). Austin's (1962:17) original idea on sincerity conditions came from an examination of performatives. Austin spoke of mis-invocations, mis-applications, and mis-executions. Searle, however, applied the idea of sincerity conditions to conventional speech acts. The degree of strength of the sincerity conditions reflects that certain speech acts have stronger sincerity conditions than others. According to Searle, request and beg are often paired, together with beg having a stronger sincerity condition than request. Similarly, assert and testify are paired, with testify having a stronger sincerity condition than assert. We might take note that the facts that make beg stronger than request are different from those that make testify stronger than assert.

3.4 Operations on the illocutionary force

Each category of speech act has an illocutionary force (IF). As we have discussed, an illocutionary force has an illocutionary point, mode of achievement, and other constraining factors (Table 3.3). Certain operations can change the illocutionary force of a speech act. That is, the illocutionary forces can be constrained in several ways. Some illocutionary forces may have more propositional content conditions than others. The example of report has more propositional content conditions than assert because its propositional content conditions only relate to past or present. Therefore, report entails assert. Some illocutionary forces have more preparatory conditions than other forces with the same point. For example, remind has more preparatory conditions than assert because it is necessary for a reminder that

Table 3.3 Operations on the illocutionary force (IF)

The assertive IF	*has the assertive illocutionary point with:*	• the mode of achievement that the speaker presents a proposition to the hearer, and propositional content conditions apply.
The directive IF	*has the directive illocutionary point with:*	• the propositional content represents a future course of action of the hearer.
The commissive IF	*has the commissive illocutionary point with:*	• the propositional content condition that the propositional content represents some future course of action of the speaker.
The declarative IF	*has the declarative illocutionary point with:*	• the mode of achievement that the speaker invokes his power to perform the declaration, with no propositional content conditions.
The expressive IF	has the expressive illocutionary point with:	• no special conditions.

the propositional content is already known to the hearer, Therefore, remind entails assert.

It is possible to add sincerity conditions to illocutionary forces to create new illocutionary forces. For example: To lament p is to assert p while expressing regret that p. Therefore, lamenting p entails asserting p.

The mode of achievement of the illocutionary point restricts the set of conditions under which the illocutionary point can be achieved. Therefore, the mode of achievement of the illocutionary point of insist varies from assert in its mode of achievement involving persistence by the speaker. Some illocutionary forces differ from others in the degree of strength with which their illocutionary point is achieved and their psychological state is expressed (Smith 1991:12). Therefore, one can convincingly argue that assert is a stronger form of suggest.

Searle (1969) outlines the conditions that are necessary and sufficient for the performance of the various speech acts, while Bach & Harnish (1979:47) observe the distinction between conditions necessary and sufficient for the successful performance of an act, and conditions necessary and sufficient for a completely non-defective or felicitous performance of the act. Bach & Harnish call these the success conditions. Therefore, the essential conditions and propositional content conditions are the success conditions. In turn, the sincerity conditions are required for the non-defectiveness of the performance of the speech act.

We next discuss the assertive speech act.

4 The assertive speech act

4.1 Introduction to the assertive speech act

In this chapter we examine the assertive speech act of Irish. We start with a review of a number of assertive verbs of Irish, after which we then examine data for each with a discussion. We explore the expression of the assertive speech act and its intended meaning, over and above what is simply said, and in this, we will appeal to belief, desire and intention as component parts of the speech act. Being a claim of fact about the state of something in the world, an assertive is either true or false. In turn, we examine the role of the situation of the utterance, context and common ground pertaining to the interlocutors of the assertive speech act. In the determination of uttered meaning, we additionally appeal to a logical form, based on the logical structures of Role and Reference Grammar (RRG), along with a predicate calculus-type notation to encode belief, desire, intention, and obligation. This assists with the formalisation of the situation, context, common ground, and the speech act, as a logical form. In this, we will adopt the convention throughout our study of denoting the speaker as S and the hearer as H, on the understanding that these roles will invariable swap during the course of a discourse exchange.

An assertive commits S to a proposition being true such that, in uttering the assertive, S asserts that proposition if S expresses a) the belief that the proposition holds, and b) the intention that H believes that proposition. An assertive is satisfied simply if its proposition is *true* at the moment the utterance is made. Core to this discussion of the assertive is the assumption that the Gricean Cooperative Principle (Grice 1957, 1969) and its associated maxims apply (1). The speech act formalisation concerns the objective conditions of satisfaction for the speech act and its utterance meaning. According to Stalnaker:

> … First, assertions have content; an act of assertion is, among other things, the expression of a proposition – something that represents the world as being a certain way. Second, assertions are made in a context – a situation that includes a speaker with certain beliefs and intentions, and some people with their own beliefs and intentions to whom the

> assertion is addressed. Third, sometimes the content of the assertion is dependent on the context in which it is made, for example, on who is speaking or when the act of assertion takes place. Fourth, acts of assertion affect, and are intended to affect, the context, in particular the attitudes of the participants in the situation; how the assertion affects the context will depend on its content .
>
> Stalnaker (1978:78–95)

In speech act theory, the name of the speech act is based on an appropriate English verb that represents the exemplar of that type of speech act. Therefore, the primitive of the set of assertive utterances is based on the English verb assert which names the illocutionary force of assert. Notwithstanding this, it is important to remember that not all assertions use an assertive verb. In English, we can say '*The black tea is delicious*', which is an assertion about the state of the tea, uttered without using an assertive verb. In fact, the use of an assertive verb here would sound distinctly odd ' ?? *I assert the black tea is delicious*'. This is true for Irish also!

(1) Gricean Cooperative Principle

i.	The maxim of quality	Speakers' contributions should be true.
ii.	The maxim of quantity	Speakers' contributions should be only as informative as the situation requires and speakers should refrain saying either too little or too much.
iii.	The maxim of relevance	Contributions should relate to the purpose of the exchange.
iv.	The maxim of manner	Contributions should avoid obscurity and ambiguity and be clear, orderly and succinct.

We now examine the assertive utterances in detail.

4.2 The assertive utterances

We start our exploration by examining a selection of assertive speech act verbs, beginning with 'assert', in various examples of utterances.

4.2.1 Assert

An example of an assertive utterance is provided in (2) which illustrates a sentence with an assertive verb of Irish. Example (3) shows an assertion made without using an assertive verb. The assertion *Dhún Aisling an bosca* 'Aising closed the box' is satisfied in this context of the utterance where it is true that the box is closed by Aisling.

(2) Assert – utterance with assertive verb

a.

Dearbhaím mo neamhchiontacht.

assert:V-PRS +1SG POSS innocence

I assert my innocence.

b. [**do'** (1SG, **assert'** (1SG, my innocence))]

c. Constructional signature: [V.TNS NP NP]

(3) Assertive – utterance without assertive verb

a.

Dúnann Aisling an bosca.

Close:V-PRS Aisling DET box:N

Aisling closes the box.

b. [**do'** (Aisling, **close'** (Aisling, box)) ∧ **be'** (box, **closed'**)]

c. Constructional signature: [V.TNS NP NP]

We provide a formalisation of these two examples in (4) and (5). In determining the assertive meaning, it will be necessary to enquire into the contribution that context makes to the utterance situation, specific to S and H, at the moment of the utterance. We will also appeal to the idea that S is motivated by a set of beliefs, desires and intentions and that this influences the discourse behaviour towards H. Importantly, in this (assertive) situation, S will make an assessment of the extent of the shared common ground with H and accordingly, through the discourse, construct the common ground and maintain it appropriately. In this formalisation, following Nolan (2022:123–178), we define the speech act construction and identify the situation (SIT) context (CONT), CommonGround.Speaker (CG.S), CommonGround.Hearer (CG.H), preconditions, proposition (PROP), belief B, desire D, intention I states, and postconditions resulting from the utterance of the assertive speech act. In our formalisation, we indicate the actor and undergoer within various logical structures, and the B, D, and I states. For B, we use a predicate

BEL' (LS), for D, we use a predicate **WANT'** (LS) and for I, we use a predicate **INTEND'** (LS).

A partial sketch is proposed of how the various dimensions needed to derive utterance meaning link together, based on our formalisation of the assertive speech act. The interlocutors are S and H. Therefore, in *this* situation of the assertive, we typically have an utterance UTT_1 containing an expression with a constructional signature of [V._{TNS} NP NP], signalling an illocutionary force of assertive.

We represent this utterance as a logical structure in the style of RRG, as:

> UTT_1: [**do'** (S, **say'** (S, EXPRESSION_1)) & CAUSE (**hear'** (H, SA))]
> where UTT is the utterance,
> EXPRESSION is the particular sentence in the utterance, and
> SA is the speech act.

This formalisation is intended to indicate that the expression is the carrier of the *what is said* and which feeds into the speech utterance in the *what is meant* meaning derivation. We reflect an initial context of the situation through a basic ontology. As part of the context, we show the initial common ground of S and common ground for H. At the event level, a simple[3] verbal predication is found in a sentence with a single clause containing a single verb and its arguments that denote a single event and the participants of that event.

The relevant contents of common ground for S and H are explicitly identified. With the example in (2), the assert speech act verb is used. Imagine a context, perhaps set in an office. There is a plate of chocolate biscuits in the office kitchen area. At some point, all the chocolate biscuits are gone. Brian is accused of eating them by his colleagues. Brian objects and asserts his innocence, as we see in example (2): *Dearbhaím mo neamhchiontacht* 'I assert my innocence'. We model this example in (5a) under the assumption that this context holds. We indicate that the initial context is as included in the model, within its ontology. The initial common ground for both S and H is represented. The proposition is that [S IS INNOCENT], and this is what is asserted by S with the utterance. H has doubts as to whether S is innocent or not. S intends to convince H that the proposition is true.

---

3 Complex predications and complex events within a situation are reported on in Nolan (2017).

For example in (3), while the common ground of H, CG.H, does not indicate content at this point, for the common ground of S, CG.S, we show this as containing two logical structures: 1) [**exist'** (box)] and 2) [**be'** (box, open')]. These act as the preconditions for S in making the assertive utterance. S BELieves the box is closed. S desires (= **WANTS'**) that H BELieve the box is closed. S therefore intends that H BELieve the box is closed as a consequence of the assertive speech act. The resulting postcondition is that H BELieves the box is closed. The proposition of the assertive is that the box is closed.

The conditions of satisfaction of different speech acts in the same class are identical. Their differences reside in the resolution of a number of pragmatic factors, e.g., the compatibility of the common ground of the agents involved and various matters of cultural convention.

We schematically identify the semantics within a logical form where the influence of the situation, context and common ground feeds into the utterance meaning derivation. The '*what is said*' is reflected in the underlying event and its semantics, while the '*what is meant*' is derived at a higher level of abstraction. We use subscript indexing to relate elements across the model. For example, in (4a) and (5b), the speech act contains $expression_1$ and this is also similarly identified within the denoted event. We apply the same subscript denotation method to arg_1, arg_2, etc. within the examples. The contribution of the lexicon and the language grammar, along with the recognition of belief, desire and intentions in the type of situation and the associated illocutionary force, cultural conventions, general, specialist, and cultural knowledge, common ground, and other sources of information are all important in communication and for representing meaning in communication.

Arriving at the meaning of a speech act in the situation requires us to consider the level of the interaction of all these dimensions. In the semantics of linguistic interaction, compositionality is a property of structures that combine information conveyed through different linguistic as well as non-linguistic means of communication. The meaning of the sentence is the meaning of its utterance in its context. Computing the meaning from a speech act is a dynamic process co-constructed in discourse and arises from the agent's intention to express and negotiate views and attitudes.

As part of the illocutionary point of the assertive, the direction of fit has the aim of getting their propositional content to match the world of the utterance (Searle & Vanderveken 1985:92). Assertive illocutionary forces have the word-to-world direction of fit, as the illocutionary point of the assertive is to sincerely represent the world as it actually is.

For both (4) and (5) we additionally represent the semantics underpinning the utterance (capturing the '*what is said*') while the pragmatic dimension reflects the '*what is meant*' in (6) and (7), respectively.

In (4) and (5), we represent the detail of the initial context and common ground explicitly, with the detail of the underlying semantic representation in (6) and (7), respectively. Later, in subsequent examples, we will revert to a reduced form of the representation for purposes of brevity, ease of exposition, and understanding.

After this part of the discussion, we will not represent the semantic side of the model on the understanding that these aspects are still there but not central to the pragmatic discussion. Specifically, then, the semantic representation of (4) is provided in (6) while the semantic representation of (5) is provided in (7).

(4) Modelling the assertive speech act (with assertive verb) in the utterance situation

Situation	*this*.SIT$_a$
UTTERANCE SIGNATURE	V.$_{TNS}$ NP NP
Pragmatics	
INITIAL CONTEXT	CONT Ontology 1. **IS_A** (innocence, thing) : INNOCENCE IS_A thing: < **ARG$_{1>}$** 2. **IS_A** (guilt, thing) : INNOCENCE IS_A thing: < **ARG$_{1>}$** 3. **IS_A** (assert, event) : ASSERT IS_A event process: <**v**$_3$>:
Common ground (CG)	CG.S 1. [**exist'** (chocolate biscuits)] ∧ 2. [**be'** (chocolate biscuits, GONE'] CG.H 1. [**exist'** (chocolate biscuits)] ∧ 2. [**be'** (chocolate biscuits, GONE')] 3. H has doubts exists as to whether S is innocent or not. 4. [**be'** (S, INNOCENT')] OR NOT [**be'** (S IS INNOCENT)]
Speaker	S

Hearer	H
Speech act	UTT$_1$: [**do'** (S, **say'** (S, EXPRESSION$_1$)) & CAUSE (**hear'** (H, SA))]
PROP	[S IS INNOCENT] [**be'**(S, INNOCENT')]
Precondition	
ILLOCFORCE (IF)	ASSERTIVE
IFID	Assertive verb used
illocutionary point (IP)	S presents PROP as representing the state of affairs of the world
degree of strength of IP	+++ 3
Mode of achievement (MoA)	S expresses his innocence in language to H
position of authority	Not a factor here
position of power	Not a factor here
Preparatory Conditions (PrepC)	S believes own innocence chocolate biscuits existed but now are gone
Sincerity Conditions (SC)	The speech act is performed by S in accordance all beliefs, desires, and intentions (BDI) and informed by shared common ground.
BELIEF	S: BEL'(S, **be'** (S, INNOCENT')) ∧ **be'** (chocolate biscuits, GONE') H: BEL'(H, **be'** (S, GUILTY')) ∧ **be'** (chocolate biscuits, GONE')
DESIRE	WANT'(S, BEL'(H, **be'** (S, INNOCENT')))
INTENTION	INTEND'(S, BEL'(H, **be'** (S, INNOCENT')))
Degree of strength of SC	=
Direction of fit (DoF)	word-to-world
Realisation	S expresses UTT to H Emergent common ground constructed
Postcondition	H interprets UTT from S Common ground updated

(5) Modelling the assertive speech act (no assertive verb) in the utterance situation

Situation	*this*.SIT$_a$
UTTERANCE SIGNATURE	V.$_{TNS}$ NP NP
Pragmatics	
INITIAL CONTEXT	CONT 1. **Is_A** (box, thing) : Ontology: BOX IS_A thing: < **ARG**$_{1>}$ 2. **Is_A** (Aisling, person) : Ontology: AISLING IS_A person: < **ARG**$_{2>}$ 3. **Is_A** (close, event) : Ontology CLOSE IS_A event process: <**v**$_3$>:
Common ground	CG.S 1. [**exist'** (box)] ∧ 2. [**be'** (box, open')] CG.H 1. __
Speaker	S
Hearer	H
Speech act	**UTT**$_1$: [**do'** (S, **say'** (S, EXPRESSION$_1$)) & CAUSE (**hear'** (H, SA))]
PROP	[**do'** (Aisling, **close'** (Aisling, box)) ∧ **be'** (box, closed')]
Precondition	
ILLOCFORCE (IF)	ASSERTIVE
IFID	ASSERTIVE
illocutionary point (IP)	S presents PROP as representing the state of affairs of the world
degree of strength of IP	+++ 3
Mode of achievement (MoA)	S expresses the fact in language to H
position of authority	Not a factor here
position of power	Not a factor here
Preparatory Conditions (PrepC)	S believes the PROP The box is closed

Sincerity Conditions (SC)	The speech act is performed by S in accordance with all BDI and informed by shared common ground.
BELIEF	BEL'(S, [**do'** (Aisling, **close'** (Aisling, box)) ∧ **be'** (box, closed')])
DESIRE	WANT'(S, [**do'** (Aisling, **close'** (Aisling, box)) ∧ **be'** (box, closed')]))
INTENTION	INTEND'(S, BEL'(H, [**do'** (Aisling, **close'** (Aisling, box)) ∧ **be'** (box, closed')])))
Degree of strength of SC	=
Direction of fit (DoF)	word-to-world
Realisation	S expresses UTT to H Emergent common ground constructed
Postcondition	H interprets UTT from S Common ground updated

(6) Semantics of the assertive speech act (with assertive verb) in the utterance situation

Semantics	
Event(s)	**EXPRESSION**$_1$: [**do'** (ARG_1, **assert**$_3$**'** (ARG_1, ARG_2)) ∧ **be'** (ARG_2, pred')] <v_3>: *dearbh* 'assert': [**do'** (x_1, **assert'** (x_1, y_2)) ∧ **be'** (y_2, GONE')]
Arguments	< ARG_1, ARG_2 >
Semantics	<*this*.SIT_a < CG.S < CG.H <[**do'** (S, **say'** (S, $\textbf{UTT}_1$)) & CAUSE (**hear'** (H, SA))] >>>>
Location.time	time
Location.space	location

(7) Semantics of the assertive speech act (no assertive verb) in the utterance situation

Semantics	

Event(s)	EXPRESSION$_1$: [**do'** (ARG$_1$, **close$_3$'** (ARG$_1$, ARG$_2$)) ∧ **be'** (ARG$_2$, pred')] <V$_3$>: *dún* 'close': [**do'** (X$_1$) **close'** (X$_1$, Y$_2$) ∧ **be'** (Y$_2$, closed')]
Arguments	< ARG$_1$, ARG$_2$ >
Semantics	<*this*.SIT$_a$ < CG.S < CG.H <[**do'** (S, **say'** (S, UTT$_1$)) & CAUSE (**hear'** (H, SA))] >>>>
Location.time	time
Location.space	location

4.2.2 Claim

To assertively claim something is to state or assert that something is the case, possibly without providing evidence or proof. It is used to claim something is true. It can be used by S to request or demand something of H, or state that one owns or has earned something. In assertively making a claim, S asserts that P, and in doing so expresses the belief that P, and the concomitant intention that H believe that P. The assertive speech act of claim is shown in (8).

(8) Claim

a.

Éilím	*mo*	*chearta.*
claim:V-PRS+1SG	POSS	rights

I claim my rights.

b. [**do'** (1SG, **claim'** (1SG, my rights))]

c. Constructional signature: [V.TNS NP NP]

(9) The assertive speech act of claim
With S uttering UTT, S claims that P to H

UTTERANCE SIGNATURE	$V._{TNS}$ NP NP
Pragmatics	
Initial Context	CONT 1. **Is_A** (rights, thing) : Ontology: RIGHTS IS_A thing: < **ARG**$_{1}$> 2. **Is_A** (claim, event) : Ontology CLAIM IS_A event process: <**v**$_3$>
Common ground	CG.S 1. [**exist'** (rights)] CG.H 1. [**exist'** (rights)]
Speaker	S
Hearer	H
Speech act	**UTT**$_1$: [**do'** (S, **say'** (S, EXPRESSION$_1$)) & CAUSE (**hear'** (H, SA))]
PROP	[S HAS RIGHTS] [**be-at'** (S, rights)]
Precondition	
ILLOCFORCE (IF)	ASSERTIVE
IFID	Assertive verb used = CLAIM
illocutionary point (IP)	S presents PROP as representing the state of affairs of the world
degree of strength of IP	+++ 3
Mode of achievement (MoA)	S claims S's rights in language to H S takes possession of S's rights in language to H
position of authority	Not a factor here
position of power	Not a factor here
Preparatory Conditions (PrepC)	S believes S's entitlement to his rights S has intention to take possession of the rights flagged in PROP
Sincerity Conditions (SC)	The speech act is performed by S in accordance all beliefs, desires, and intentions (BDI) and informed by the shared common ground.

BELIEF	S: BEL'(S, **be-at'** (S, rights))
DESIRE	WANT'(S, BEL'(H, (S, **be-at'** (S, rights))))
INTENTION	INTEND'(S, BEL'(H, (S, **be-at'** (S, rights))))
Degree of strength of SC	=
Direction of fit (DoF)	word-to-world
Realisation	S expresses UTT to H Emergent common ground constructed
Postcondition	H interprets UTT from S Common ground updated

The assertive speech acts of claim, affirm, confirm, and state name the same illocutionary force and they have the same illocutionary point, mode of achievement, degree of strength, propositional content conditions, preparatory conditions, and sincerity conditions as assert. Both claim and assert are connected with the rights of the speaker.

4.2.3 Affirm, confirm

When one uses the speech act of affirm/confirm, one states emphatically or publicly that something is the case, and that one accepts or confirms the validity of a judgement, agreement, or fact, and ratifies this to be the case. One can also affirm/confirm one's support for something, and thereby offer someone emotional support or encouragement. Affirm (10) is the opposite of deny.

(10)affirm / confirm

a.

Dearbhaím	*an*	*cás*	*ar*	*dtús.*
affirm/confirm:V-PRS+1SG	DET	case	at:PREP	start

I affirm/confirm the case first.

b. at.the.start'[do' (1SG, **affirm'** (1SG, the case))]

c. Constructional signature: [V.TNS NP NP]

(11)The assertive speech act of affirm/confirm

With S uttering UTT, S affirms to H that P

PROP	P

Precondition

ILLOCFORCE (IF)	ASSERTIVE

IFID	Assertive verb used = **AFFIRM/CONFIRM**
illocutionary point (IP)	S presents PROP as representing the state of affairs of the world
degree of strength of IP	++ 2
Mode of achievement (MoA)	S affirm/confirms PROP in language to H
position of authority	Not a factor here
position of power	Not a factor here
Preparatory Conditions (PrepC)	S believes PROP Intention of S: [INTEND'(S, BEL'(H, PROP))] Affirm: PROP is true and H does not know PROP Confirm: PROP is true and H may already know PROP
Sincerity Conditions (SC)	The speech act is performed by S in accordance all beliefs, desires, and intentions (BDI) and informed by the shared common ground.
BELIEF	S: BEL'(S, **do'** (S **affirm'** (S, PROP)))
DESIRE	S: WANT'(S, BEL'(H, PROP))
INTENTION	S: INTEND'(S, BEL'(H, PROP))
Degree of strength of SC	+ The expression of affirm/confirm has intensity and is emphatic
Direction of fit (DoF)	word-to-world
Realisation	S expresses UTT to H Emergent common ground constructed
Postcondition	H interprets UTT from S Common ground updated

4.2.4 State

To use the assertive speech act of state is to indicate something definitely as being the case, in order, for example, specify the facts of something for consideration. Making a statement typically involves a series of assertive acts as, for example, when a politician states / gives a full account of something.

(12) State

a.

Luaim *d'ainm* *leis.*
State:V-PRS +1SG POSS+name with:PREP+3SG.M
I state your name to him.

b. [**do'** (1SG **state'** (1SG, your name))] ∧ [**be-at'** (your name, 3SG.M)]

c. Constructional signature: [V.TNS NP NP PP]

(13) The assertive speech act of state
With S uttering UTT, S states to H that P

Prop	P: [**be-at'** (your name, 3SG.M)]
Precondition	
IllocForce (IF)	Assertive
IFID	Assertive verb used = STATE
illocutionary point (IP)	S presents Prop as representing the state of affairs of the world
degree of strength of IP	+++ 3
Mode of achievement (MoA)	S states the Prop in language to H
position of authority	Not a factor here
position of power	Not a factor here
Preparatory Conditions (PrepC)	S believes the facts H may/may not know Prop
Sincerity Conditions (SC)	The speech act is performed by S in accordance all beliefs, desires, and intentions (BDI) and informed by shared common ground.
Belief	S: Bel'(S, **do'** (S, **state'** (S, Prop)))
Desire	Want'(S, Bel'(H, Prop))
Intention	Intend'(S, Bel'(H, Prop))
Degree of strength of SC	=
Direction of fit (DoF)	word-to-world
Realisation	S expresses UTT to H Emergent common ground constructed
Postcondition	H interprets UTT from S Common ground updated

4.2.5 Assure

To assure is to tell someone something positively, with a high level of confidence, in order to dispel any doubts that may have existed about the condition of something or some end-result. To assure is to assert with the perlocutionary intention to convince the hearer of the truth of the propositional content in the world of the utterance. The perlocutionary intention increases the degree of strength of the illocutionary point. It determines the preparatory condition that the hearer has doubts about the truth of the proposition.

(14) Assure (= assertive promise)

a.

Geallaim	*duit*	*go*	*bhfuil*	*an*	*obair déanta.*
promise:V-PRS+1SG	to:PREP+2SG	that	be:AUX	DET	work done

I assure (promise) you that the work is done.

b. [**do'** (1SG, **assure'** (1SG, 2SG))] ∧ [**be'** (work, [done'])]

c. Constructional signature: [V.TNS NP NP THAT RP]

(15) The assertive speech act of assure

With S uttering UTT, S assures H that P

PROP	P: [**be'** (work, [done'])]
Precondition	
ILLOCFORCE (IF)	ASSERTIVE
IFID	Assertive verb used = ASSURE
illocutionary point (IP)	S presents PROP as representing the state of affairs of the world
degree of strength of IP	++ 2
Mode of achievement (MoA)	S assures PROP in language to H S projects confidence in PROP to H
position of authority	Not a factor here
position of power	Not a factor here
Preparatory Conditions (PrepC)	S believes PROP
Sincerity Conditions (SC)	The speech act is performed by S in accordance all beliefs, desires, and intentions (BDI) and informed by shared common ground.

BELIEF	S: BEL'(S, **do'** (S, **assures'** (S, PROP)))
DESIRE	WANT'(S, BEL'(H, PROP))
INTENTION	INTEND'(S, BEL'(H, PROP))
Degree of strength of SC	+
Direction of fit (DoF)	word-to-world
Realisation	S expresses UTT to H Emergent common ground constructed
Postcondition	H interprets UTT from S Common ground updated

4.2.6 Argue

To put forward an argument, to argue, is to give reasons or cite evidence in support of a proposition, idea, action, or theory, typically with the aim of persuading others to share one's view. To argue is to attempt to persuade someone to (not) do something while potentially giving supporting reasons. When one argues that P, one is asserting that P while providing supporting reasons as to why P holds. The perlocutionary intention of S is to convince H of P.

(16) Argue (assertive)

a.
Áitím go bhfuil an ceart agam.
argue:V-PRS+1SG that be:AUX DET right at:PREP+1SG
I argue (prove) that I am right.

b. [**do'** (1SG, **argue'** (1SG, [**be'** (1SG, [right'])])))]

c. Constructional signature: [V.TNS NP THAT RP]

(17) Argue

a.
Áitíonn *Pól go mbainfeadh an leasú molta an bonn d'Airteagal 41 den Bhunreacht.*
Áitíonn *Pól go mbainfeadh an leasú molta*
Argues:V-PRS Paul that remove:V-COND DET amendement proposed
an bonn d'Airteagal 41 den Bhunreacht.
DET basis Article 41 of:PREP+DET Constitution
Paul argues that the proposed amendment would undermine Article 41 of the Constitution.

b. [**do'** (1SG, **argue'** (1SG, LS.RP))]

c. Constructional signature: [V.TNS NP THAT RP]

Where [LS.RP] means the logical structure (LS) of a referring phrase (RP) that, in this example, includes an embedded clause.

(18) The assertive speech act of argue
With S uttering UTT, S argues to H that P

PROP	P: [**be'** (1SG, [right'])]
Precondition	
ILLOCFORCE (IF)	ASSERTIVE
IFID	Assertive verb used = ARGUE
illocutionary point (IP)	S presents PROP as representing the state of affairs of the world
degree of strength of IP	+++++ 5
Mode of achievement (MoA)	S argues for PROP in language to H S provides compelling reasons in support of the view that PROP holds
position of authority	Not a factor here
position of power	Not a factor here
Preparatory Conditions (PrepC)	S believes PROP H may not believe PROP
Sincerity Conditions (SC)	The speech act is performed by S in accordance all beliefs, desires, and intentions (BDI) and informed by shared common ground.
BELIEF	S: BEL'(S, **do'** (S, **affirm'** (S,X)))
DESIRE	WANT'(S, BEL'(H, X))
INTENTION	INTEND'(S, BEL'(H, X))
Degree of strength of SC	+
Direction of fit (DoF)	word-to-world
Realisation	S expresses UTT to H Emergent common ground constructed
Postcondition	H interprets UTT from S Common ground updated

4.2.7 Rebut

The assertive speech act of rebut is related to argue. To rebut is to claim or prove that a proposition, idea, action, theory, evidence, or accusation is false and incorrect. To rebut is to argue against evidence or arguments, previously introduced in dialogue, to counter, disprove, or contradict the other interlocutor's proposition as to the state of affairs. Therefore, to rebut is to argue that NOT PROP holds. Therefore, rebut is to argue against P.

(19) Rebut

a.
Bhreabaim na cáineadh sin.
rebut:V-PRS+1SG DET.PL criticisms those
I rebut those criticisms.

b. [**do'** (1SG, **rebut'** (1SG, those criticisms))]

c. Constructional signature: [V.TNS NP NP]

(20) The assertive speech act of rebut
With S uttering UTT, S rebuts the P to H

PROP	P
Precondition	
ILLOCFORCE (IF)	ASSERTIVE
IFID	Assertive verb used = REBUT
illocutionary point (IP)	S presents PROP as representing the state of affairs of the world
degree of strength of IP	+++++ 5
Mode of achievement (MoA)	S rebuts PROP in language to H = S argue that NOT PROP in language to H
position of authority	Not a factor here
position of power	Not a factor here
Preparatory Conditions (PrepC)	S believes NOT PROP holds
Sincerity Conditions (SC)	The speech act is performed by S in accordance all beliefs, desires, and intentions (BDI) and informed by shared common ground.
BELIEF	S: BEL'(S, **do'** (S, **rebuts'** (S, NOT PROP)))

DESIRE	WANT'(S, BEL'(H, NOT PROP))
INTENTION	INTEND'(S, BEL'(H, NOT PROP))
Degree of strength of SC	+
Direction of fit (DoF)	word-to-world
Realisation	S expresses UTT to H Emergent common ground constructed
Postcondition	H interprets UTT from S Common ground updated

4.2.8 Inform, notify

To inform and notify is to tell, or give someone facts or information. Both inform and notify are directed towards H by S. They are hearer-directed. Specifically, for S to inform/notify is to assert to H with the preparatory condition that H does not already know P. While H may actually know P, there may be a legal or some formal requirement on S to inform/notify H of P. That is, S may have an obligation to inform H of P.

(21) Inform, notify

a.
Cuirim in iúl duit

Put:V-PRS+1SG in:PREP expression to:PREP+2SG
go bhfuil sí ag imeacht.
that BE-AUX 3SG.F at leaving:VN
I inform you that she's leaving.

b. [**do'** (1SG, **put'** (1SG, [**be-at'** (knowledge, 2SG)]))] & [**be'** (3SG.F, [leaving'])]

c. Constructional signature: [V.TNS NP PP PP THAT RP]

(22) Inform, notify

a.
Cuirim an buaiteoir ar an eolas
Put:V-PRS+1SG DET winner on:PREP DET knowledge
trí ríomhphost agus téacs.
through email and text
I notify the winner of the information by e-mail and text.

b. **via.email.and.txt'**[**do'** (1SG, **put'** (1SG, [**be-on'** (knowledge, the winner)])))]
c. Constructional signature: [V.TNS NP NP PP (PP)]

The Irish verb *cuir* is one of the most polysemous in Irish, with a multitude of meaning senses. These non-exhaustively include: bury, cast, cause, engage, follow, give, inform, lay, make, moult, notify, pass, place, plant, propel, propound, put, wage, score, seek, send, set, shed, slough, sow. With this verb, both the syntactic and pragmatic context of use is crucial to a determination of the intended meaning.

(23) The assertive speech act of inform / notify
With S uttering UTT, S informs/notifies H that P

PROP	P
Precondition	
ILLOCFORCE (IF)	ASSERTIVE
IFID	Assertive verb used = INFORM/NOTIFY
illocutionary point (IP)	S presents PROP as representing the state of affairs of the world
degree of strength of IP	++++ 4
Mode of achievement (MoA)	S informs/notifies PROP in language to H
position of authority	Not a factor here
position of power	Not a factor here
Preparatory Conditions (PrepC)	S believes PROP H does not know PROP S may have a model obligation to inform H of PROP
Sincerity Conditions (SC)	The speech act is performed by S in accordance all beliefs, desires, and intentions (BDI) and informed by shared common ground.
BELIEF	S: BEL'(S, **do'** (S, **inform'** (S, PROP)))
DESIRE	WANT'(S, BEL'(H, PROP))
INTENTION	INTEND'(S, BEL'(H, PROP))
Degree of strength of SC	=

Direction of fit (DoF)	word-to-world
Realisation	S expresses UTT to H Emergent common ground constructed
Postcondition	H interprets UTT from S Common ground updated

4.2.9 Remind

The assertive speech act of remind is used to cause some H to remember someone or something, or to cause H to remember of an obligation to be fulfilled, or to take note of something. For S to remind H of P is to assert to H with the preparatory condition that H may have once know the propositional content P, but might have since forgotten it.

(24) Remind

a.

Meabhraím duit tábhacht na haclaíochta.
Remember:V-PRS+1SG to:PREP+2SG (DET) importance (of) DET exercise
Lit: I remember to you the importance of fitness.
I remind you of the importance of fitness.

b. [**do'** (1SG, **remember'** (1SG, [**be-at'** (the importance of fitness, 2SG)]))]

c. Constructional signature: [V.TNS NP PP RP]

(25) Remind

a. *Meabhraím do m'iníon go gcaithfidh muid a bheith sa bhaile faoi ocht.*

Meabhraím do. m'iníon go gcaithfidh muid
Remember:V-PRS+1SG to:PREP my:POSS+daughter that must 3PL
a bheith sa bhaile faoi ocht
PRT BE:AUX at:PREP home under eight
Lit: I remember to my daughter that we must be at home by eight.
I remind my daughter that we must be home by eight.

b. [**do'** (1SG, **remember'** (1SG, [**by.eight'** [**be-at'** (home, my daughter)]]))] & <MODAL.OBLIGATION<[**by.eight'** [**be-at'** (home, 1PL)]]

c. Constructional signature: [V.TNS NP PP THAT (MODAL.OBLIGATION) RP]

(26) Remind

a. <u>*Cuirim i gcuimhne*</u> *do dhaoine cé chomh tábhachtach agus atá aclaíocht.*

Cuirim *i* *gcuimhne do* *dhaoine cé* *chomh*
Put:V-PRS+1SG in:PREP memory to:PREP people how as
tábhachtach agus atá *aclaíocht*
importance and BE-AUX.PRS exercise
I remind people as to how important exercise is.

b. [**do'** (1SG, **put'** (1SG, [**be** '(important.exercise, [**be-in'** (memory, people)])]))]

c. Constructional signature: [V.TNS NP PP PP RP]

(27) The assertive speech act of remind

With S uttering UTT, S reminds H that P

PROP	P
Precondition	
ILLOCFORCE (IF)	ASSERTIVE
IFID	Assertive verb used = REMIND
illocutionary point (IP)	S presents PROP as representing the state of affairs of the world
degree of strength of IP	++ 2
Mode of achievement (MoA)	Using language, S reminds H of PROP as representing known facts Transfer of a memory of PROP by S to H
position of authority	Not a factor here
position of power	Not a factor here
Preparatory Conditions (PrepC)	S believes PROP H already knowns PROP, but may have forgotten it
Sincerity Conditions (SC)	The speech act is performed by S in accordance all beliefs, desires, and intentions (BDI) and informed by shared common ground.
BELIEF	S: BEL'(S, **do'** (S, **remind'** (S, PROP)))
DESIRE	WANT'(S, BEL'(H, PROP))
INTENTION	INTEND'(S, BEL'(H, PROP))

Degree of strength of SC	–
Direction of fit (DoF)	word-to-world
Realisation	S expresses UTT to H Emergent common ground constructed
Postcondition	H interprets UTT from S Common ground updated

4.2.10 Predict

The assertive speech act of predict is used to say or estimate that a specified thing will happen in the future or will occur as a consequence of some event. To predict is to assert with the propositional content condition that the propositional content P is to occur or be true in the future with respect to the utterance time T. S has (or should have) evidence in support of P.

(28) Predict

a.

Tuaraim	*stoirm*	*sneachta*	*amárach.*
Predict V-PRS+1SG	storm	snow	tomorrow

I predict a snowstorm tomorrow.

b. [**do’** (1SG, [**tomorrow’** (**predict’** (1SG, snow storm))])]

c. Constructional signature: [V.TNS NP RP]

(29) The assertive speech act of predict

With S uttering UTT, S predicts the P to H

PROP	P
Precondition	
ILLOCFORCE (IF)	ASSERTIVE
IFID	Assertive verb used = PREDICT
illocutionary point (IP)	S presents PROP as representing the state of affairs of the world
degree of strength of IP	+++ 3
Mode of achievement (MoA)	S predicts PROP in language to H S expresses confidence in the future occurrence of PROP at time T > now

position of authority	Not a factor here
position of power	Not a factor here
Preparatory Conditions (PrepC)	S believes PROP
Sincerity Conditions (SC)	The speech act is performed by S in accordance all beliefs, desires, and intentions (BDI) and informed by shared common ground.
BELIEF	S: BEL'(S, **do'** (S, **predict'** (S, PROP)))
DESIRE	WANT'(S, BEL'(H, PROP))
INTENTION	INTEND'(S, BEL'(H, PROP))
Degree of strength of SC	–
Direction of fit (DoF)	word-to-world
Realisation	S expresses UTT to H Emergent common ground constructed
Postcondition	H interprets UTT from S Common ground updated

4.2.11 Report

To report is to give an account of a particular matter that one has observed, heard, done, investigated, or that one has arrived at a particular place or is ready to do something. To report is to assert with the propositional content condition that the propositional content is about the past with respect to the time of utterance. That is: I report what *has* happened and I predict what *will* happen.

(30)Report

a.

Tuairiscím go bhfuil an obair críochnaithe.

Report:V-PRS+1SG that BE-AUX DET work finished

I report that the work is complete.

b. [**do'** (1SG, [**report'**(1SG, [**be'** (work, [complete'])])])]

c. Constructional signature: [V.TNS NP THAT RP]

(31)Report

a.

Tuairiscím chuig d'athair thú.

Report:V-PRS+1SG to:PREP POSS+father 2SG
I report you to your father.
b. [**do’** (1SG, [**report’** (1SG, [**be-to’** (father, 2SG)])])]
c. Constructional signature: [V.TNS NP PP RP]

(32) The assertive speech act of report
With S uttering UTT, S reports the P to H

Prop	P
Precondition	
IllocForce (IF)	Assertive
IFID	Assertive verb used = REPORT
illocutionary point (IP)	S presents Prop as representing the state of affairs of the world
degree of strength of IP	++ 2
Mode of achievement (MoA)	S reports Prop in language to H S expresses confidence in past occurrence of Prop at time T < now
position of authority	Not a factor here
position of power	Not a factor here
Preparatory Conditions (PrepC)	S believes Prop
Sincerity Conditions (SC)	The speech act is performed by S in accordance all beliefs, desires, and intentions (BDI) and informed by shared common ground.
Belief	S: Bel’(S, [**do’** (S, **report’** (S, the case))])
Desire	Want’(S, Bel’(H, Prop))
Intention	Intend’(S, Bel’(H, Prop))
Degree of strength of SC	=
Direction of fit (DoF)	word-to-world
Realisation	S expresses UTT to H Emergent common ground constructed
Postcondition	H interprets UTT from S Common ground updated

4.2.12 Recommend

To assertively recommend is to put forward something as having one's approval as being beneficial, or suitable for a particular purpose or role, To recommend is to present something or someone as worthy of confidence, acceptance, or use. One can assertively recommend that a particular action should be done. An example of an assertive recommend is indicated in (22). The assertive recommend is oriented towards H.

(33) Recommend

a.

Molaim	*duit*	*an*	*post*	*a*	*chríochnú.*
Recommend:V-PRS+1SG	to:PREP+2SG	DET	job	PRT	finish:VN

I recommend you finish the job.

b. [**do'** (1SG, BECOME **finish'** (2SG, job)]

c. Constructional signature: [V.TNS NP PP NP PRT VN]

(34) The assertive speech act of recommend

With S uttering UTT, S recommends P to H

PROP	P
Precondition	
ILLOCFORCE (IF)	ASSERTIVE
IFID	Assertive verb used = RECOMMEND
illocutionary point (IP)	S presents PROP as representing the state of affairs of the world
degree of strength of IP	+++ 3
Mode of achievement (MoA)	S recommend the facts in language to H
position of authority	Not a factor here
position of power	Not a factor here
Preparatory Conditions (PrepC)	S believes the facts
Sincerity Conditions (SC)	The speech act is performed by S in accordance all beliefs, desires, and intentions (BDI) and informed by shared common ground.
BELIEF	S: BEL'(S, [**do'** (S, **recommend'** (S, PROP))])

Desire	Want'(S, Bel'(H, Prop))
Intention	Intend'(S, Bel'(H, Prop))
Degree of strength of SC	+
Direction of fit (DoF)	word-to-world
Realisation	S expresses UTT to H Emergent common ground constructed
Postcondition	H interprets UTT from S Common ground updated

4.2.13 Suggest

With the assertive suggest, S puts something forward to H for consideration. The assertive suggest by S causes H to think that something exists, is the case, or is worth doing. The assertive suggest (23) and assertive insist (24) are directed towards H. They differ from assert in their degree of strength. Insist has special mode of achievement of persistence in its illocutionary point. Both suggest and insist have an assertive and a directive use. However, we are concerned with the assertive use here. The assertive suggest has only the belief by S that there is reason to believe that P or that, because it is possible that P is true, H should consider P. The assertive suggest that P is not an expression of belief that P. In suggesting that P, S merely expresses the belief that there is reason to believe that P, but not any sufficient reason to believe it.

(35) Suggest

a.

Comhairlím	*duit*	*an*	*oigheann*	*a*	*sheiceáil.*
suggest:V-PRS+1SG	to:PREP+2SG	DET	oven	PRT	check:VN

I suggest you check the oven.

b. [**do'** (1SG, BECOME **check'** (2SG, oven))]

c. Constructional signature: [V.TNS NP PP NP PRT VN]

(36) The assertive speech act of suggest

With S uttering UTT, S suggests the P to H

Prop	P

Precondition

IllocForce (IF)	Assertive

IFID	Assertive verb used = SUGGEST
illocutionary point (IP)	S presents PROP as representing the state of affairs of the world
degree of strength of IP	+ 1
Mode of achievement (MoA)	S suggests the facts in language to H
position of authority	Not a factor here
position of power	Not a factor here
Preparatory Conditions (PrepC)	S believes the facts
Sincerity Conditions (SC)	The speech act is performed by S in accordance all beliefs, desires, and intentions (BDI) and informed by shared common ground.
BELIEF	S: BEL'(S, [**do'** (S, **suggest'** (S, PROP))])
DESIRE	WANT'(S, BEL'(H, PROP))
INTENTION	INTEND'(S, BEL'(H, PROP))
Degree of strength of SC	–
Direction of fit (DoF)	word-to-world
Realisation	S expresses UTT to H Emergent common ground constructed
Postcondition	H interprets UTT from S Common ground updated

4.2.14 insist

The speech act insist is used to assertively by S to forcefully demand that H do something X while not accepting a refusal. It is likely to be the case that H disagrees with or opposes what S say. Therefore, the assertive insist is more forceful in that S demand something of H forcefully, not accepting refusal. With the assertive insist, S demands of H forcefully to have (something), or have something done.

(37) Insist

a.

Áitíonn *mé go gcríochnóidh tú an post.*

Insist:V-PRS 1SG to:PREP finish:V 2SG DET job
I insist that you finish the job.
b. [**do'** (1SG, [**insist'** (2SG, **finish'** (2SG, job))])]
c. Constructional signature: [V.TNS NP that RP]

(38) Insist (stand)
a.
Seasann mé go ndéanann tú é seo.
stand:V-PRS 1SG to:PREP do-make:V-PRS 2SG 3SG.M this
Lit: I stand that you do this.
I insist that you do this.
b. [**do'** (1SG, **stand'** (1SG, [CAUSE BECOME **do-make'** (2SG, this)]))]
c. Constructional signature: [V.TNS NP THAT RP]

(39) The assertive speech act of insist
With S uttering UTT, S insists on P to H

PROP	P
Precondition	
ILLOCFORCE (IF)	ASSERTIVE
IFID	Assertive verb used = INSIST
illocutionary point (IP)	S presents PROP as representing the state of affairs of the world
degree of strength of IP	+++++ 5
Mode of achievement (MoA)	S insist the facts in language to H
position of authority	Not a factor here
position of power	Not a factor here
Preparatory Conditions (PrepC)	S believes the facts
Sincerity Conditions (SC)	The speech act is performed by S in accordance all beliefs, desires, and intentions (BDI) and informed by shared common ground.
BELIEF	S: BEL'(S, [**do'** (S, **insist'** (S, PROP))])
DESIRE	WANT'(S, BEL'(H, PROP))
INTENTION	INTEND'(S, BEL'(H, PROP))

Degree of strength of SC	+
Direction of fit (DoF)	word-to-world
Realisation	S expresses UTT to H Emergent common ground constructed
Postcondition	H interprets UTT from S Common ground updated

4.2.15 Testify

To testify is to assert in a formal/legal sense of being a witness and under oath. To testify is to tell what one knows about a matter in a court of law after having officially promised to tell the truth. The mode of achievement increases the degree of strength of the assertion and required the preparatory condition that S has witnessed the event/ knows the facts of the testimony.

(40)

a.

Fianaím *i do bhfabhar*
testify:V+PRS+1SG in your favour
I testify in your favour.

b. **[in.your.favour' [do'** (1SG, **testify'**(1SG))]]

c. Constructional signature: [V.TNS NP PP]

(41)

a.

Tugaim *fianaise don* *chúirt go bhfaca said* é.
testify:V+PRS+1SG evidence to:PREP+DET court that see:V-PST 3PL 3SG.M
Lit: I give evidence to the court that they saw him/it.
I testify to the court that they saw him/it.

b. **[to.the.court'[do'** (1SG, **give'** (1SG, evidence))]]

c. Constructional signature: [V.TNS NP NP PP THAT RP]

(42) The assertive speech act of testify

With S uttering UTT, S testifies that P to H

PROP	P

Precondition

ILLOCFORCE (IF)	ASSERTIVE

IFID	Assertive verb used = TESTIFY
illocutionary point (IP)	S presents PROP as representing the state of affairs of the world
degree of strength of IP	++++ 4
Mode of achievement (MoA)	S affirm/confirms the facts in language to H
position of authority	Not a factor here
position of power	Not a factor here
Preparatory Conditions (PrepC)	S believes the facts
Sincerity Conditions (SC)	The speech act is performed by S in accordance all beliefs, desires, and intentions (BDI) and informed by shared common ground.
BELIEF	S: BEL'(S, **do'** (S, **testify'** (S, evidence)))
DESIRE	WANT'(S, BEL'(H, the case facts))
INTENTION	INTEND'(S, BEL'(H, the case facts))
Degree of strength of SC	+
Direction of fit (DoF)	word-to-world
Realisation	S expresses UTT to H Emergent common ground constructed
Postcondition	H interprets UTT from S Common ground updated

4.2.16 Boast/lament

To boast is to talk with a sense of excessive pride and self-satisfaction about one's achievements, possessions, or abilities. One can boast about a person, place, or something that one possesses or that has a feature which is a source of pride. To lament is to express sorrow, regret, or disappointment about something, or to mourn. Both boast and lament have assertive and expressive uses. In the assertive sense, to boast that P is to assert that P while expressing pride. We examine the expressive use of lament later in the chapter on expressives. Boast has no performative use.

(43) Boast

a.

Maím gur mór is fiú an obair
boast:V-PRS+1SG that big COP worth DET work
atá ar bun agam.
BE-AUX.PRS up at:PREP+1SG
I boast that the work I am doing is well worth it.

b. [**do’** (1SG, **boast’** (1SG, work is worth it))]

c. Constructional signature: [V.TNS NP THAT RP]

(44) Boast

a.

Maím go raibh aithne aige orm.
boast:V-PRS+1SG that BE-AUX.PST knowledge at:PREP+3SG ON:PREP+1SG
I boast that he knew me.

b. [**do’** (1SG, **boast’** (1SG, [**be-on’** ([**be-at’** (knowledge, 3SG)], 1SG)]))]

c. Constructional signature: [V.TNS NP RP]

(45) The assertive speech act of boast

With S uttering UTT, S boasts that P to H

PROP	P
Precondition	
ILLOCFORCE (IF)	ASSERTIVE
IFID	Assertive verb used = BOAST
illocutionary point (IP)	S presents PROP as representing the state of affairs of the world
degree of strength of IP	++++ 4
Mode of achievement (MoA)	S boasts X in language to H
position of authority	Not a factor here
position of power	Not a factor here
Preparatory Conditions (PrepC)	S believes the facts
Sincerity Conditions (SC)	The speech act is performed by S in accordance all beliefs, desires, and intentions (BDI) and informed by shared common ground.

BELIEF	S: BEL'(S, **do'** (S, **boast'** (S, X)))
DESIRE	WANT'(S, BEL'(H, X))
INTENTION	INTEND'(S, BEL'(H, X))
Degree of strength of SC	–
Direction of fit (DoF)	word-to-world
Realisation	S expresses UTT to H Emergent common ground constructed
Postcondition	H interprets UTT from S Common ground updated

In contrast to boast, to lament P is to assert P while expressing sadness or sorrow that P.

(46) Lament

a.

Is trua liom an obair caillte.

COP sorrow with:PREP+1SG DET work lost

I lament the lost work.

b. [**be'** (**be-on'** (sorrow, 1SG), the lost work))]

c. Constructional signature: [COP.TNS NP NP NP]

(47) Lament

a.

Is trua liom do chás agus

COP sorrow with:PREP+1SG your situation and

is trua liom do chaill.

COP sorrow with:PREP+1SG your loss

I lament your situation and lament your loss.

b. [**be'** (**be-on'** (sorrow, 1SG)), your situation)] ∧ [**be'** (**be-on'**(sorrow, 1SG), your loss)]

c. Constructional signature: [COP.TNS NP NP NP]

(48) The assertive speech act of lament

With S uttering UTT, S laments the P to H

PROP	P
Precondition	
ILLOCFORCE (IF)	ASSERTIVE
IFID	Assertive verb used = LAMENT

illocutionary point (IP)	S presents PROP as representing the state of affairs of the world
degree of strength of IP	++++ 4
Mode of achievement (MoA)	S laments X in language to H
position of authority	Not a factor here
position of power	Not a factor here
Preparatory Conditions (PrepC)	S believes the facts
Sincerity Conditions (SC)	The speech act is performed by S in accordance all beliefs, desires, and intentions (BDI) and informed by shared common ground.
BELIEF	S: BEL'(S, **do'** (S, **lament'** (S, X)))
DESIRE	WANT'(S, BEL'(H, X))
INTENTION	INTEND'(S, BEL'(H, X))
Degree of strength of SC	+
Direction of fit (DoF)	word-to-world
Realisation	S expresses UTT to H Emergent common ground constructed
Postcondition	H interprets UTT from S Common ground updated

4.3 Some comments on assertives

For the assertive clause we examined, we have found the following syntactic patterns, the constructional schemas (49). With the clausal structure of the assertive, there appears to be a robust consistency in the syntactic pattern consists of small variations on (50) where the leftmost NP is S, the actor of the utterance. The speaker S is the actor with the assertives.

(49) The syntactic patterns of the assertive speech acts

Speech act	IFID/SA Verb	Constructional schema
Assertive	assert	[V.TNS NP NP]
	claim	[V.TNS NP NP]
	affirm/confirm	[V.TNS NP NP]
	state	[V.TNS NP NP NP]
	assure	[V.TNS NP NP THAT RP]
	argue	[V.TNS NP THAT NP]
	argue	[V.TNS NP THAT RP]
	rebut	[V.TNS NP NP]
	inform	[V.TNS NP PP PP THAT RP]
	notify	[V.TNS NP NP PP (PP)]
	remind	[V.TNS NP PP RP]
	remind	[V.TNS NP PP THAT (OBLIGATION) RP]
	remind	[V.TNS NP PP PP RP]
	predict	[V.TNS NP RP]
	report	[V.TNS NP THAT RP]
	report	[V.TNS NP PP RP]
	recommend	[V.TNS NP PP NP PRT VN]
	suggest	[V.TNS NP PP NP PRT VN]
	insist	[V.TNS NP THAT RP]
	testify	[V.TNS NP PP]
	testify	[V.TNS NP NP PP THAT RP]
	boast	[V.TNS NP NP]
	lament	[COP.TNS NP NP NP]

(50)

[V.TNS:PRS ^{ACTOR}NP (NP|PP) (NP|PP) (THAT) (OBLIGATION) RP]

We have seen that an ASSERTIVE commits S to a proposition being true such that, in uttering the assertive, S asserts that proposition if S expresses a) the belief that the proposition holds, and b) the intention that H believes that proposition. An assertive is satisfied simply if its proposition is *true* at the moment the utterance is made. With an assertive, it is the intention of S that H form the belief that P. That is, at the time of utterance, S presumes that H does not believe that P. This involves a notion of illocutionary presumption (Bach & Harnish 1979:42). In S's illocutionary intention, S presumes that q if the truth of q is necessary for the rationality of his illocutionary intention. In speaking of the rationality of illocutionary intentions, we mean that is that there may be a good reason to believe that the intention will be fulfilled by being recognised. Generally, for an illocutionary act with a presumption, the truth of that presumption is necessary for the success of that act. It is argued by Bach & Harnish that, with this notion of illocutionary presumption, we can distinguish some of the other kinds of assertives partly in terms of what is presumed.

In this analysis, we have proposed the following relative degrees of strength of the assertives discussed in this chapter: 5: argue, rebut, insist; 4: testify, boast, lament, inform/notify; 3: assert, claim, recommend, predict, state; 2: affirm, confirm, remind, report, assure; 1: suggest. Additionally, for each assertive, we indicated the relative degree of strength of the sincerity condition as one of + (strong), = (moderate), or - (weak).

The various assertives differ in the belief(s) expressed and in the expressed intention. When one asserts something, one's expressed belief and intention are very strong.

In contrast, when one alleges that something is the case, the belief and intention expressed are weaker. The evidential, as a form of assertive speech act, provides a mechanism whereby S can provide evidence or indicate a level of commitment to the veracity of the assertion. At the weaker pole, this can involve epistemic judgements. We examine the evidential in the next chapter.

5 The evidential utterance as a type of assertive speech act

5.1 Introduction to the evidential of Irish as an assertive speech act

In this chapter we consider the evidential as a type of assertive speech act, as it occurs in modern Irish. The formulation of the Irish evidential has several characteristics worthy of note. Firstly, Irish does not have a grammaticalised evidential system, in the sense defined by Aikhenvald (2003:15), but instead uses an evidential strategy. In this account, in support of our discussion of the pragmatic aspects of evidentiality as a type of assertive speech act, we utilise elements of the RRG model to characterise certain syntactic and semantic dimensions of evidentiality as it is found in Irish. Within the evidentiality strategy of Irish, a combination of lexical, syntactic, and potentially adverbial means are used to flag information and knowledge source. Context and common ground both play a role in the meaning determination. The pragmatic and syntactic dimensions of evidentiality in Irish are considered, along with the pragmatic functions. Importantly, with the evidential, the language has a rich repertoire of evidential adverbials that are also frequently deployed and which potentially gives the evidential an epistemic quality. In the evidential strategy of Irish, the evidential reporting of facts in the world based on a knowledge source is facilitated and understood as stating the fact plus the existence of a source of evidence for some information, including that i) there is evidence, and ii) specifying the actual type of evidence.

As a conceptual domain, evidentiality is defined by Aikhenvald as:

> … understood as stating the existence of a source of evidence for some information; that includes stating that there is some evidence, and also specifying what type of evidence there is.
>
> Aikhenvald (2003:1)

The lexical means include judicious use of verbs of perception related to the senses, and verbs of cognition, while the syntactic means avail of a range of syntactic structures that allow for a speaker to denote some knowledge source as fact with a possible graded commitment. The adverbial means allow the speaker to overtly hedge their commitment to the veracity of the knowledge source. While both evidentiality and epistemic modality are to do with knowledge, they are quite different and not at all the same. Evidentiality is about identifying a source of knowledge or information (the *evidential channel*) and specifying the actual type of information (the *knowledge*), while epistemic modality (Nolan 2008) records a speaker's *stance* on some piece of knowledge (De Haan 1999).

The pragmatic and syntactic dimensions of evidentiality in Irish are now considered. Evidentiality allows S to qualify their stance as to the reliability of information communicated via assertion by S to H. A feature of the evidential utterance is that it specifies the source of evidence on the asserted statement is based, the degree of precision or probability, along with various expectations concerning the information.

What then are the pragmatic functions of evidentiality? The evidential utterance is fundamentally an assertive speech act, an illocutionary act, and, as such, has pragmatic dimensions. As a form of assertive speech act, the evidential has important pragmatic dimensions to do with the commitment of the speaker to the exactness of the information expressed via the particular evidential channel chosen. That is, it is a type of illocutionary speech act with a sincerity condition attached. It signals the source of information, but also the actual information in the evidence channel. The information delivered via the evidence channel contains the new information. Irish employs an evidential strategy which uses lexical, syntactic, and adverbial means to encode the appropriate level of evidentiality that S requires. The evidential hierarchy plays a role in the execution of the pragmatically informed evidential strategy for Irish. We will discuss the evidential hierarchy shortly.

In addition, the evidential has pragmatic nuances across an evidential and epistemic continuum with respect to both the stance on the mode of knowing and the knowledge characterised in the utterance. We will see this reflected in the evidential hierarchy.

The perspective of S is encoded in the evidential utterance, and this must be evaluated and unpacked by H. The choice of information source signalled may depend on the speaker's perspective of the situation.

As the function of the evidential is pragmatic in nature, it allows the speaker's degree of commitment to the information communicated to be modulated. As an assertive speech act (Searle 1979:1–29), S is committed, with varying degrees of strength, to the veracity of the proposition expressed. Assertive speech acts commit S, in varying degrees of strength, to the truth of the utterance's proposition. Assertive speech acts assert that p, where p is the proposition.

According to Searle, an assertive can be evaluated on a true-false dimension, and S specifies the extent to which they commit to the truth of the proposition expressed. However, as argued by Searle (1979:12–13), S may make a strong or weak commitment to the proposition expressed. This commitment can be explicitly signalled in the speech act by virtue of the use of the assertive evidential speech act.

As an assertive speech act, the evidential is subject to a number of important conditions. The preparatory or precondition condition is that S has an ACCESSIBLE REASON for presenting the asserted proposition as true. The essential condition is that S POSSESSES EVIDENCE that the proposition represents an actual state of affairs. Additionally, the sincerity condition is that S believes the evidence expressed by an utterance. As sincerity conditions come with varying degrees of strength, evidentials therefore provide a linguistic means of expressing the degree of strength of the sincerity conditions on the assertive. This is reflected within the evidential hierarchy.

Evidentials therefore can be examined in terms of their pragmatic function of modulating S's degree of certainty and commitment to the information communicated to H. The utterance form helps signal the pragmatic attitude of S to towards the information communicated, and hence the degree of certainty or evidential strength on the quality of the information. The degrees of commitment of S can be pragmatically inferred by H from the choice of information source-channel, as reflected in the evidential hierarchy across over some specific supporting clausal form, and also by the choice of adverbial used in an utterance.

The pragmatic functions of evidential adverbials are that they can be utilised to indicate the source or the strength of the S's evidence, by virtue of the adverbial used. They may also be indicators of the kind, or amount, of evidence that S has for the utterance. Importantly, they are indicative of S's degree of commitment.

Evidential adverbials function differently to hearsay adverbials. Hearsay adverbials indicate that the source of knowledge is not S. They flag information for which S has less, or no, evidence than if it was experienced first-hand and are therefore reveal a diminished commitment on behalf of S.

(1) The evidential of Irish as an assertive speech act
With S uttering UTT, S states to H that P

Prop	P: <EVID<[**verb of perception or cognition'**(1SG, [LS])]>> Where [LS] is some logical structure
Precondition	
IllocForce (IF)	Assertive
IFID	VERB OF PERCEPTION | VERB OF COGNITION AND POSSIBLE use of evidential adverbials
illocutionary point (IP)	S presents Prop as representing the state of affairs of the world
degree of strength of IP	+++ 3
Mode of achievement (MoA)	S states the Prop in language to H S utilises a verb of perception or verb of cognition, possibly with an evidential adverbials, to indicate S's level of commitment to the Prop to H
position of authority	Not a factor here
position of power	Not a factor here
Preparatory Conditions (PrepC)	S believes the facts H may/may not know Prop
Sincerity Conditions (SC)	The speech act is performed by S in accordance all beliefs, desires, and intentions (BDI) and informed by shared common ground.
Belief	S: Bel'(S, **do'** (S, **state'** (S, Prop)))
Desire	Want'(S, Bel'(H, Prop))
Intention	Intend'(S, Bel'(H, Prop))
Degree of strength of SC	=
Direction of fit (DoF)	word-to-world
Realisation	S expresses UTT to H Emergent common ground constructed
Postcondition	H interprets evidential UTT from S Common ground updated

The constructional schema of the evidential is given in (2):

(2)
<EVID<[**verb of perception or cognition'**(1SG, [LS])]>>

The evidential strategy of Irish, therefore, indicates information source, through a set of lexical and syntactic means which may include any of the dimensions of visual, non-visual sensory, inference, assumption, reported speech, and quotative functions. The choice of information source signalled may depend on the speaker's perspective of the situation. The scope of an evidential is the clause. An evidential does not have any bearing on the truth, value, or utility of a the information expressed, and it is possible, for example, to lie on purpose using an evidential strategy. Consequently, an evidential statement can be questioned by an interlocutor in a dialogue.

Evidentiality encodes the perspective of the clausal actor or experiencer, that is, the speaker S. In Irish, a reportative strategy is used whereby the experiencer S uses a lexical verb of perception to record that some fact or situation has been made known. The motivation to express information about facts clearly and with precision may be a factor for using an evidential strategy. The use of an evidential therefore connects with a desire to make visible in speech a transparency as to how one knows certain facts.

While evidentiality is concerned with knowledge, it is concerned in a different way than epistemic modality which is also concerned with knowledge. The difference is that evidentiality identifies the *source* of some information or knowledge, whereas epistemic modality records one's *stance* on some knowledge. Evidentiality is therefore not the same as epistemic modality, even though both are to do with different dimensions of knowledge. Evidentiality is understood as stating the existence of a source of evidence for some information, including that there is evidence, and specifying the actual type of evidence. For Irish, the means of expressing the source of information or knowledge includes lexical means, via verbs of perception ('see', 'hear', 'smell') and cognition ('know', 'understand', and so on). Evidential adverbials are also used in certain contexts. These verbs of perception and cognition are used in what is called a reportative function (Wiemer 2010:95) that carries the evidential meaning. The types of information source, the information channel, include those in (3).

(3) Information source types (based on Aikhenvald 2018:57)
   a. VISUAL covers information acquired through sight.
   b. NON-VISUAL / sensory information obtained through hearing, smell, touch and taste.
   c. INFERENCE based on visible or tangible results.

d. QUOTATIVE for information with an explicit reference to the quoted source author.
e. REPORTED for information with no reference to who reported it.
f. ASSUMPTION based on reasoning, assumption, or knowledge in common ground.

It is possible to specify whether the speaker saw the event happen, heard it, didn't see it but heard it, smelt it, inferred it based on visual evidence, reasoning, knowledge in common ground, or was somehow informed about it. The preferences for the expression of evidential choices (Aikhenvald 2018:76) is given in (4), with the evidential strength residing in the left pole, the visual.

(4) VISUAL < NON-VISUAL < INFERRED < REPORTED < ASSUMED

In Irish, the main verb identifies the evidential channel (see, hear, etc.), whereas the subordinate clausal complement describes the information fact or situation. A change in the complement clause distinguishes between an actual credible receipt of the information and a non-evidential hearsay meaning with the status of opinion or rumour (Aikhenvald 2003:33).

The evidential hierarchy is introduced next as a tool to explain the central characteristics of linguistic evidentiality and how evidentiality is a discrete semantic-functional domain that is different from epistemic modality. We will provide an analysis showing how the Irish data reflects the evidential strategy. The data has examples of use of lexical verbs of perception and cognition, and indicates a variety of syntactic organisations that support evidentiality. Evidential adverbials are included in this analysis. We will then provide a formalisation of evidentiality as an assertive speech act, as an instance of language in use, encompassing the situation of utterance, context, actor, knowledge, and the information-source-type.

5.2 The central characteristic of linguistic evidentiality

The primary characteristic of linguistic evidentiality (Diewald & Smirnova 2010:8) is the explicit encoding of information plus a source for that information or knowledge which S asserts when producing the utterance. One may distinguish between different degrees of classification within an evidential strategy (Figure 5.1), ranging over an evidential hierarchy that

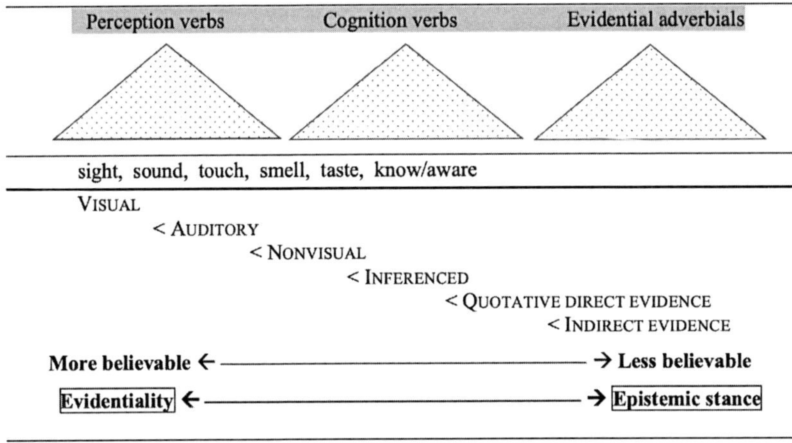

Figure 5.1 The evidential hierarchy and the credibility of information expressed

signals more credibility relating to the information expressed at the direct/visual pole and less credibility towards the indirect pole.

De Hann (1999:6) proposes such a hierarchy based on credibility of the information expressed, ranging from evidentiality at one pole to epistemic stance at the other. The expression of knowledge may actually reflect i) a speaker's reliability, ii) an epistemic stance with respect to the information, and iii) a speaker's actual knowledge within some social and cultural context. Consequently, an evidential may, or may not, have additional meanings of an epistemic nature. Specifically, evidentiality codes a person's source of information in an utterance, while epistemic modality relates to a speaker's judgemental stance on a relevant piece of information. They are different but related, in that both concern knowledge (Schenner 2010:167). There is a clear semantic distinction (5) between evidential marking of the source of the information and the epistemic degree of commitment that a speaker places in their utterance (De Haan 1999:3). Epistemic modality involves the speaker's assessment of the epistemic status of an event, that is, the expression of different degrees of speaker certainty regarding the conception or likelihood of the occurrence of the event. Stance taking via means of epistemic modality involves the expression of the speaker attitudes, belief, or evaluation concerning events and their commitment to the communicated proposition. The taking of an epistemic stance allows the speaker to assess the proposition and the validity of the utterance, or to distance themselves and reduce their commitment for the propositional content.

(5) Evidentiality and epistemic modality differ in their semantics:
- Evidentials assert the nature of the evidence for the information in the sentence.
- Epistemic modals evaluate the speaker's commitment for the statement.

For Irish, as we will see, evidentiality may indeed reflect S's stance by virtue of the type of construction chosen, since the specification of the source, and mode of access to the knowledge, may carry an indication of S's attitude and commitment towards the validity of the communicated information (Marín Arrese, Haßler & Carretero 2017:8). Some information may signalled as be more, or less, believable, depending on the evidential hierarchy, as we have indicated in Figure 5.1. Notwithstanding this, evidentiality is considered to be a semantic-functional domain in its own right, and not a subdivision of epistemic modality (Diewald & Smirnova 2010:9–10).

In Role and Reference Grammar (RRG), a functional-cognitive model of grammar, evidentiality is considered as an operator on the clause and the clause is argued to have a layered structure. The various operators have

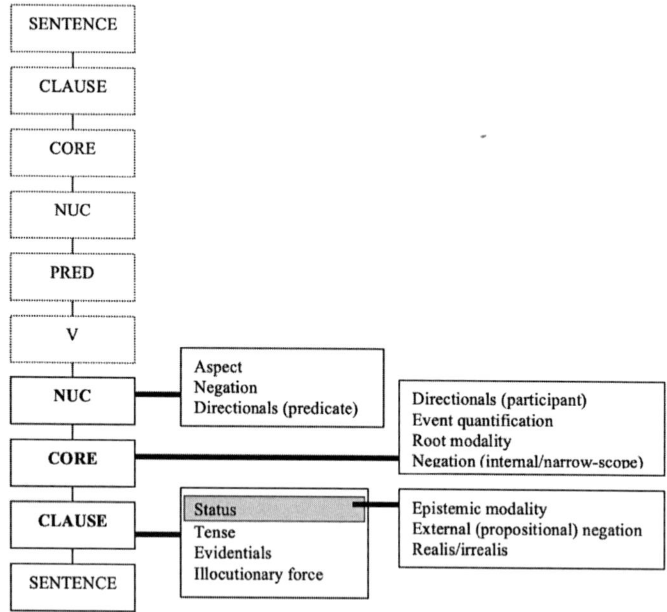

Figure 5.2 The operator projection in the layered structure of the clause

different scopes depending on their type. Evidentiality is shown to outrank modality (6) in the hierarchy posited by Van Valin & LaPolla (1997:49). The kinds of operator recognised within RRG are indicated in Figure 5.2.

(6)

[CLAUSE] **ILLOCUTIONARY FORCE**

> [CLAUSE] **evidentiality**

> [CLAUSE] STATUS: **epistemic**

> [CORE] deontic/root.

In RRG, then, an evidential is encoded as a clause level operator, along with Status (epistemic modals, external negation, realis/irrealis), tense, and illocutionary Force. Essentially, this reflects that evidentially has wide scope over the full clause.

5.3 Analysis of the Irish assertive evidential

5.3.1 Evidential use of verbs of perception in Irish

It is the case that the Irish data on evidentiality makes extensive use of verbs of verbs of perception and cognition within its evidential strategy. A verb of perception is a verb that conveys the evidence delivered via the experience of one of the physical senses. Verbs of cognition designate mental processes that involve S, an actor-experiencer, who *senses* or *cognises* and an object of knowledge or belief, and S, as cogniser, *knows*, *thinks*, *feels*, *believes*, and so on, while what is sensed or cognised is typically denoted in the form of a complement clause. Verbs of perception and cognition are found to be involved in a variety of constructions in Irish. The verbs of perception describe the actual perception of some entity by S, and these verbs take a variety of complements. The verbs *taste* and *smell* do not show as frequently in the data, possibly because only a limited range of things can be apprehended through the sense of taste and smell.

The lexical verbs of perception and cognition either encode evidentiality. They may also perform an epistemic function. The evidentiality encoded by such verbs identify the source of information received via the cognitive-sensory evidential channel. Investigating the use of verbs of perception and cognition enables us to understand how we frame our own ideas, and how linguistic forms encode our attitudes toward the conceptual worlds of others. The use of verbs of cognition in a language refers to the mental state indicated by the verb, but may be indicative of an expression of S's stance. Verbs of cognition such as *think*, *believe*, *know*, and so on have subtle meanings that warrant analysis at the pragmatic and discursive levels of language in order to be fully understood. However, they pose challenges to an analysis of their evidential and modal status. Visual evidence is a form of direct evidence (De Hann 2001:92). Other direct evidentials include auditory evidentials. Nonvisual sensory evidence denotes that the action was perceived by any of the senses except sight. Perception verbs consist of those verbs signifying sight, sound, touch, smell, and taste. These are recognised as being ideal candidates for carriers of evidential meaning. Much of what we *know* and *believe* is based on what we *perceive*. Before we proceed with the analysis, it is necessary to make some observations regarding the coding of propositions in the Irish data. There is one proposition in the ASSERTION in example (7). However, in example (8), there are two propositions: i) Aifric is swimming, and ii) S sees Aifric swimming. In (8), the first proposition in carries the illocutionary force of ASSERTION but the second proposition carries evidential meaning. This is by virtue of the fact that S, through their visual evidence, can support the expressed claim, i.e. (8): Aifric is reported by S to be swimming.

(7) Visual: see

a.

Feicim *Aifric.*
see:V-PRS+1SG Aifric
I see Aifric.
see' (1SG, Aifric)

(8)

a.

Feicim *Aifric* *ag* *snamh.*
see:V-PRS+1SG Aifric at:PREP swim:VN
I see Aifric swimming.
see' (1SG, Aifric) & **be-at'** (Aifric, [swimming'])

b.

Feicim Aifric + *Aifric ag snamh.*
[I see Aifric] + [Aifric is swimming]

We now provide typical examples of these evidential clauses initially for visual and aural, and then, later, continue with a discussion of the sense and cognitive modes. We start with a discussion of VISUAL and AURAL examples. Each of these VISUAL and AURAL examples has certain things in common. The leftmost first verb encodes the evidential channel by which the reported fact was determined. The second verb encodes the reported event.

(9) Visual: see

a.

Feicim *an fear ag* *casadh* *isteach sa* *chaolsráid.*
See.V-PRS+1SG DET man at:PREP turn:VN into DET alley
I see the man turning into the alley.

b.

[*Feicim an fear*$_1$] + [*an fear*$_1$ *ag casadh isteach sa chaolsráid*]
I see the man$_1$ + the man$_1$ turns into the alley
<EVID<[**see'** (1SG, [into.the.alley' [**turn'**(the man)]])]>>

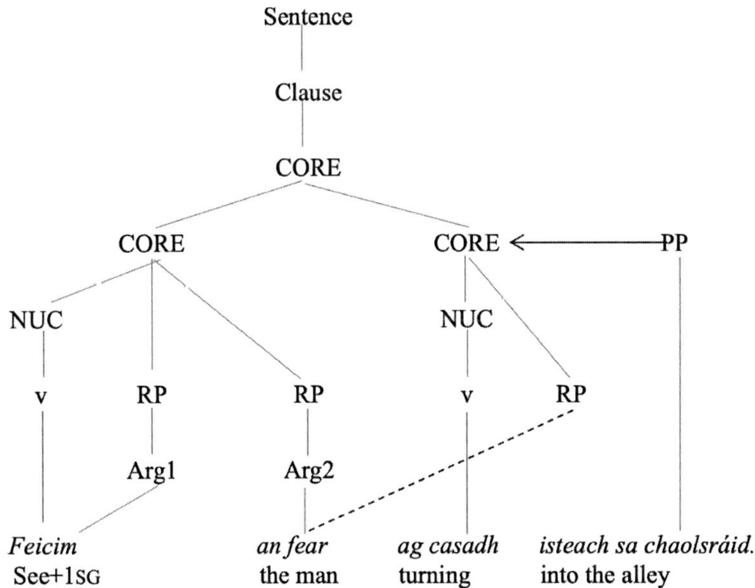

Figure 5.3 Shared argument between clauses in Subordination in the LCS

(10) Aural: hear

a.

Cloisim anois <u>iad</u> ag <u>labhairt</u> Rómainise
Hear.V-PRS+1SG now 3PL at:PREP speak:VN Romanian
ar a gcuid teileafóiníní.
on:PREP 3PL.POSS some telephones
I now hear them speaking Romanian on their phones.
<EVID<[**hear'** (1SG, [means: on.their.phones'[**speak'** (3PL, Romanian)]])]>>

b.

[*Cloisim anois <u>iad</u>*] + [*<u>iad</u> ag <u>labhairt</u> Rómainise ar a gcuid teileafóiníní*].
[I hear <u>3PL</u> now] + [<u>3PL</u> speak Romanian on their phones]

5.3.2 Non-evidential use of verbs of perception in Irish

In evidentiality, a different meaning of the utterance can be revealed by S through use of a clausal complement associated with the information source. Specifically, for example, the THAT complement clauses in the (11)–(13), where the examples can be seen to distinguish between a) an *actual* evidential hearing and b) a non-evidential *hearsay* meaning of the verb 'hear'. This type of phenomena has been observed for other languages (Aikhenvald 2003:33), and is not all unique to Irish. In the non-evidential *hearsay* examples, the complementisers (COMP) *go bhfuil* (to:PREP be:AUX) and *go mbeidh* (to:PREP be:AUX.FUT) are glossed to 'that'.

(11)

a. Implies actual hearing
Cloisim **éan** *ag <u>teacht</u> isteach.*
Hear.V-PRS+1SG bird at:PREP come:VN in:PREP
I hear a bird coming in.
<EVID<[**hear'** (1sg, [**come' (be-in' (**<u>bird</u>))])]>>

b. Implies hearsay
Cloisim <u>go bhfuil</u> **éan**
Hear.V-PRS+1SG COMP/to:PREP be:AUX.PRS bird
tar **éis** *<u>teacht</u> isteach.*
after:PREP come:VN in:PREP
Lit: I hear that a bird is after coming in.
I hear that a bird has come in

<[**hear'** (1SG, [**that-be'**(a bird has come in)])]>

(12)

a. Implies actual hearing

Cloisim tú ag obair ar
Hear.V-PRS+1SG 2SG at:PREP work:VN on:PREP
dhlúthdhiosca de do chuid amhrán.
CD of:PREP 2SG.POSS some songs
I hear you working on a CD of your songs.
<EVID<[**hear'** (1SG, [**do'** (2SG, **work**' (2SG, CD of your songs))])]>>

b. Implies hearsay

Cloisim go bhfuil tú ag obair
Hear.V-PRS+1SG COMP/to:PREP be:AUX-PRS 2SG at:PREP work:VN
ar dhlúthdhiosca de do chuid amhrán.
on:PREP CD of:PREP of 2SG.POSS some songs
I hear that you are working on a CD of your songs.
<[**hear'** (1SG, [**that-be' (do'** (2SG, **work**' (2SG, CD of your songs)))])]>

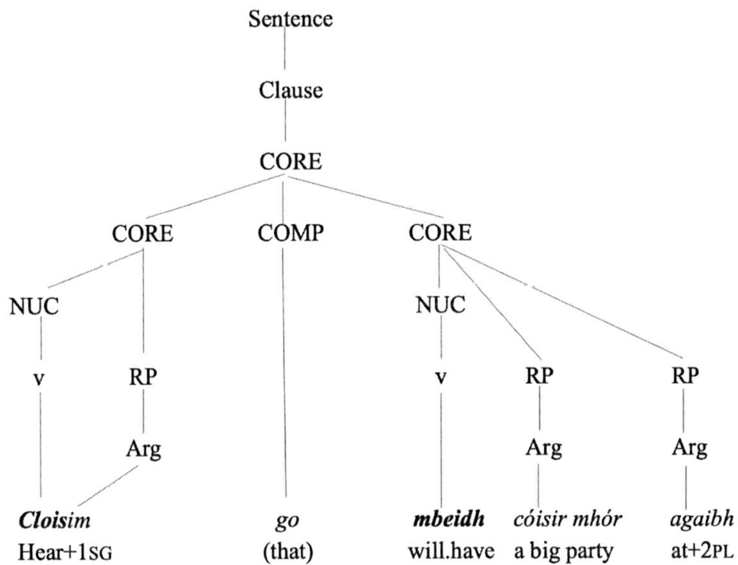

Figure 5.4 Hearsay (non-evidential) complement structure in LCS

(13)

a. Implies actual hearing

Cloisim an cóisir mhór ag ceiliúradh.
I hear.V-PRS+1SG DET party big at:PREP celebrating:VN
I hear the big party celebrating.
< **evid** <[**hear’** (1SG, **celebrate**’ (the big party))]>>

b. Implies hearsay

Cloisim go mbeidh cóisir mhór agaibh
Hear.V-PRS+1SG COMP/to:PREP be:AUX-FUT party big at:PREP+2PL
ar an Satharn
on:PREP DET Saturday
I hear that you will have a big party on Saturday.
<[**hear’** (1SG, [**that-be’** (**have.on.Saturday**’ (2SG, a big party))])]>

5.3.3 Sense and cognition

For the SENSE and COGNITION examples, the clausal encoding is rather different than that which is found with the visual and aural modes, but reflecting the speaker’s experience of what is sensed [x_{RP} SENSES y_{RP}] or perceived [x_{RP} PERCEIVES y_{RP}], where y is an RP of some kind. We see this in (14)–(15).

(14) Sense: Smell

Bolaíonn muid do chraiceann banana
smell.V-PRS 1PL 2SG.POSS skin banana
ar chúl an ghluaisteáin.
on back DET car
We smell [your banana peel in the back of the car]$_{RP}$
We smell your banana peel in the back of the car.
<**EVID**<[**smell’** (1PL, (**be-on’** [banana skin, [inside.car’]]))]>>

(15) Cognitive: Aware

Fuair mé boladh uafásach deataigh.
Get.V-PST 1SG smell terrible (of) smoke
Lit: I got a terrible smell of smoke.
I became aware of [a terrible smell of smoke]$_{RP}$.
I became aware of a terrible smell of smoke.
<**EVID**<[**perceive’**(1SG, [terrible smell of smoke])]>>

It can be seen clearly that the clausal organisation contains just one CLAUSE, one CORE and one NUC with one verb. While the first argument is the senser

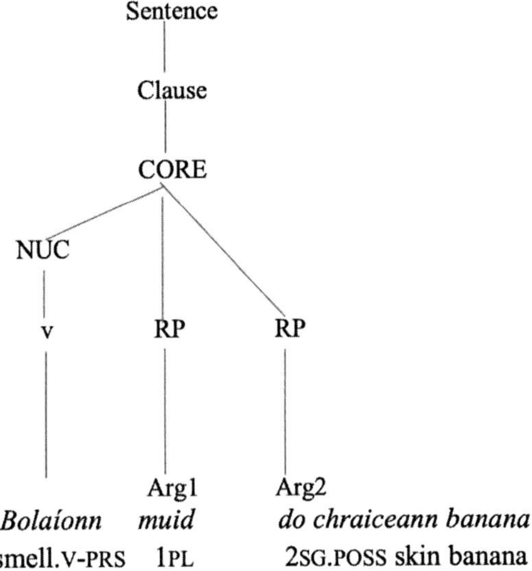

Figure 5.5 Evidential *sense* and *cognition* structure of LCS

or perceiver RP, the second argument is an RP that captures what it was that came to one's attention via the particular channel or mode.

5.3.4 Evidential adverbials

Having examined the evidential strategy with clauses of Irish and their use of verbs of perception and cognition, we now discuss the evidential application of adverbials. Before we take on this task, it is necessary to say some words regarding the general classification of an adverbial, and later, the type of adverbials that exist in Irish and how they are formed. In the introduction to their volume on *Adverbs: Functional and Diachronic Aspects*, Pittner, Elsner, & Barteld (2015:8) note that adverbs have typically been characterised as intractable and confusing. They have been described as both elusive and vast by van der Auwera (1998:3) and, by Haspelmath (2001:16543), as the 'most problematic major word class'. It is uncontroversial that the most characteristic function of adjectives is to modify nouns. For adverbs, a widely held view (Huddleston & Pullum 2002:563) is that '[a]dverbs characteristically modify verbs and other categories except nouns, especially adjectives and adverbs'.

Schachter & Shopen (2007:20) pose the question as to whether there is sufficient similarity among the various types of 'adverbs' to justify their assignment to a single parts-of-speech class, along with a caveat that adverbs must be assigned to separate subclasses. The subclass designations for these would include 'sentence adverb' (*unfortunately*), 'directional adverb' (*home*), 'degree adverb' (*extremely*), 'manner adverb' (*slowly*), and 'time adverb' (*yesterday*). Adverbs are typically identified them as modifiers of verbs, adjectives, or other adverbs, but is probably more appropriate to consider them as functioning as modifiers of constituents other than nouns. Sentence modifiers, for example, typically express the speaker's attitude toward the event spoken of; modifiers of verbs commonly express time, place, direction, or manner, and modifiers of adjectives and adverbs commonly express degree. In many languages, manner adverbs are derivable from adjectives by means of productive processes of derivational morphology. In Irish, phrases consisting of a preposition plus a noun or noun phrase can be used to express a wide range of adverbial meanings, including time, place, direction, manner, and so on.

Adverbs have been treated in the context of a discussion of adverbial functions, due to their close connection to a syntactic function, along with the adverbial internal structure (Pittner, Elsner, & Barteld 2015:9). Adverbs are closely related to adjectives and to the function of adverbials. A delimitation of these two word classes has been necessary after the category of adjective had been established in linguistic theory as a discrete word class. Both categories (adjective and adverb) are frequently held to have a modifying function.

According to Pittner, Elsner, & Barteld (2015:11), one of the reasons defining adverbs is difficult is that these are entwined to the function(s) of an *adverbial*. These adverbial functions may be syntactic or pragmatic. Adverbial expressions may be usefully differentiated not only by how they are constructed, but also by their semantic contribution to the sentence in which they occur. It is necessary to distinguish between the lexical category *adverb* and the syntactic function *adverbial*. The term adverb is refers to a lexical category whereas adverbial refers to a certain function expressed through phrases used adverbially.

Some of the syntactic adverbial functions (Van Valin 2005:230) are concerned with: the *manner* in which a motion event is carried out, the *motion* accompanying another action, a *position or stance* while doing an action, or the *means* by which an action is carried out. Others are concerned with qualifying, informing, or providing additional information of some dimension of: *direct perception* and the unmediated apprehension of some act, event or situation through the senses, *indirect perception* and the deduction of some act, event, or situation from evidence of it, *propositional attitude* concerning the expression of a participant's attitude, judgment, or opinion regarding a state of affairs, *cognition*, with an expression of knowledge or mental activity, *indirect discourse* and the expression of reported speech, or *direct discourse* and the direct quotation of a speech event. These adverbial functions reflect adjustments onto different points on the utterance (16).

Simply, adverbials of Irish are used to qualify, or add additional information, to verbs, adjectives, and other adverbs, rather than just modify. In fact, the claim that an adverbial has a modification function is probably a misnomer that mis-classifies what an adverbial actually does. In turn, while we generally refer to an adverb as a part of speech, this is simply a convenient term that, for Irish, does not map to a lexical category. In relation to Irish, it is more appropriate to talk of adverbials with particular functions. Indeed, adverbials in Irish generally have a phrasal quality and are constructed, in the main, from a preposition and adjectives. An adverbial can be created from an adjective by adding *go* before it [*go*: PREP 'to' ADJ]. Often, though, the [*go*: PREP 'to'] is omitted. If the adjective begins with a vowel, *h* is added before it the adjective within the adverbial. Adverbials can often be created from nouns by putting a preposition before them [PREP N]. An adverbial can describe relation to *time* or *place*. In any event, various phrases can be used in an adverbial function, as we will see in our discussion of evidential adverbials. As regards adverbial functions, an adverbial of Irish can express a relative location to another thing/person. An adverbial can be used in *questions*, or can be used for *negation.* An adverbial can express an *emotional attitude*. An adverbial can express a *directional orientation*. Importantly, in Irish, an adverbial can have an evidential function that maps along the evidential-epistemic hierarchy.

(16) Adverbial functions

Manner	do (x, [motion (x)] . . . ∧ [manner.of.motion (x)])
Motion	do (x, [motion (x)] . . . ∧ [**pred'** (x, (y))])
Position	do (x, [stance (x)] ∧ [**pred'** (x, (y))])
Means	do (x, [. . .] ∧ [**pred'** (x, y)])
. . .	
Direct perception	**perceive'** (x, [LS ... y . . .])
Indirect perception	**perceive'** (x, [LS])
Propositional attitude	**believe'** ((x,) [LS])
. . .	
Cognition	**know'** (x, [LS])
Indirect discourse	do (x, [**say'** (x, [LS TNS ...])])
Direct discourse	do (x, [**say'** (x, [LS IF ...])])

In Irish, evidential adverbials are used by S to deliver indirect evidential meaning. An indirect evidential meaning refers to information about actions or events which the speaker did not personally witness, or the nature of the speakers commitment to the quality of the information reported. It has two subtypes: i) information which comes to the speaker from another source; it is generally called the reportative evidential, and ii) inference, where the speaker draws the conclusion that a certain action has occurred based on evidence available.

They may also reflect the commitment of S towards the veracity of the knowledge in some way. That is, these evidential adverbials may reveal a stance in the speaker's commitment towards the information given, and so should be considered as primarily evidential, but also allowing for possible epistemic readings under a particular context. In modern Irish, evidential adverbials are used in this function.

As we will see, evidential adverbials signal a mode of *knowing*, including those based on probability or likelihood, certain of the evidence, or a speaker's own direct knowledge. None of these evidential adverbials imply an absolute truth or certainty, unless something is known only to the speaker, which is in turn dependent on the specific contextual situation. We can now examine a representative selection of these evidential (phrasal) adverbials (*más fíor* 'allegedly', *de réir dealraimh* 'apparently', *mar dhea* 'supposedly', *i mo thuairim* 'in my opinion', *is léir* 'clearly', *is cosúil* 'it seems', *is dócha* 'likely'), noting their similarities and differences, and some evidential and epistemic connotations. Some adverbials (17)–(20) leave open the possibility that the information provided may not be accurate, or the information source may be unreliable. In all of these adverbials, the scope is the full clause. The adverbial in (20) appeals to direct visual evidence as the information source, but with the stance that the evidence may not be accurate.

(17) Allegedly
Haiceáladh a guthán, más fíor.
Hack:ADJ 3SG.F.POSS phone if true
Allegedly, her phone was hacked.

(18) Supposedly
Le bheith ag cuidiú a bhí siad ann, mar dhea.
With be:AUX-PST at:PREP help:VN REL BE.AUX-PST 3PL DET supposedly
They were supposedly there to help.

(19) Apparently/According to appearances

Beidh leabhar ag teacht uaithi gan mhoill,
Be.AUX-PRS book at:PREP come:VN from:PREP+3SG.F soon
de réir dealraimh.
according appearances
She apparently has a book coming out soon.

(20)Apparently/According to appearances
Ba eisean an t-úinéir, de réir dealraimh.
COP him-EMP DET owner according appearances
It was him (that was) the owner, according to appearances.

That the information source is S, drawing on their own knowledge resources, is revealed by the adverbial used in (21). Opinion adverbials express a wide range of opinion about a situation, including: certainty, reality, sources, limitations and precision of the situation. The evidential adverbial in (22) reveals that the knowledge source is S's own knowledge resources. This sentence has an embedded complement consisting of a lexical verb and the verb arguments. The complement is indicative that the information source, while not *hearsay*, may be contradicted. The subjunctive impersonal passive coding on the verb denotes an irrealis mood, and it indicates the speaker's attitude toward the event. The subjunctive deals with actions whose actual fulfilment are not an established certainty or given fact in the mind of the speaker.

(21)Of the opinion
I mo thuairim féin, tá sé an-stuama.
In:PREP my opinion SELF BE:AUX-PRS 3SG.M very-prudent
In my own opinion, he/it is very prudent.

(22)Of the opinion
Táim den tuairim go mbronntar stádas ró-ard ar an tuairim.
Táim den tuairim go mbronntar
Be:AUX.PRS+1SG of:PREP+DET opinion to:PREP award:V-SBJN.IMP-PASS
stádas ró-ard ar an tuairim.
status too-high on:PREP DET opinion.
I am of the opinion that one awarded too high a status to the judgement.

Typically, the copula codes an established fact and the speaker is vouching for that fact. The evidential adverbial in (23) employs a copula in its syntactic structure, with an embedded THAT complement. This evidential adverbial strikes a tone that the evidence speaks for itself. Notwithstanding this, the THAT complement is indicative that the information source, while not *hearsay*, may be contradicted.

(23) Clearly
Is léir ***go*** *gcaithfimid feabhsú.*
COP clear to:PREP need:V-FUT+1PL improvement
Lit: It is clear that we will need improvement.
Clearly, we need improvement.

The adverbial example in (24) is suggestive of certainty with respect to the evidence of the information source. However, this adverbial hedges on the possibility that the information may not actually be what appears to be the case. The sentences involve a copula structure with an embedded THAT complement indicative that the information source may be contradicted. Here, the embedded THAT complement allows for a good deal of variation. Example (24a) involves an RP in the THAT complement, while example (24b) has a lexical verb and its arguments in VSO order in the RP in the THAT complement.

(24) Seems
a.
Is cosúil go bhfuil fios
COP seem COMP/to:PREP BE.AUX.PRS know
do ghnó agatsa!
2SG.POSS business at:PREP+2SG.EMP
It seems that you know your business!

b.
Is cosúil gur inis sé dalladh scéalta
COP seem COMP told.V-PST 3SG.M blindly stories
don duine sin.
to:PREP+DET person DET
It seems that he blindly told stories to that person.

The evidential adverbial in (25) indicates that the information source is the available evidence, and is based on the probability that the information provided by the evidence is correct, while allowing that it may not.

(25) Likely
Is dócha go bhfuair sé bás ón bhfuacht.
COP likely COMP/to:PREP get:V-PST 3SG.M death from:PREP cold
It is likely that he died from the cold.

Overall, we can see that these examples of evidential adverbials reveal a stance in S's commitment towards the information given, but allow for possible epistemic readings. As we have seen, these signal the source of information knowledge, but also reflect the commitment of the speaker towards the veracity of the knowledge in some way. We have seen that these variously include:

i. The possibility that the information provided may not be accurate, or the information source may be unreliable.
ii. The information source can be the speaker, drawing on their own knowledge resources.
iii. Revealing that the knowledge source is the speaker's own knowledge resources. the information source may be contradicted.
iv. Appealing to direct visual evidence as the information source, but with the stance that the evidence may not be accurate.
v. Coding an established fact and the speaker is vouching for that fact.
vi. Striking a tone that the evidence speaks for itself.
vii. Suggesting a level of certainty with respect to the evidence of the information source.
viii. Hedging on the possibility that the information may not actually be what appears to be the case. Therefore, the information source may be contradicted.

These examples of evidential adverbials are evidence that the evidential hierarchy accurately reflects the situation with Irish in that they move S's commitment towards the information into a more epistemic direction.

5.4 Some comments on the evidential as an assertive speech act

We have found important facts on how evidentiality is expressed in Irish as a type of assertive speech act. The primary insight is that the evidential strategy of Irish has pragmatic dimensions and that the language employs a range of means to code evidentiality, including those that are lexical, syntactic, and adverbial. We have seen that evidentiality is to do with signalling the source of the information delivered in the in the evidence channel. The clause complement type reflects a meaning difference between direct evidential strategy and marking of hearsay. With visual and aural modes, the verb in the first clause identifies the information channel, while the verb in the second clause identifies the reported event or information. With the sense and cognitive modes, the clause organisation differs from that found in the visual and aural modes. Here, there is only one clause and the second argument encodes an RP encapsulating the sense of perceived information. An evidential hierarchy plays a guiding role in the evidential strategy with one pole (see, hear), coding more credibility, with (smell, taste) towards in the centre of the continuum, followed by the verbs (aware, know), then followed by adverbials towards the other pole and coding less believable information. One of the evidential hierarchy poles, that with less believable information, overlaps with an epistemic stance on the knowledge, reflecting the level of the speaker's commitment on the uttered statement. The expression of evidentiality may have epistemic connotations. This evidential overlap with an epistemic stance has been reported as something found in European languages. The 'reported' term may have a connotation of 'unreliable' information. The evidential may be used to indicate surprise at unexpected admissions or new information. Finally, the evidential hierarchy is productive in use of the language.

6 The directive speech acts

6.1 Introduction to the directive speech act

In the context of Irish, this chapter examines how the aim of a directive speech act by S is to cause the hearer H of the directive utterance to perform some action. This communicative function of a directive speech act is essential to our human interaction. Directives express the speaker's attitude toward some prospective action by the hearer. That is, a directive expresses an attitude of S toward some prospective action by H and reflects the intention of S that the utterance, or the attitude it expresses, is to be taken as a reason for H to undertake the action. The term directive is due to Searle (1975b:344–369). According to Searle, directive speech acts are satisfied, indeed, are complied with, if the world comes to match its propositional content. That is, they have a world-to-word direction of fit. This match must result from the performance of the directive itself. In order to comply with a directive 'mow the lawn', then my mowing of the lawn must be caused by this request in order to count as compliance. Searle posits that a directive necessarily constitutes an expression of S's desire that this directive be satisfied. Following Alston (2000:99–102), one might then define directives as an attempt by S to get H to modify the context in such a way that H has an obligation to bring about the truth of the propositional content or to provide some appropriate reason for not doing the directed action.

However, some problematic but interesting issues are presented by the directives involving permission, advice, and warning. It is the case, for example, that many speech acts which are classified as directives are not necessarily expressions of desire. While Searle & Vanderveken (1985:198) classify permission and advice as directives, we can note that both types of act can be performed without S having the desire that the propositional content of the speech act become true. One may, for example, grant permission to H to do some action X while having a strong desire that, instead, H should really do some other action Y. One can advise H to do some action without having any desire that H actually do that action. S may advise but not care all that much if at all about the outcome by H. In turn, one may give advice or issue a warning without caring much whether or not H takes that advice or heeds the warning. Moreover, it is not certain that any advice or warning actually imposes an obligation on H. Though, it may be the case that issuing even some apparently disinterested advice may commit S to have a weak preference that H follows the advice (2). This motivates us to consider permission, warning, and advice as members of the class of directives (Aikhenvald 2010:201–203; Jary & Kissine 2014:64–65).

(1)

Question S:	*Conas is féidir liom dul go dtí an stáisiún bus?*
	How do I get to the bus station?
Answer H:	*Tóg an chéad chasadh eile ar chlé tar* éis *na soilse tráchta.*
	Take the first turn next on the left after the traffic lights.

Bach & Harnish (1979:47–49) define directives as expressing S's intention that their utterance be taken as a reason to act. Kissine (2013, chapter 4) also defines directives as reasons to act. In Kissine's account, the status of reason to act is outlined in terms of the utterance's inferential status relative to the conversational background.

We can say, then, that the primitive speech act direct is an attempt to get the hearer to do something X while (possibly) remaining neutral about the outcome.

Directives have the propositional content constraint that the propositional content represents a future course of action by H, and also have the preparatory conditions that H must be capable of carrying out the action X specified in the propositional content.

Directive illocutionary forces have the world-to-word direction of fit. A consequence of the illocutionary point of the directive illocutions is that S, by virtue of their utterance, creates reasons for H to change the world by acting in such a way as to bring about success in achieving the direction of fit (Searle & Vanderveken 1985:94). Many illocutionary points can be achieved with different degrees of strength in the world of the utterance. The degree of strength is determined by the mode of achievement of the illocution.

The degree of strength of commanding and ordering H to do X is stronger than (merely) requesting or asking H to do X. The increased degree of strength comes from the application of some position of power or position of authority by S over H. There are many interrelationships between the factors of preparatory conditions, mode of achievement, and degree of strength. For example, a command has the preparatory condition that S must be in a position of authority over H to achieve the illocutionary point. The mode of achievement of the directive illocutionary point is that S achieves the illocutionary point in the application of authority. A command has a degree of strength stronger than that of a request. Also, like a command, an order has a degree of strength stronger than a request because of the respective modes of achievement. We indicate this relative degree of strength as: command > order > request > ask.

S succeeds in issuing a felicitous command to H when the following hold:

i. The illocutionary point of the utterance is to attempt to get H do X, where X is some act.
ii. The mode of achievement of this attempt to get H do X is made by applying the position of authority of S over H, with a strong degree of strength.
iii. The propositional content condition is that S expresses the proposition that H will do X as a future act.
iv. S proposes that (s)he is in a position of authority over H with respect to the future act X, and that H has the ability to do X.
v. S presupposes all of the propositional presuppositions that may be applicable. These presuppositions reflect preparatory conditions.
vi. The sincerity condition is that S expresses the desire that H do X with an appropriate degree of strength.

Sentence forms that encode directive situations have an irrealis quality that reflects the distinction between actualised and non-actualised states of affairs. Directives, then, will not have any past tense marking on the matrix verb as the directive is current in present time where [T = now] and all directed proposed/prospective actions are to occur in some future time of [T > now].

Directive situations are those in which S desires a state of affairs (SoA) to become true and directs/orders/commands, or otherwise appeals to H to make the SoA true. The desired SoA has not occurred yet. Hence, directives encode situations that are not yet actualised and, as such, have an irrealis status. In many languages this is frequently encoded by irrealis markers, but this is not the case in Irish.

There is a significant overlap in the domain of the directive speech act and the imperative as a mood. Therefore, it is essential to clarify what is meant by the two terms directive and imperative as they are not always used in the same way. For Van Olmen & Heinold (2017:2), the term directive is traditionally taken to refer to any linguistic form which counts as 'an attempt … by the speaker to get the hearer to do something' (Searle 1976:11). The term imperative is usually employed for the grammatical form in a language that is dedicated to the expression of directivity (Searle 1969:121; van der

Auwera 2006:565). Mauri & Sansò (2011:3491) reserve the label directives for forms which encode that 'the speaker wishes a state of affairs (SoA) to become true and conveys an appeal to the addressee(s) to help make this SoA true'. The term imperative is used for particular linguistic forms that prototypically call upon the addressee(s) to help realise some state of affairs and 'directive strategy' for any linguistic form that can fulfil the same function. Aikhenvald (2010:1–2) defines the imperative as the form that is dedicated to prototypically conveying a command, and understood as an attempt to get an addressee to act. The assumption that the imperative's core function is to issue directives in the traditional sense of speech act theory is appealing. Jary & Kissine (2016) propose a concept of imperative as follows:

> A sentence-type whose only prototypical function is to provide the addressee(s) with a reason to act, that is suitable for the performance of the full range of directive speech acts, and whose manifestations are all morphologically and syntactically homogeneous with the second person even in English, the use of the imperative as a permission, for instance, is very infrequent and highly dependent on contextual clues such as *yes* and the fixed expression *go ahead.* … It is also clear from the type of modality involved that permissions differ substantially from more prototypical uses like orders: the former set up a possibility whereas the latter create a necessity.
>
> Jary & Kissine (2016:132)

The label *imperative* is (typically) reserved for directive speech acts in which the H coincides with the performer of the directed action (as in [H do X]).

The imperative of Irish is reported on by Ó Baoill (2010:274ff). He indicates that the imperative mood is used with commands, requests or various incitements, with different characteristics depending on the type of relationship pertaining between S and H or prospective agent. In positive forms there is no common imperative marker, but there is a specific ending for all persons including an impersonal marker.

According to Ó Baoill, the imperative is restricted regarding the number of semantic distinctions expressed and their use with different tenses because of the nature of commands and requests. The 2SG is regarded as the unmarked directive, with zero marking. Imperatives present a course of action in which S desires H to fulfil. The directive force will depend on the immediate context in which it is given and the authority of S over H. The 2SG imperative is identical with the root of the verb in Irish (see Table 6.1 for 2SG form). The use of impersonal/autonomous forms of all verbs including

Table 6.1 Imperative verbal conjugations (Ó Baoill 2010:275)

	***ól* 'drink'**	***bris* 'break'**	***ordaigh* 'order'**	***éirigh* 'rise'**
1sg	*ólaim*	*brisim*	*ordaím*	*éirím*
2sg	***ól***	***bris***	***ordaigh***	***éirigh***
3sg	*óladh sé/sí ó*	*briseadh sé/sí*	*ordaíodh sé/sí*	*éiríodh sé/sí*
1pl	*laimis*	*brisimis*	*ordaímis*	*éirímis*
2pl	***ólaigí***	***brisigí***	***ordaígí***	***éirígí***
3pl	*ólaidís*	*brisidís*	*ordaídís*	*éirídís*
Aut/Impass	*óltar*	*bristear*	*ordaítear*	*éirítear*

bí 'be', as imperatives is a feature of Irish grammar (2)–(3). Verbs of saying and telling (4)–(5) are often used in directive requests for information.

(2)

a.
Óltar *an* *tae* *seo*!
Drink:V-IMPASS DET tea this
Lit: Someone should drink this tea.
Drink this tea!

b. Constructional signature: [V.TNS.IMPASS NP]

(3)

Bítear *ag an* *obair* *ar* *a* *hocht ar maidin.*
Be:V-PRS.IMPASS at DET work on PRT eight on morning
Let everyone be at work at eight in the morning.

(4)

Abair *liom* *cá* *bhfuil* *an* *cruinniu.*
Say:V-PRS.2SG to:PREP+1SG where is DET meeting
(You.SG) tell me where the meeting is taking place.

(5)

Insígí *rud* *beag* *dom.*
Tell:V-PRS.2PL thing small to:PREP+1SG
(You.PL) tell something small to me.

A directive situation is rooted in the deictic here-and-now of the utterance and requires both S and H to take part in the speech act. Moreover, the typical directive situation is reflective of a manipulative or coercive speech act in which S may have authority or power over H, and, additionally, S has expectations of H regarding the eventual fulfilment of S's intention, and desire, that H do X (Givón 1990:806ff).

6.2 The directive utterances

6.2.1 Direct

The primitive directive is direct, which is used as the name for the set of directives, and also names the directive illocutionary force. We examine *direct* first then progress to a selection of other directives of Irish. Note that the various verbs of Irish may have a somewhat different semantics to their English counterpart. In any event, the clause structure is definitely different in that it is verb initial.

The directive has a mode of achievement of its illocutionary point whereby the attempt by S to get H to do something may allow H the option of a refusal. Alternatively, it may have a mode of achievement where a refusal is not allowed to H. For example, when I direct you to do something then you are not allowed to refuse, but if I ask you to do something, I allow you the possibility of a refusal as part of my speech act.

(6) The directive speech act of direct
With S uttering UTT, S directs H to do X

Precondition	Illocutionary force	Directive
	IFID	use of direct
	Intention of S:	Get H to do X
	Desire of S:	S wants H to do X
	Authority of S:	S has authority over H
	Power of S:	S may or may not have power over H
	Degree of Strength:	++ 2
	Mode of Achievement:	H must do X
	Mode of Achievement:	No refusal is allowed by H
	Obligation:	Modal obligation on H to do X
	Ability:	H has the ability to do X
	Core common ground established	

Realisation	S directs H to do X S expresses the BELIEF that P of UTT S intends that H do X because of S's utterance S's authority over H is sufficient reason for H to do X Emergent common ground constructed
Postcondition	H does X Common ground updated

(7)

a.
Treoraím do chuid iarrachtaí i dtreo
Guide:V-PRS+1SG your part efforts in:PREP direction
an toraidh deiridh.
DET result final
I direct your efforts towards the final result.
b. Constructional signature: [V.TNS NP RP]

(8)

a.
Tugtar treoir duit leis seo clárú láithreach.
V-PRES.IMPASS guide to:PREP+2SG with:PREP this register immediately
You are directed to register immediately.

(9)

a.
Tá tú dírithe leis seo chuig X.
Be:AUX-PRS 2SG direct:VA with:PREP this towards X
You are hereby directed to X.

6.2.2 Require

A requirement reflects the belief and the intention that S is presuming that S has the authority over H (be it physical, psychological, or institutional authority) that gives power to the utterance, and therefore increases the degree of strength. Requirements reflect expressed intention of S that H take S's utterance as a sufficient reason to act.

Requirements do not necessarily involve S's expressing any desire at all that H act in a certain way. It might be quite clear that S couldn't care less. Instead, what S expresses is the belief that his utterance constitutes sufficient reason for H to perform the action. To require has the preparatory condition of need that X is to be done by H. There is typically a particular reason for requiring H to do X.

(10) The directive speech act of require

With S uttering UTT, S requires H to do X

Precondition	Illocutionary force	Directive
	IFID	use of require
	Intention of S:	Get H to do X
	Desire of S:	S wants H to do X
	Authority of S:	S has authority over H
	Power of S:	S may or may not have power over H
	Degree of Strength:	+++++ 5
	Mode of Achievement:	H must do X
	Mode of Achievement:	No refusal is allowed by H
	Obligation:	Modal obligation on H to do X
	Ability:	H has the ability to do X
	Core common ground established	
Realisation	S directs H to do X	
	S expresses the BELIEF that P of UTT	
	S INTENDS that H do X because of S's utterance	
	S's authority over H is sufficient reason for H to do X, and	
	Emergent common ground constructed	
Postcondition	H does X	
	Common ground updated	

(11)

a.

Teastaíonn *cabhair uaim* *láithreach.*

Require:V-PRS help from:PREP+1SG immediately

I require-help immediately.

b. Constructional signature: [V.TNS NP NP]

(12)

a.

Ceanglaítear *ort* *faoin* *dlí* *clárú.*

Bind:V-PRS-IMPASS on:PREP+2SG under law registration

You are required under law to register.
b. Constructional signature: [V.TNS NP NP]

(13)
a.
Tá an chúirt ag ordú duit bheith i láthair.
Be:AUX.PRS DET court at:PREP ordering:VN to:PREP+2SG be:AUX attendance
Lit: The court is ordering to you (to) be in attendance.
The court orders you to attend.
b. Constructional signature: [V.TNS NP NP]

(14)
a.
Tá mé ag iarraidh ort
Be:AUX.PRS 1SG at:PREP try:VN on:PREP+2SG
bheith umhal dom.
be:AUX obedient to:PREP+1SG
Lit: I am requiring of you (to) be obedient to me.
I require you to obey me.
b. Constructional signature: [V.TNS NP NP]

(15)
a.
Tá cabhair ag teastáil uainn. láithreach bonn.
Be:AUX.PRS help at:PREP need:VN from:PREP+1PL immediately now
Lit: Help is requiring from us immediately now.
We require immediate assistance.

(16)
a.
Tá ceangal dlí ort clárú.
Be:AUX.PRS connection law on:PREP+2SG registration
Lit: Law binds on you to register.
You are legally required to register.

Requirements, such as ordering, should not be confused with requests, no matter how strong the request might ones. In a request, S expresses the intention that H take S's expressed desire as a reason to act. The intention of S is to get H to do X while the desire of S is that S wants H to do X and that this is sufficient as a reason to act.

(17)

a.

Iarraimid *do* *chúnamh* *láithreach.*
Request:V-PRS+1PL your assistance immediately
We request your immediate assistance.

b. Constructional signature: [V.TNS NP NP]

6.2.3 Command, order

There are some subtle differences between a command and an order. A command requires that S be in a position of authority and not simply a position of power over H. With a command, for S to direct H by invoking a position of authority or power commits S to not allowing or permitting H the option of a refusal.

(18) The directive speech act of command

With S uttering UTT, S commands H to do X

Precondition	Illocutionary force	Directive
	IFID	use of command
	Intention of S:	Get H to do X
	Desire of S:	S wants H to do X
	Authority of S:	S has authority over H
	Power of S:	S may have power over H
	Degree of Strength:	+++++ 5
	Mode of Achievement:	H must do X.
	Mode of Achievement:	No refusal is allowed by H
	Obligation:	Modal obligation on H to do X
	Ability:	H (probably) has the ability to do X
	Core common ground established	
Realisation	S directs H to do X	
	S expresses the BELIEF that P of UTT	
	S INTENDS that H do X because of S's utterance	
	S's authority over H is sufficient reason for H to do X	
	S's potential power over H is sufficient reason for H to do X	
	S gives H permission to do X	
	Emergent common ground constructed	

Postcondition	H does X
	Common ground updated

An order requires an institutional structure of authority (Searle and Vanderveken 1985:201). One can also order someone to do something by virtue of one's position of power, whether that power is institutionally sanctioned or not. Being in a position of authority entails being able to give *permission* and therefore, order entails permit. To issue an order without being able to grant permission renders the order infelicitous. Both command and order have a strong degree of strength associated with them and invoke a position of power or authority over H. The mode of achievement commits S to not giving H the option of refusing by virtue of directing H by invoking a position of authority or power.

(19) The directive speech act of order
With S uttering UTT, S orders H to do X

Precondition	Illocutionary force	Directive
	IFID	use of order
	Intention of S:	Get H to do X
	Desire of S:	S wants H to do X
	Authority of S:	S has authority over H
	Power of S:	S has power over H
	Degree of Strength:	+++++ 5
	Mode of Achievement:	H must do X.
	Mode of Achievement:	No refusal is allowed by H
	Obligation:	Modal obligation on H to do X
	Ability:	H has the ability to do X
	Core common ground established	
Realisation	S directs H to do X	
	S expresses the BELIEF that P of UTT	
	S INTENDS that H do X because of S's utterance	
	S's authority over H is sufficient reason for H to do X	
	S's potential power over H is sufficient reason for H to do X	
	S permits H to do X	
	S gives H permission to do X	
	Emergent common ground constructed	

Postcondition H does X
Common ground updated

(20)
a.
Cuirtear iallach ort an tsíocháin a choinneáil.
put:V-PRS.IMPASS force on:PREP+2SG DET peace REL keep:VN
You are commanded/forced to keep the peace.
b. Constructional signature: [V.TNS NP NP]

(21)
a.
Ordaítear duit an tsíocháin a choinneáil.
Order:V-PRS.IMPASS on:PREP+2SG DET peace REL keep:VN
You are ordered to keep the peace.
b. Constructional signature: [V.TNS NP NP]

(22)
a.
Ordaím dóibh imeacht.
Order:V-PRS+1SG to:PREP+3PL leave:VN
I order them to leave.
b. Constructional signature: [V.TNS NP NP]

(23)
a.
Ordaím go ndíbreofaí iad.
Order:V-PRS+1SG to:PREP expel:V-COND.IMPASS 3PL
Lit: I order/command that one would expelled them.
I order that they be expelled/deported.
b. Constructional signature: [V.TNS NP NP]

6.2.4 Forbid

Forbid, as a prohibitive, essentially has the requirement that H not do a certain thing. To forbid H to do X means to *order NOT*, and is the negation of ordering. Permissives, like requirements, and prohibitives like forbid, presume the authority of S. They express S's belief, and his intention that H believe that S's utterance constitutes sufficient reason for H to (not) do a certain action.

(24)The directive speech act of forbid
With S uttering UTT, S forbids H to do X

Precondition	Illocutionary force	Directive
	IFID	use of forbid
	Intention of S:	Get H to not do X
	Desire of S:	S wants H to not do X
	Authority of S:	S has authority over H
	Power of S:	S has power over H
	Degree of Strength:	+++++ 5
	Mode of Achievement:	H must not do X
	Mode of Achievement:	Permanent over time: T.now … T>now
	Mode of Achievement:	No refusal is allowed by H
	Obligation:	Modal obligation on H to not do X
	Ability:	H has the ability to do X
	Core common ground established	
Realisation	S directs H to do X	
	S expresses the BELIEF that P of UTT	
	S INTENDS that H do X because of S's utterance	
	S's authority over H is sufficient reason for H to do X	
	S's potential power over H is sufficient reason for H to do X	
	S does not permit H to do X	
	S does not give H permission to do X	
	Emergent common ground constructed	
Postcondition	H does not do X	
	Common ground updated	

(25)

a.

Coiscim	*duit*	*méar*	*a*	*leagan*	*air.*
Forbid:V-PRS+1SG	to:PREP+2SG	finger	PRT	lay:VN	on:PREP+3SG.M

I forbid you to lay a finger on him.

b. Constructional signature: [V.TNS NP NP TO RP]

To prohibit is to forbid something with the propositional content condition that ranges over an extended period of time.

(26)

a

Toirmiscim a chuid cruinnithe.

prohibit:V-PRS+1SG POSS group meetings

I prohibit their meetings.

b. Constructional signature: [V.TNS NP PRT VN]

(27)

a.

Cuirim cosc a chruinnithe.

put:V-PRS+1SG stop POSS meetings

Lit: I put a ban/stop on their meetings.

I prohibit their meetings.

b. Constructional signature: [V.TNS NP PRT VN]

(28) The directive speech act of prohibit

With S uttering UTT, S prohibits H to do X

Precondition	Illocutionary force	Directive
	IFID	use of prohibit
	Intention of S:	Get H to not do X
	Desire of S:	S wants H to not do X
	Authority of S:	S has authority over H
	Power of S:	S has power over H
	Degree of Strength:	++++ 5
	Mode of Achievement:	H must not do X.
	Mode of Achievement:	Permanent over time: T.now … T>now
	Mode of Achievement:	No refusal is allowed by H
	Obligation:	Modal obligation on H to not do X
	Ability:	H may or may not have the ability to do X
	Core common ground established	

Realisation	S directs H to do X S expresses the BELIEF that P of UTT S INTENDS that H not do X because of S's utterance S's authority over H is sufficient reason for H to not do X S's potential power over H is sufficient reason for H to do X S does not permit H to do X S does not give H permission to do X Emergent common ground constructed
Postcondition	H does not do X Common ground updated

6.2.5 Permit

Permit is placed within the directive class of speech act verbs and is built upon the primitive speech act verb direct. To grant permission to H to do X is to perform the illocutionary act of NOT forbidding H to do X. Issuing permission to do some action entails that S prefers the realisation of the propositional content by H over some other incompatible state of affairs. Both warning and advice constitute a reason for H to act in a certain way, though not necessarily one that provides a sufficient reason to cause this action. Also, by removing an obstacle to action, permission establishes a reason for H to act, that may be independent of S's desires. The reasons for issuing a permissive are either to grant (a request for) permission or to remove some restriction against the action in question. It would seem, therefore, that S presumes either that such a request has been made or that such a restriction exists. Some of the verbs of permitting are highly specialised, such as dismiss (= permit to leave), excuse (= permit not to make amends), and release (= permit not to fulfil an obligation) (Bach & Harnish 1979:44).

(29) The directive speech act of permit

With S uttering UTT, S permits H to do X

Precondition	Illocutionary force	Directive
	IFID	use of permit
	Intention of S:	Get H to do X
	Desire of S:	S wants H to do X
	Authority of S:	S has authority over H
	Power of S:	S has no power over H

Degree of Strength:	+ 1
Mode of Achievement:	Permanent over time: T.now … T>now
Mode of Achievement:	H may or may not do X.
Mode of Achievement:	Refusal is allowed by H
Obligation:	No obligation on H to do X
Ability:	H may or may not have the ability to do X
Core common ground established	

Realisation S permits H to do X
S transfers permission to H to do X
S gives H permission to do X
S expresses the BELIEF that P of UTT
S INTENDs that H may (or may not) do X because of S's utterance
S's authority over H is sufficient reason for H to do X
Emergent common ground constructed

Postcondition H may or may do X
S is not interested in either the outcome or whether H actually does X
Common ground updated

Order, forbid, and permit are related. To order H to do X by invoking a position of authority or power commits S to not giving H the option of refusing to do X. To forbid H to do X means to *order* NOT, and is the propositional negation of ordering, and permission to do X is not granted. To permit H to do X is to perform the illocutionary act of NOT forbidding H to do X, and permission to do X is granted. The granting of permission, via permit, to carry out X is not entailed by a suggestion to do X. In suggesting X, one is just stating an opinion on how H might proceed. It makes no claims as to whether X is permissible or not. We now consider allow and the transferring of permission to H to do X.

(30) The directive speech act of allow
With S uttering UTT, S allows H to do X

Precondition	Illocutionary force	Directive
	IFID	use of allow

	Intention of S:	Get H to do X
	Desire of S:	S wants H to do X
	Authority of S:	S has authority over H
	Power of S:	S has no power over H
	Degree of Strength:	+ 1
	Mode of Achievement:	H may or may not do X
	Mode of Achievement:	Permanent over time: T.now … T>now
	Mode of Achievement:	Refusal is allowed by H
	Obligation:	No obligation on H to do X
	Ability:	H has the ability to do X
	Core common ground established	
Realisation	S allows H to do X S transfers permission to H to do X S gives H permission to do X S removes barrier from H to do X S expresses the BELIEF that P of UTT S INTENDS that H may or may not do X because of S's utterance S's authority over H is sufficient reason for H to consider doing X Emergent common ground constructed	
Postcondition	H may or may do X S is not interested in the outcome S is not interested whether H does X Common ground updated	

One example of the use of allow is shown in (31). We will compare the semantics of this with permit shortly and see the difference of use within a speech act.

(31)

a.

Ligeann *Alice Walker* *don* *aistriúchán*
Allow:V-PRS Alice Walker to:PREP+DET translation
ar 'The Purple Colour'
on 'The Colour Purple'
go *iliomad teangacha.*
to:PREP many languages.

Alice Walker allows the translation of 'The Purple Colour' into many languages.

b. Constructional signature: [V.TNS NP NP]

We can consider in some more detail the speech act verb permit, which lexicalises the granting or giving of permission, versus allow and permit. For Searle & Vanderveken (1985:202), 'to grant permission to someone to do something is to perform the act of illocutionary denegation of forbidding him to do it'. It is both interesting and useful to briefly examine some of the semantic characteristics of permit. In Irish, the verb *ceadaigh* lexicalises the concept of PERMIT within its lexical semantics to include GIVE PERMISSION as a transfer of permission construction , and we contrast *give* vs. *allow* vs. *permit* in (32). These characteristics are important to the speech act pragmatics. We set out the event chains that are encoded within this construction, reflecting times T_1, T_2, (and T_3), and these are indicated in (33).

(32)

GIVE PERMISSION	ALLOW	PERMIT
	S allows H to do X	S permits H to do X
Transfer of permission	Removal of a barrier to action	Transfer of authorisation
	Event not impeded	Barrier to action not placed

(33) Event chains reflecting times T_n

a. TRANSFER: TRANSFER of theme to a recipient or location
[Event$_1$] ______ ALLOW ____ [Event$_2$ (& *potential* Event$_n$)]]
[T_1 __________ <later> ___ T_2]

b. Give permission: Transfer of permission and purpose of permission explicit
[Event$_1$] BEFORE [Event$_2$] PURP [Event$_3$]
T_1 _________ <trigger> __ T_2 ________ < immediate> T_3

c. ALLOW: REMOVAL of a barrier to action and event not impeded
[[Event$_1$] BUT _____ [Event$_2$] _________ [Event$_3$]]
T_1 _______________ T_2 ________________ T_3

d. PERMIT: TRANSFER OF AUTHORISATION and a barrier to action not placed
[[Event$_1$]_______ PERMIT [Event$_2$]]
T_1_____________ <later> T_2

Within the verb *cheadaigh*, shown here in the past tense form of the verb, the concept of PERMIT also lexicalises the transfer of authority from the 'x' Actor to the 'z' Recipient (34). In speech act terms this transfer of authority to do X is from S to H. As a construction, this has two variants and we give examples of each following. The first variant, shown in examples (35) and (36) of the construction, consists of a single event encoded with a single verb. The second construction variant consists of a complex multi-event with two verbs and argument sharing. We show first the single event/single verb construction.

(34) *Ceadaíonn*: V.TNS xNP yNP zPP :construction signature

(35)

a.

Ceadaíonn an réiteoir cúl don Mhí.

Permit:V-PRS DET referee goal to:PREP+DET Meath:N

The referee permits the goal to Meath.

xNP yNP zPP

b. Constructional signature: [V.TNS NP NP PP]

(36)

a.

Ceadaíonn an chúirt an dlí um

Permit:V-PRS DET court DET law about:PREP

íosphá i Washington

low-pay:N in:PREP Washington:N

The court permits the minimum-wage law in Washington.

xNP yNP zPP

b. Constructional signature: [V.TNS NP NP PP]

The second variant, with a constructional signature (37), consists of a complex multi-event with two verbs and argument sharing (38)–(39). This is a complex multi-event construction with two verbs. Argument sharing occurs with the event encoded by V2 being the permitted action. The event encoded by V2 is reflected as a VN in the syntax. The V1 verb is a form of *ceadaigh* 'permit'.

(37)

Ceadaíonn xNP zPP yNP a VN : construction signature

V_1 ____________________ V_2

[[$Event_1$]____ PERMIT [$Event_2$]]

T_1________________ <later> T_2

(38)

Ní cheadófar do mhúinteoirí na Dála
NEG permit:V-FUT-IMPERS to:PREP teachers (of) DET Dáil
an jab scoile
DET job:N school:N
a choimeád oscailte.
REL keep:VN open:VN
Lit: *One* will not permit teachers within the Dáil to keep open the school job.
Teachers in the Dáil will not be permitted to keep **open** their school jobs.
xNP zPP yNP a VN
b. Constructional signature: [V.TNS NP PP NP PRT VN]

(39)

a.
Ceadaíonn Kennedy don CIA ionradh náireach
permit:V-PRS Kennedy to:PREP+DET CIA:N invasion:N shameful:ADJ
a dhéanamh ar Chúba.
REL do:VN on:PREP Cuba
Lit: Kennedy permits the CIA to do.make the infamous invasion on Cuba.
Kennedy permits the CIA to **make** the infamous invasion of Cuba.
xNP zPP yNP a VN
b. Constructional signature: [V.TNS NP PP NP PRT VN]

That permit is related to forbid is demonstrated by (40) where the act is not permitted, that is, it is forbidden, over persistent time.

(40)

a.
Ní ceadóidh Alice Walker 'The Colour Purple' a aistriú.
NEG permit:V-FUT Alice Walker 'The Colour Purple' REL translate:VN
go hEabhrais.
to:PREP Hebrew:N
Alice Walker will not permit 'The Colour Purple' to be translated to Hebrew.
Alice Walker will forbid 'The Colour Purple' to be translated to Hebrew.
b. Constructional signature: [V.TNS NP PP NP PRT VN]

(41)

NEG **[do'** (AW, CAUSE.PERMIT **[do'** (Ø) **translate_to'** (TCP, Hebrew)])]

An alternative way of indicating forbid in Irish is shown in (42), 'X puts a stop on RP'.

(42)

a.

Cuireann Alice Walker cosc ar 'The Colour Purple' a aistriú .
Put:V-PRS Alice Walker block on 'The Colour Purple' REL translate:VN
go hEabhrais.
to:PREP Hebrew:N
Alice Walker forbids the translation of 'The Colour Purple' into Hebrew.

b. Constructional signature: [V.TNS NP NP]

6.2.6 Insist

Insist is a strong directive while advise is a weak directive. It has a different mode of achievement of the illocutionary point, that of persistence. Here, we examine insist, and advise following this.

(43) The directive speech act of insist

With S uttering UTT, S insists H do X

Precondition	Illocutionary force	Directive
	IFID	use of insist
	Intention of S:	Get H to do X
	Desire of S:	S wants H to do X
	Authority of S:	S may or may not have authority over H
	Power of S:	S may or may not have power over H
	Degree of Strength:	++++ 4
	Mode of Achievement:	Permanent over time: T.now … T>now
	Mode of Achievement:	H may or may not do X.
	Mode of Achievement:	Refusal is allowed by H

	Obligation:	No obligation on H to do X
	Core common ground established	
Realisation	S insists H do X S expresses the BELIEF that P of UTT S expresses the DESIRE that H do X S INTENDS that H may do X because of S's DESIRE Emergent common ground constructed	
Postcondition	H may or may do X S is definitely interested in the outcome and that H actually do X Common ground updated	

(44)

a.

Áitím *go roghnóimid an t-iarrthóir*
Insist:V-PRS+1SG that select:V-PRS+1PL DET candidate
don agallamh.
to:PREP+DET interview
I insist we select the candidate for the interview.

b. Constructional signature: [V.TNS NP THAT RP]

6.2.7 Advise

Advise is a weak directive. According to Bach & Harnish (1979:49), to advise is where S expresses the belief that H doing X is a good idea and that it is in H's interest to do the action, rather than S expressing a desire that H do a certain action. S expresses the intention that H should take S's belief as a reason to act. The directive advise varies in strength of the expressed belief.

Furthermore, some imply a reason that the recommended action is a good idea. In a warning, for example, S presumes the presence of some source of danger or trouble for H, and that H should do a certain action that is beneficial to H (Bach & Harnish 1979:44). As a directive, advise may imply a reason as to why the recommended action is a good idea. While it is possible, of course, that S does not actually care one way or another whether H takes the advice. As a directive:

S's intentions are that
H understands that S believes that
S has the attitudes expressed and that
H should do the action X that
H is being advised to perform.

(45) The directive speech act of advise
With S uttering UTT, S advises H do X

Precondition	Illocutionary force	Directive
	IFID	use of advise
	Intention of S:	Get H to either do X or favour X
	Desire of S:	S wants H to do X
	Authority of S:	S has no authority over H
	Power of S:	S has no power over H
	Degree of Strength:	+ 1
	Mode of Achievement:	H may or may not do X.
	Mode of Achievement:	Refusal is allowed by H
	Obligation:	No obligation on H to do X
	Core common ground established	
Realisation	S advises H to do X	
	S expresses the BELIEF that P of UTT	
	S expresses the DESIRE that H do X	
	S INTENDS that H consider doing X because of S's DESIRE	
	Emergent common ground constructed	
Postcondition	H may or may do X	
	S is not interested in the outcome	
	S is not interested whether H does X	
	Common ground updated	

(46)

a.

Comhairlím go dtógfadh. sí sos ón obair.
Advise:V-PRS+1SG that take:V-FUT 3SG.F break from:PREP+DET work
I advise that she take a break from the work.

b. Constructional signature: [V.TNS NP THAT RP]

(47)

a.

Cuirim comhairle don iarrthóir
Put:V-PRS+1SG advice. to:PREP+DET candidate
cur isteach ar an bpost.
put:VN in on DET job
I advise the candidate to apply for the post.

b. Constructional signature: [V.TNS NP NP THAT RP]

6.2.8 Recommend

To recommend is to advise with the preparatory condition that the state of affairs represented by the proposition is good in general and good for H. When one recommends, one recommends a course of action, or person, or thing to H, with a view to H then doing the recommended action X and favouring the person or thing/X.

(48) The directive speech act of recommend
With S uttering UTT, S recommends H do X

Precondition	Illocutionary force	Directive
	IFID	use of recommend
	Intention of S:	Get H to favour or consider X
	Desire of S:	S wants H to favour or consider X
	Authority of S:	S has no authority over H
	Power of S:	S has no power over H
	Degree of Strength:	++ 2
	Mode of Achievement:	H may or may not do X.
	Mode of Achievement:	Refusal is allowed by H
	Obligation:	No obligation on H to do X
	Core common ground established	The state of affairs represented by the proposition is good and beneficial to H
Realisation	S recommends that H favour or consider X	
	S expresses the BELIEF that P of UTT	
	S expresses the BELIEF that the effect is beneficial to H	
	S expresses the DESIRE that H favour or consider X	
	S INTENDS that H to favour or consider X	
	Emergent common ground constructed	

Postcondition H may or may do X
S is not interested in the outcome
S is not interested in whether H favour or consider X
Common ground updated

(49)
a.
Molaim an t-iarrthóir don phost.
Recommend:V-PRS+1SG DET candidate for:PREP+DET job
I recommend the candidate for the job.
b. Constructional signature: [V.TNS NP NP]

(50)
a.
Molaimid duit comhairle dhlí a fháil.
Recommend:V-PRS+1PL to:PREP+2SG advice legal REL obtain:VN.
We recommend to you that legal advice be obtained.
b. Constructional signature: [V.TNS NP TO NP THAT RP]

6.2.9 Request

The set of requests express S's desire that H do something (Bach & Harnish 1979:48). Moreover, they express S's intention (or, if compliance is not mandatory, S's desire or wish) that H take this expressed desire as reason to act. According to Bach & Harnish, the perlocutionary intentions of S are that S intends that H believe that S has the desire and the intention expressed and that S intends that H perform the action requested.

In this regard, verbs of requesting vary in strength of the attitude expressed, as between *invite* and *insist* and between *ask* and *beg*. The stronger ones convey a sense of intensity, earnestness, or urgency. They can convey both an appeal to H's sympathy and have a special manner of performance. Some verbs of requesting are rather specialised in scope. For example, *summon* refer to requests for H's presence while *beg* and *solicit* apply to requests for contributions or favours. Some convey a sense of earnestness or urgency, while others convey both an appeal to the hearer's sympathy and some special manner of performance. A request is a directive illocution that has a polite mode of achievement of its illocutionary point and which allows for the possibility of a grant or refusal by H.

(51) The directive speech act of request
With S uttering UTT, S requests H do X

Precondition	Illocutionary force	Directive
	IFID	use of request
	Intention of S:	Get H to do X
	Desire of S:	S wants H to do X
	Authority of S:	S has no authority over H
	Power of S:	S has no power over H
	Degree of Strength:	+++ 3
	Mode of Achievement:	S is polite
	Mode of Achievement:	H may or may not do X.
	Mode of Achievement:	Refusal is allowed by H
	Obligation:	No obligation on H to do X
	Ability:	H may not have the ability to fulfil the request
	Core common ground established	
Realisation	S requests H to do X	
	S expresses the BELIEF that P of UTT	
	S expresses the DESIRE that H do X	
	S INTENDS that H do X because of S's DESIRE	
	Emergent common ground constructed	
Postcondition	H may or may do X	
	S is interested in the outcome and that H do X	
	Common ground updated	

Example (52) is the polite form of a directive, issued as a request.

(52)

a.
Táthar ag iarraidh. ar an bpobal gan siúl
Be:AUX.PRS.IMPASS at request:VN on DET public not walk:VN
ar an bhféar.
on DET grass
Lit: One is requesting on the public not walk on the grass.
The public are requested to not walk on the grass.
[= Do not walk on the grass!]

b. Constructional signature: [V.TNS.IMPASS AT VN RP]

6.2.10 Beg

To beg is to request in a humble manner while expressing a strong desire for something, because of a strong need. The mode of achievement is the humble manner. The degree of strength is strong.

(53) The directive speech act of beg

With S uttering UTT, S begs H do X

Precondition	Illocutionary force	Directive
	IFID	use of beg
	Intention of S:	Get H to do X
	Desire of S:	S wants H to do X
	Authority of S:	S has no authority over H
	Power of S:	S has no power over H
	Degree of Strength:	++ 2
	Mode of Achievement:	S is humble
	Mode of Achievement:	S is intense in the begging request
	Mode of Achievement:	H may or may not do X.
	Mode of Achievement:	Refusal is allowed by H
	Obligation:	No obligation on H to do X
	Core common ground established	
Realisation	S begs H to do X	
	S expresses the BELIEF that P of UTT, and that this is due to a strong need	
	S expresses the DESIRE that H do X	
	S INTENDS that H do X because of S's DESIRE	
	Emergent common ground constructed	
Postcondition	H may or may do X	
	S is interested in the outcome and that H do X	
	Common ground updated	

(54)

a.

Impím *ort* *ar airgead.*

implore:V-PRS+1SG from:PREP+2SG for money

I implore you for money.

b. Constructional signature: [V.TNS NP NP FOR NP]

(55)

a.

Guím *airgead* *ort.*
Beg:V-PRS+1SG money from:PREP+2SG
I beg you for money.

b. Constructional signature: [V.TNS NP NP FOR NP]

6.2.11 Ask

Asking questions are special cases of requests, in that what is requested is that H provide S with certain information. There are differences between the different questions types. Also, Bach & Harnish (1979:44) note that the form of questioning known as *interrogate* suggests duress in a way that the more usual *ask* does not.

Ask has two distinct uses: 1) asking someone to *do something*, and 2) asking a *question*. We consider the first possibility here, asking someone to *do something,* and address the second possibility in the next chapter given its significant complexity.

(56) The directive speech act of ask

With S uttering UTT, S ask H do X

Precondition	Illocutionary force	Directive
	IFID	use of ask
	Intention of S:	Get H to do X
	Desire of S:	S wants H to do X
	Authority of S:	S may or may not have authority over H
	Power of S:	S may or may not have power over H
	Degree of Strength:	++ 2
	Mode of Achievement:	H may or may not do X
	Mode of Achievement:	Refusal is allowed by H
	Obligation:	No obligation on H to do X
	Core common ground established	

Realisation	S asks H to do X S expresses the BELIEF that P of UTT S expresses the DESIRE that H do X S INTENDS that H should do X because of S's DESIRE Emergent common ground constructed
Postcondition	H may or may do X S is interested in the outcome and that H do X Common ground updated

(57) Asking someone to do something

a.

Iarraim ort gan siúl ar an bhféar.
Ask:V-PRS+1SG on:PREP+2SG not walk:VN on DET grass
I ask you (to) not walk on the grass.

b. Constructional signature: [V.TNS NP NP RP]

(58) Asking someone to do something

a.

Iarrtar ort gan siúl ar an bhféar.
Ask:V-PRS.IMPASS on:PREP+2SG not walk:VN on DET grass
One asks you (to) not walk on the grass.

b. Constructional signature: [V.TNS.IMPASS NP RP]

(59) Asking someone to do something

a.

Iarrtar ort an féar a choimeád.
Ask:V-PRS.IMPASS on:PREP+2SG DET grass REL keep:VN
One asks that you preserve the grass.

b. Constructional signature: [V.TNS.IMPASS NP NP THAT RP]

(60) Asking someone to do something

a.

Iarrtar ort meabhrú do do pháiste gan rith isteach an geata ar maidin (dea-homhartha é seo don scoil ach níl sé go maith ó thaobh sábháilteachta de!) agus gan siúl ar an bhféar.

One asks of you to remind your child not to run into the gate in the morning (this is a good sign for school but not good for safety!) and not to walk on the grass.

(61)

a.

Iarrtar ort gan dul ar shuíomh na scoile de bharr na tógála atá ar siúl faoi láthair.
One asks of you to not visit the school site due to the construction currently underway.

We already mentioned that a question is an instance of a request in that H is requested to provide S with certain information. There are differences between questions, as we will see in the next chapter. However, for this particular discussion, question forms such as examination type questions and the various rhetorical questions are not important. We will examine in detail the speech act of asking a question in the next chapter, while also identifying the various question types along with their purpose and function.

6.3 Some comments on directives

The directive speech acts are seen to typically reflect the following degrees of strength: 5: require, command, order, forbit/prohibit; 4: insist; 3: request; 2: direct, recommend, beg, ask; 1: permit/allow, advise.

The directives have the syntactic patterns, the various constructional schemas, indicated by the various examples (62). These can be generalised to (63). The directive can sometimes involve use of the impersonal passive form where the actor/grammatical subject is backgrounded within the directive. The present tense is recorded on the verb as the directive is delivered in real time by S to H.

(62) The syntactic patterns underpinning the directive speech acts of Irish

Speech act	IFID/SA Verb	Constructional schema
Directive	drink	[V.TNS.IMPASS NP]
	direct	[V.TNS NP RP]
	require	[V.TNS NP NP]
	request	[V.TNS NP NP]
	order	[V.TNS NP TO RP | THAT RP]
	forbid	[V.TNS NP NP (TO RP)]
	permit	[V.TNS NP NP TO RP]
	prohibit	[V.TNS NP PRT VN]
	allow	[V.TNS NP NP]
	permit	[V.TNS NP NP PP]
	permit	[V.TNS NP PP NP PRT VN]
	insist	[V.TNS NP THAT RP]
	advise	[V.TNS NP THAT RP]
	advise	[V.TNS NP NP THAT RP]
	recommend	[V.TNS NP NP]
	recommend	[V.TNS NP TO NP THAT RP]
	request	[V.TNS.IMPASS AT VN RP]
	beg	[V.TNS NP NP FOR NP]
	ask	[V.TNS NP NP RP]
	ask	[V.TNS.IMPASS NP RP]

(63)

[V.TNS: PRS ^{actor}NP NP|RP (TO NP | AT VN | FOR NP | PRT VN | THAT RP]

We summarise, across Table 6.2a and 6.2b, the various dimensions of the directive speech act.

In the next chapter, we examine more closely the (directive) speech act of asking a question, the various question types and clausal syntactic underpinning, and their purpose and function.

Table 6.2a The directive speech act dimensions – part 1

IL: Directive	Direct	Require	Command	Order	Forbid/prohibit	Permit/allow	Insist
Intention of S				Get H to do X			
Desire of S				S wants H to do X			
Authority of S over H				Y			?
S power over H	–		?		Y	N	?
Deg. of Strength	**2**			**5**		**1**	**4**
Mode of Achievement	H must do X	H must do X	H must do X	H must do X	H must not do X. Lasting over time: No refusal is allowed by H	Lasting over time. H may or may not do X. H may refuse	Lasting over time. H may or may not do X. H may refuse
Obligation on H			Y			N	
Permission given			Y	Y	N	Y	–
Permission transferred					N	Y	–
Barrier removed					N	Y	–
S interest in result			Y			N	Y

Table 6.2b The directive speech act dimensions – part 2

IL: Directive	Advise	Recommend	Request	Beg	ask
Intention of S	Get H to favour X	Get H to favour or consider X		Get H to do X	
Desire of S	S wants H to do X	S wants H to favour or consider X		S wants H to do X	
Authority of S over H		N			?
S power over H		N			?
Deg. of Strength	1	2	3		2
Mode of Achievement	H may or may not do X. H may refuse.	H may or may not do X. H may refuse.	S is polite. H may or may not do X. H may refuse.	S is humble. S is intense. H may or may not do X. H may refuse.	H may or may not do X. H may refuse.
Obligation on H		N			
Permission given	–	–	–	N	–
Permission transferred	–	–	–	N	–
Barrier removed	–	–	–	N	–
S Interest in result	N			Y	

7 The question as a type of directive speech act

This chapter characterises in detail the pragmatic dimensions of the question forms of Irish while also looking at the supporting syntax, and the various functions of these questions. A question is an instance of a directive request speech act in that H is requested to provide S with certain information. There are differences between questions types. Specifically, Irish has three questions forms: alternate, polar yes-no interrogatives, and information questions. We examine each of these question forms of Irish in turn, looking at their syntactic and semantics structure, and their pragmatics in use in a questioning situation. Questions are best understood as part of a dialogue with a chain of speech acts. Therefore, to gain a more complete insight into the question forms and their functions, we also consider the nature of the answers given to each. As mentioned, questions are directive speech acts and, as such, are an attempt by S to get H to provide an answer to the question. In the sense of *ask a question*, S requests that H perform a speech act by way of providing an answer-response to S's question. Importantly, the form of the response is determined by the propositional content of the question. The required response to one of these question forms may be constrained in certain ways depending on the nature of the question.

The speech act of requesting information is associated with interrogative forms (1). These interrogative sentences fall into three major classes depending on their syntactic and semantic properties. The required response to one of these question forms may be constrained in certain ways depending on the nature of the question.

(1) Types of questions

Alternative questions	The answer must be based on one of the *options* presented within the question.
Polar yes-no questions	The answer can only contain an *affirmation or negative.*
Information questions (WH-questions)	The answer is guided by the wh-word used, which serves to target a *specific information gap*, allowing an open set of possible but relevant replies.

If the question is an alternative questions then the answer to it is constrained to only allow a choice of one from the list of options presented within the actual question. If the question is a yes-no question, S expresses the propositional content of the answer in the asking of the question, and seeks an affirmative or negative response. In such a case, all that H needs to do is affirm or deny the propositional content. In information questions the form of the question contains a propositional function by virtue of the particular question particle (WH-particle) used by S, such that H is requested to fill in a value of a free variable.

The primary function of questioning is to seek information and, during our discourses, it is quite natural and normal to seek information from our partner in conversation. Similar to other language, Irish has different strategies for soliciting diverse kinds of information. These question forms of Irish act as signalling cues for the various kinds of information required, and therefore the questioning strategies require sentences with different structural forms. We see this with the IFID in (2) where the cue is the syntactic clausal schema. Another important core function of questioning is the maintenance of common ground between the interlocutors. The construction and maintenance of common ground is crucial to the retrieval of pragmatic meaning from the speech act.

(2) The directive speech act of ask a question
With S uttering UTT, S asks H to do X (= answer a question)

Precondition	Illocutionary force	Directive
	IFID	• use of the constructional schema: QPRT:*an* V-PRS NP NP (*nó* 'or' NP) → indicates an alternative question • use of the constructional schema: QPRT:*nach* V-PRS NP NP or QPRT:*nar* V-PST NP NP → indicates a polar yes-no question • use of the constructional schema:

		QPF REL V.TNS NP Where QPF is a question proform that interrogates for the kind of knowledge gap → indicates an information question (The proforms are: *Cé, Cé leis, Cé aige, Cád, Céard, Cén, Cá, Cén* áit/*Cén háit, Cathain, Cén uair, Cá huair, Cén t-am, Cén fáth, Conas, Cad é mar, Cé mhéad, Cá mhéad*)
	Intention of S:	Get H to do X
	Desire of S:	S wants H to do X
	Authority of S:	S may or may not have authority over H
	Power of S:	S may or may not have power over H
	Degree of Strength:	++ 2
	Mode of Achievement:	H may or may not do X
	Mode of Achievement:	Refusal is allowed by H
	Obligation:	No obligation on H to do X
	Core common ground established	
Realisation	S asks H to do X (=provide an answer) S expresses the BELIEF that P of UTT S expresses the DESIRE that H do X S INTENDS that H should do X because of S's DESIRE Emergent common ground constructed	
Postcondition	H may or may do X S is interested in the outcome and that H do X Common ground updated	

A central assumption is that information is freely exchanged under the Gricean Cooperative Principle (Grice 1957, 1969) and that its associated maxims apply. The Gricean Cooperative Principle Maxims are i) Quality: Speakers' contributions should be true; ii) Quantity: Speakers' contributions should be only as informative as the situation requires and speakers should refrain from saying either too little or too much; iii) Relevance:

Contributions should relate to the purpose of the exchange; iv) Manner: Contributions should avoid obscurity and ambiguity and be clear, orderly and succinct. To support the question forms and their inherent signalling cues, Irish uses a variety of syntactically significant question particles in the formation of its different question forms.

The use of question particles are common in the world's languages as a cue in the syntactic structure of interrogatives Dryer (2005:470). Other elements of the grammar of Irish have been reported on in Nolan (2008, 2012, 2013, 2017). Within dialogue in language, the use of questions and answers is common while essential (Coulthard 1992, Dayal 2018, Dryer 2005, Hamblin 1973, Holmberg 2015).

In order to ask a question, certain things must be appropriate in the context in which the speech act is uttered. As well as a sentence being grammatical, it must also be felicitous. The felicity conditions necessary for the successful realisation of the speech act of requesting information are made under the assumption that information is freely exchanged under a Gricean presumption of cooperation, already mentioned.

Certain felicity conditions apply to the questioning speech act, and these are described in (3), where the speaker = S and hearer = H, and P = some proposition.

(3) Felicity conditions on speech act of questioning

FELICITY CONDITIONS:	QUESTION
PROPOSITIONAL CONTENT:	Any proposition P
PREPARATORY CONDITION:	S questions H about proposition P *iff* (i) S does not KNOW the truth about P. (ii) S WANTS to KNOW the truth about P. (iii) S BELIEVES H KNOWS the truth about P that S wants. (iv) It is not obvious that H will provide the information without being asked
SINCERITY CONDITION:	S WANTS this information
ESSENTIAL CONDITION:	A question counts as an attempt to elicit this information

A felicitous use of a question speech act requires that S: i) not be aware of the information requested and ii) S believes that H has knowledge of that information. As part of the felicity conditions of a question, we typically presuppose ignorance, or an information gap, on the part of the speaker, and a presumption of knowledge on the part of H. Of course, S may already possess the relevant information but can still felicitously pose the question to H (as in some examination context), if H's knowledge is considered to be in doubt.

An utterance is identified as an interrogative questioning form because it has certain morphosyntactic form that provide *cues* (Dryer 2005:470–473). Consequently, it has an illocutionary force that requires an answer, or some appropriate response, from H.

The speech act formalisation concerns the objective conditions of satisfaction for the speech act and its utterance meaning. In the discourse chain, H's response to the question depends on whether H believes that S is obeying Grice's maxim of quality. If H believes that S *is* obeying the maxim of quality in asking the question, then H can conclude that S really does not know the answer. The most cooperative response from H is to simply inform S of the answer, replying as appropriate to the particular question form. If H believes that S is not obeying the maxim of quality, then H can conclude that S does actually know the answer to the question, or that an answer is not actually required. Also, H can interpret S's question rhetorically, as if it were meant only to bring the answer into the discourse.

7.1 The alternative question

In this section we examine the alternative question and its structure. Alternative questions are formulated such that they list a set of options within the question from which H must select in H's response. They do not allow for yes-no answers. Instead, an appropriate answer must contain one selection from the alternative choice options listed in the framing of the question. Alternative questions are dependent on the presence of disjunction.

In posing a simple question, it is the case that certain question particles are used that are actually common to both alternate or yes-no question forms (Table 7.1). The forms of the question particle can vary according to the morphosyntactic context and may have morphosyntactic consequences (see Table 7.2).

On occasion, in casual speech, the question particle may be omitted. The alternative questions may involve the copula.[4] While the question particle,[5] *an* is used as a marker for the alternate question, it can also be used to support a variety of simple queries, including polar questions.

Alternative questions are formulated such that they list a set of options within the question from which H must select in H's response. Alternative questions do not allow for yes-no answers and they are formulated such that the answer yes, or no, is not possible. Instead, an appropriate answer must contain one of a selection from the alternative choice options listed in the framing of the question.

As a consequence of this, the set of alternative propositions framed within the question is equal to the set of possible answers defined by virtue of the form of the question. The answer to an alternative questions has the primary quality that they only allow felicitous answers which choose one out of the set of alternatives listed in the question. Of course, an exception to this is that H may declare a lack of interest in any of the listed alternatives. That is, alternative questions list the set of alternatives as option-1, option-2, and so on, within the formulation of the question. In the alternative question, the allowed alternatives are explicitly stated within the question clause. These alternative questions of Irish takes the schematic format in (4).

---

[4] The copula is described (Doherty 1996:11) as an inflectional particle that has a paradigm for combination with various 'presentential particles' (a). Ó Sé (1990:2–4) considers the way in which various verbal grammatical categories are represented in the Irish copula, with only two basic forms of the copula occurring in Modern Irish, *is* and *ba*, that fuse with negative and interrogative particles. Linguists are not yet in complete agreement regarding the full status of the Modern Irish copula and its characteristics.

(a)

	Present/Future	Past/Conditional
INTERROGATIVE + COPULA	*an*	*ar / arbh*
negation + copula	ni/chan	nior(bh) / char(bh)
subordination + copula	gur / gurb	gur / gurbh

[5] The following works have been consulted: *An caighdeán oifigiúil* 2017; Bennett, et al. 2015; Christian Brothers 1997; de Bhaldraithe 1987; Collins Irish Grammar 2011. Doherty 1996; Doyle 2001; McCloskey 1991; McGonagle 1991; Ó Dónaill 1981; Ó Mianáin 2020, Ó Sé 1990; Ó Siadhail 1989, Ward 1974.

Data is used from the websites:

https://en.wikipedia.org/wiki/Irish_conjugation#Interrogative_particles, www.teanglann.ie/ga/, https://www.gaois.ie/en/corpora/monolingual/, www.nualeargais.ie/gnag/kopul1.htm.

Table 7.1 The appropriate question particle

present tense	affirmative	*An* + verb + subject + object$_1$ + object$_2$ *An* ólann *tú fuisce nó caife?* Do you drink whiskey or coffee?	Alternative question
	negative	*Nach* + verb + subject + object *Nach n*-ólann *tú fuisce?* Don't you drink whiskey?	Polar question
past/ preterit tense	affirmative	*Ar* + verb + subject + object$_1$ + object$_2$ *Ar* ól *tú fuisce nó caife?* Did you drink whiskey or coffee?	Alternative question
	negative	*Nár* + verb + subject + object *Nár* ól *tú fuisce?* Didn't you drink whiskey?	Polar question

Table 7.2 The morphosyntax of the question particle

Tense	Affirmative particle	Lenition/ Eclipsis[6]	Negative particle	Lenition/Eclipsis
Present	*an*	E	*nach*	E
Past/preterit	*ar*	L	*nár*	L

(4) The schematic format of an alternative question

Present tense Constructional schema: QPRT:*an* V-PRS NP NP (*nó* 'or' NP)

Past tense Constructional schema: QPRT:*ar* V-PST NP NP (*nó* 'or' NP)

[6] Lenition (called *séimhiú* in Irish) is an initial mutation that affects the spelling and pronunciation of words that begin with the letters *b*, *c*, *d*, *f*, *g*, *m*, *p*, *s*, and *t*. The word meaning does not change. Lenition is represented in written text with a letter *h* placed after the first letter of a word. Lenition is also referred to as aspiration (source: http://www.nualeargais.ie/gnag/lenition.htm).

Eclipsis, also known as nasalisation, is the substitution of the unvoiced consonants with the corresponding voiced ones (*c* becomes *g*, *f* becomes *bh*, *t* becomes *d*, *p* becomes b). Voiced consonants are then replaced with nasals (*b* becomes *m*, *d* becomes *n*, *g* becomes *ng*) (source: http://www.nualeargais.ie/gnag/eklipse.htm).

Consonant	eclipsed	spoken	consonant	eclipsed	spoken
b	*mb*	*[m]*	*g*	*ng*	*[ng]*
c	*gc*	*[g]*	*p*	*bp*	*[b]*
d	*nd*	*[n]*	*t*	*dt*	*[d]*
f	*bhf*	*[v]/[w]*			

The alternative question (5) is posed by S is used to ascertain which of the specific alternatives listed as options holds for H. The alternative question may be posed in different ways but the format of the answer remains the same, and is constrained to one of the listed alternative options.

(5) The alternative question can have different formulations

a.

An fearr leat tae nó caife?

QPRT prefer with:PREP+2SG tea or coffee

Do you prefer tea or coffee?

b.

An ólann tú tae nó caife?

QPRT drink:V-PRS 2SG tea or coffee

Do you drink tea or coffee?

In (6) and (7), a set of alternatives is proposed in the alternative question by S and, as a response, a selection from these alternatives is requested from H. There can be many options listed (*option-1, …, option-n*) and they are not limited to two. The background context generally assumed is that, before the question is answered, S is unclear as to whether H wants option-1 or option-2. For convenience, in (8), we label these options as Y_1 and Y_2. Only one of these is selected by H within the answer .

(6) Alternative question with responses

Question:

An ólann tú tae nó caife?

QPRT drink:V-PRS 2SG tea or coffee

Do you drink tea or coffee?

P=YOU DRINK TEA OR COFFEE

Answer 1:

Ólaim tae.

drink:V-PRS+1SG tea

I drink tea.

Answer 2:

Caife.

Coffee.

([~~I drink~~][ellipsis]) coffee.

(7) Alternative question
Question:
An ólann sí tae nó caife?
QPRT drink:V-PRS 3SG.F tea or coffee
Does she drink tea or coffee?
P=SHE DRINKS TEA OR COFFEE

Answer 1:
Ólann sí caife.
drink:V-PRS 3SG.F coffee
She drinks tea.

Answer 2:
Tae.
Tea.
([she drinks]^{ellipsis}) tea.

The internal semantics, including the logical structure, of the alternative question and possible answers is represented in (8). The elided elements are flagged in the logical structure representation of the asserted answer – these are in the common ground of S and H as referents because they were introduced within the question.

As a response to the question, the answer is a speech act of assertion. The semantic structure of the alternative question and answer is indicated in (8); the X argument is not spoken, it is elided, but is retrievable from context. Neither the verbal predicate or the X argument is spoken, both are elided, but again retrievable from context. With alternative questions, the disjunctive set of possible responses is constrained by the list of alternative options that are specifically listed in the question. The hearer picks one of these options in the construction of the answer.

(8) The semantic structure of the alternative question
Logical structure of the alternative question and answer
Question: **Q.**$_{\textbf{Alternative}}$ [**do'** (x, **PRED'** (x, $y_1 \vee y_2$))]
Answer [**ASSERT'** (**do'** (X, **PRED'** (X, Y1)))]
[**ASSERT'** (**do'** (x^{ellipsis}, **pred**^{ellipsis}**'** (x^{ellipsis}, Y1)))]
P=(YOU DRINK TEA OR COFFEE, tea | coffee)
CONTEXT BEFORE QUESTION
S: **KNOW'** (p, ?)
CONTEXT AFTER ANSWER

S: **BEL'** (p, tea) OR S: **BEL'** (p, coffee)
S: **KNOW'** (p, tea) OR S: **KNOW'** (p, coffee)

Subject to pragmatic context, there is a reading of an alternative question that licences a polar question interpretation (9). In this context, the [*tae nó caife*]$_{NP}$ is viewed as a single complex NP rather than a list of choices. In addition, it is possible to view the alternative question as a disjunction of two (or more) polar questions (10). In this view, in the second disjunct, the question particle, verbal predicate, and subject argument are all elided in the syntactic realisation.

Therefore, we have two perspectives on the nature of the alternative question form. In the first view, we can treat the alternative question as a distinct question form that contains a list of options (two or more) from which H, in their answer, must make a single selection. In the second view, we can consider the alternative question as a realisation of the polar question but reflecting disjunction across two (or more) clauses within the sentence. Ellipsis occurs in the second clause. Here, the negative proposition, is an implicit 'option'. This second view considers the alternative question form as an underlyingly disjoined polar question.

(9)

Alternative question:
An ólann tú [tae]$_{NP}$ *nó [caife]*$_{NP}$*?*

Polar question:
An ólann tú [tae nó caife]$_{NP}$*?*
QPRT drink:PRS 2SG [tea or coffee]
Do you drink [tea or coffee]?
P=YOU DRINK [TEA OR COFFEE] | ¬P

(10)

Disjunct polar question:
An ólann tú tae nó [~~an ólann tú~~]$_{elided}$ *caife?*
QPRT drink:PRS 2SG [tea] or [QPRT drink:PRS 2SG]$_{elided}$ coffee
Do you drink tea or [~~do you drink~~]$_{elided}$ coffee?
P=YOU DRINK TEA | YOU DRINK COFFEE | ¬P

The characteristics of the alternative questions of Irish are that:

i. A specific question particle is used.

ii. A specific syntactic form is employed with alternative questions.
iii. The alternative question form contains a list of options such that H must select from one of these in H's answer.
iv. The alternative question form may involve instances of ellipsis.
v. The answer to an alternative question contains ellipsis of the material following the verb.
vi. The answer to an alternative question may optionally contain ellipsis of the verbal predicate as well as the subject argument.
vii. The alternative question form can be viewed as a realisation of two (or more) disjunct polar questions.

We will next examine the polar yes-no questions of Irish.

7.2 The polar yes-no question

We have considered alternative questions as an interrogative form where S proposes a set of alternatives and a selection from amongst those is requested from H, the interlocutor. In contrast, the utterance of a polar yes-no question by S denotes a set consisting of a proposition and its negation, and S requests a confirmation or negation of the proposition from H. Polar yes-no questions are typically used to inquire about the truth or falsity of the proposition they express.

(11) The schematic format of a polar question

Lexical verb form:	Present tense	QPRT:*nach* V-PRS NP NP
	constructional schema:	QPRT:*nar* V-PST NP NP
	Past tense constructional schema:	
Copula verb form:	Constructional schema:	QCOP:*an* NP PN NP

As well as a positive confirmation or negative type answer, answers to polar questions can, of course, typically also assume any value on a scale between 'true' and 'false', as, for example, 'maybe', 'I don't know', 'perhaps', 'possibly', and other such responses.

Essentially, a polar question has a set of two propositions, P and ¬P, but frames just one of these, P, in the question. The ¬P option is implicit and salient but not syntactically stated. A polar question cannot denote a singleton set and the negative proposition is always (implicitly) available. With Irish, there are two syntactic constructional forms (12) and (13) for the polar yes-no question.

The first form has a matrix lexical verb while the second utilises a copula verb form. Across both forms of polar yes-no questions, the morphosyntax require that the clausal form have the question particle placed at the front-left of the clause.

(12) Polar question – lexical verb form
Question:
An *ólann* *sé* *tae?*
QPRT drink:V-PRS 3SG.M tea
Does he drink tea?
Proposition: P = (HE DRINKS TEA)
Negative of Proposition: ¬P = (HE DOES NOT DRINK TEA)

(13) Polar question – copula form
Question:
An *dochtúir* *í* *Aisling?*
QCOP doctor 3SG.F.ACC Aisling
Is Aisling a doctor?
Proposition: P = (AISLING IS A DOCTOR)
Negative of proposition: ¬P = (AISLING IS NOT A DOCTOR)

A feature of the polar yes-no question is that it can be *biased* towards a particular polarity, positive or a negative, within the answer. This happens through the use of forms such as 'someone', for example, within the question, which bias the question towards a positive orientation, as in (14), which indicates that S believes that the answer is positive and is seeking confirmation from H.

(14) Polar question with positive orientation
Question:
Ar *thug* éinne *cuairt* *aréir*?
QPST give.V-PST anyone visit last night
Lit: Did anyone give a visit last night?
Did someone visit last night?
Proposition: P = (SOMEONE VISITED LAST NIGHT)

A polar yes-no question specifically favours the core proposition framed by the question. This is the property of polar questions that makes them amenable to a yes-no response. Polar questions therefore make salient the affirmative, along with the implicit negative version of a proposition. The truth-conditional aspect of the meaning of a polar question is simply the set of the truth-conditional meanings of the possible answers to the question. Pragmatically, however, a polar question may also reveal information about the S's bias towards a particular answer. S's bias may be with regard to evidence present in the conversational context, that is, an evidential bias.

Any contextual evidence is mutually available to the participants in the discourse situation and typically forms part of the present shared common ground. Evidential bias is about contextual information available to all conversational participants, in the shared common ground and inherently public. In contrast, any epistemic bias that may occur is grounded on the speaker's own private beliefs, and need not be shared by other conversational participants. Typically, we expect that some contextual evidence influences what S believes, and determines their stance on it. Posing a question requires that H identify S's intention. Given the context dependency, the evidential or epistemic bias of a polar question assists H in determining what type of information the questioner S is seeking. Specifically, the polar question establishes a relation between the propositional content of the question and S's attitude, and whether the proposition P is in S's belief set.

The strategy that Irish employs in answers to the first form of the polar yes-no questions (with a lexical verb) is a verb-echo strategy. In many languages (Dryer 2005), polar yes-no questions are answered, not by an affirmative or negative particle, but by echoing the matrix verb of the question for positive answers and echoing the verb of the question plus a negation marker of some kind for negative answers. An affirmative answer is an echo of the matrix lexical verb in the question, while the negative answer is an echo of the matrix lexical verb in the question additionally combined with a sentential negation. Regarding the structure of these answers, within the answer in Irish to the first form of the polar yes-no questions, the tense-marked verb form is used with an explicit nominal argument (14). When a synthetic verb form is used, a pronominal appears in the grammatical relation of nominative subject within the answer. In the synthetic form, the PN is conflated on the end of the verb as a suffix. Additionally, in negative polarity answers, the negative particle is also used.

(15)

Question:
An *ólann* *tú* *bainne?*
QPRT drink:V-PRS 2SG.M milk
Do you drink milk?

Answer 1:
Ólaim. [Affirmative response]
Drink:V-PRS+1SG
Lit.: drink I
Yes.

Answer 2:
Ní ólaim. [Negative response]
NEG drink:V-PRS+1SG
Lit.: not drink I
No.

A grammatical subject may be used when the speaker chooses an emphatic affirmation or denial (16 Answer 2, in comparison to 16 Answer 1).

(16)
Question:
An ólann sé uisce?
QPRT drink:V-PRS 3SG.M water
Does he drink water?

Answer 1:
Ní ólann. [Negative response]
NEG drink:V-PRS
Lit.: Not drink
No.

Answer 2:
Ní ólann sé ar chor ar bith! [Emphatic negative response]
NEG drink:V-PRS 3SG.M at all
Lit: He doesn't drink at all!
No.

An answer to the first form of the polar yes-no questions can allow for a non-specific response indicating a lack of precise knowledge (17). Additionally, a response indicting uncertainty allows elements of the actual question to be embedded in the response (18).

(17)

Question:
An raibh na feirmeoirí orgánacha sásta?
QPRT BE.AUX.PST DET.PL farmers organic satisfied
Werc the organic farmers satisfied?

Answer 1:
Bhí siad.
BE.AUX.PST 3PL
They were (satisfied)!

Answer 2:
Níl a fhios agam.
NEG REL know at:PREP+1SG
Lit: Knowledge is not at me.
I don't know.

(18)

Question:
An mbeidh mórán daoine anseo?
QPRT BE.AUX.FUT many people DET+here
Will there be many people here?

Answer:
Níl mé cinnte an mbeidh mórán daoine anseo.
NEG 1SG certain QPRT BE.AUX.FUT many people DET+here
I am not certain how many people will here.

An answer to the first form of a polar yes-no question has several characteristics worthy of note. The lexical verb within the answer is echoed from the question and inflected for tense. As tense is a clausal category that locates the time of the event denoted by a clause in relation to the time of utterance, this is evidence that the answer is a clause. Within the answer to a polar yes-no question, pronominal subject marking implies the presence of a subject, hence also the presence of a clause.

In the answer to a polar yes-no question, ellipsis occurs with respect to the arguments of the verb. Ellipsis can also occur with respect to the verb itself in an alternative question form, as we have seen earlier with examples (6)–(10).

The VSO word order of the answer is maintained and a pronominal constituent is case-marked for the grammatical function of subject in the canonical position post-verb. As context to a polar yes-no question, before the question is answered, S may be uncertain as to whether the proposition is true, or false. Only one of (P | ¬P) holds.

The evidence supports the view that answers to polar yes-no questions have a sentential structure even when they consist of just one pronounced word. The elided material is in common ground and retrieved when needed by the hearer H for meaning resolution. Specifically, the elided (unpronounced) material is retrieved from the clausal content in the question.

A representative example of the first form of the polar question and a typical answer is indicated in (19), with the logical structure and associated semantics indicated in (20).

(19) Polar question

Question:

An	*ólann*	*sé*	*bainne?*
QPRT	drink:V-PRS	3SG.M	milk

Does he drink milk?

P=YOU DRINK MILK | YOU DO NOT DRINK MILK

Answer:

Ólann. [Positive response]

Drink:V-PRS

Lit.: drink

Yes.

(20) Logical structure of the polar question and answer

Question:

Q.$_{\text{polar}}$ [**do'** (x, **pred'**(x, y)]

Answer:

[**ASSERT'** (**do'** (**x**^{ellipsis}, **PRED'** (x^{ellipsis}, y^{ellipsis})))]

P=(HE DRINKS MILK, P | ¬P)

CONTEXT BEFORE QUESTION

S: **BEL'** (P, *true* | *false*)

S: **KNOW'** (P, ?)

CONTEXT AFTER ANSWER

S: **BEL'**(P, *true* | *false*)

S: **KNOW'**(P, *true* | *false*)

The second form of the polar question involves use of the copular form, indicated in (21). An interesting fact of Irish is that the language does not have any exact words which directly correspond to English *yes* or *no* and so the language necessarily employs a different strategy where a yes-no answer is required. To formulate an answer to the copula-form polar question, equivalent to a yes or no of English, the copula-derived phrases *sea* (COP+3SG = 'be-it') and *ní hea* (NEG.COP *3SG* = 'NEG be it') are used. These function as logically equivalent to 'yes' and 'no', respectively. The *sea* / *ní hea* can be used in formulating a response to a question with either a M or F referent. Like the first form of the polar question with the lexical verb, this second form also inquires after the truth value of a proposition.

(21)[Copula construction]

a.
Question:
An dochtúir é Lorcán?
QPRT doctor 3SG.M.ACC Lorcan
Is Lorcan a doctor?

b.
Question:
An dochtúir í Aifric?
QPRT doctor 3SG.F.ACC Aifric
Is Aifric a doctor?

Answer 1:
Sea. (= is_{cop}+$ea_{3SG.NEUT}$) [Affirmative response]
COP+3SG.NEUT
Lit: Be (s)he.
Yes.

Answer 2:
Ní hea. [Negative response]
NEGCOP 3SG.NEUT
Lit: Not be (s)he.
No.

In these question forms, the copula is used with an interrogative purpose by S, to elicit information from H. With an interrogation function, the copula clause uses a different questioning structure for classification vs identification, based on the copula structure indicated in (22).

(22) The general structure of the Irish Copula clause
  a) Classification: COP PREDICATE Subject
  b) Classification: COP $\text{PREDICATE}_{\text{PART-1}}$ Subject $\text{PREDICATE}_{\text{PART-2}}$
  c) Identification: COP PREDICATE Subject_1
  d) Ownership Identity: COP $[\text{Preposition } \textit{le} \text{ 'with' + NP}]_{\text{PREDICATE}}$ Subject
  e) Emphasis: COP PREDICATE Subject_1
  Where
  $\text{PREDICATE}_{\text{PART-2}}$ may contain a relative clause
  Subject_1 may be either [NP] or [NP + a relative clause]

Copula sentences are essentially equational units which establish an identity between a known or presupposed piece of information or entity, and a focused entity that presents new information of some kind. The copula of Modern Irish, as a marked focusing construction that brings particular terms into focus, is examined in Nolan (2012:192–217). These terms may be an NP, an adverb, an adjective, an adposition or other constituent including the verb. The copula predicate contains the new focused information and the copula subject contains the given topic.

Whenever S delivers an utterance in a particular context it is done with a communicative intent, and H must be able to unpack the utterance given the shared context. S has to distinguish three facets of knowledge with respect to H for the utterance: a) That knowledge which is computable from the context; b) That knowledge which is available from what has already been said; c) That knowledge which is available from common ground.

In an identifying copula, which takes the generalised schematic form:[x IS y], the identifying expression in focus is the 'x', and this is most likely to be definite ([DEF +]). The 'y' term is the topic of the construction, and represents the entity or information already available to the addressee. With the alternative and polar question forms, the copula is used with an interrogative purpose. T

The classification copula sentence (with copula + indefinite noun + pronoun) will require an indefinite noun while the copula in the identification function (with copula + pronoun/definite noun + pronoun/definite noun) will have a subject that is both specific and definite (Ó Siadhail 1991:224–225).

The *Collins Irish Grammar* (2011:114–115) informs us that *an* changes to *ar* for past tense and lenites/aspirates the predicate, but does not change before vowels. In turn, *ar* correspondingly changes to *arbh* for past tense before the pronouns é, *í* and *iad*. The negative forms apply here also (identification*: nach → nár*, classification: *nach → nárbh*).

Examples of the copula classification are found in (23) and identification interrogative functions in (24).

(23)Classification function

a.
An duine cliste é?
QCOP person clever 3SG.M.ACC
Is he a clever person ?

b.
An amharclann í?
QCOP theatre 3SG.F.ACC
Is it a theatre?

c.
Ar dhuine cliste é?
QCOP.PST person clever 3SG.M.ACC
Was he a clever person ?

d.
Ar amharclann í?
QCOP.PST theatre 3SG.F.ACC
Was it a theatre?

(24)Identification function

a.
An é Dónal do chara ?
QCOP 3SG.M.ACC Dónal your friend
Is Dónal your friend?

b.
An í Tara an cailín fionn?
QCOP 3SG.F.ACC Tara DET girl blond
Is Tara the blonde girl?

c.
Arbh é Dónal do chara?
QCOP.PST 3SG.M.ACC Dónal your friend
Was Dónal your friend?

While the function of polar questions is to elicit confirmation, some polar yes-no questions have a rhetorical force (25) that arises when conditions supporting the felicitous use of the speech act of questioning are not met. These questions do not seem to expect a positive or negative answer and are rhetorical in nature. Indeed, responses to the rhetorical polar questions would go against common ground knowledge. Rhetorical polar yes-no questions are actually a particular kind of information seeking question that masquerade as a polar form but they do not facilitate a yes or no answer. They contain cues from syntax and context which alerts us that the speaker is taking a rhetorical stance.

(25)

Ní	*féidir*	*leat*	*mo cheist*	*a*	*fhreagairt,*	*an*	*féidir?*
NEG	able	with:PREP+2SG	my question	REL	answer,	QPRT	able

You can't answer my question, can you?

We have seen that polar questions do not overtly provide a selection of answer possibilities in either of the forms found in Irish. Alternative questions do not inquire the truth value of a proposition, but rather ask which listed option from among a set of alternatives is most appropriate in a given context. With an alternative question, knowing the meaning of the question is knowing its possible answer. The purpose of the polar question is about confirming the truth value of a proposition. The polar yes-no question is a disjunction of p and ¬p. The polar yes-no question is also used in managing the belief status of knowledge in common ground, and to update the information gap in S's common ground from information provided within the answer by H. Common ground acts as a kind of decentralised knowledge system supporting the cognitive activation of relevant contextual knowledge. Context contributes to the meaning resolution, and to the resolution of any evidential or epistemic bias that may exist.

The answers to polar yes-no questions of Irish contain instances of ellipsis and, as such, represent full clausal expressions with a complete semantics where the elided elements are from the question part of the question-answer pair. To formulate an answer to the first form of the polar yes-no question, the grammar of Irish uses a verb-echo strategy whereby the matrix verb of the polar yes-no question is used in the answer. Nominal argument ellipsis of one or two arguments also occurs. The success of this strategy requires the construction and maintenance of common ground for the retrieval of elided arguments.

The answer to a polar yes-no question has several significant characteristics:

i. The lexical verb within the answer is echoed from the question and inflected for tense. As tense is a clausal category that locates the time of the event denoted by a clause in relation to the time of utterance, this is evidence that the answer is a clause.
ii. When it occurs in the answer to a polar yes-no question, pronominal subject marking implies the presence of a subject, hence also the presence of a clause.
iii. In the answer to a polar yes-no question, ellipsis occurs with respect to the arguments of the verb, but not the verb itself.
iv. The VSO word order of the answer is maintained and a pronominal constituent is case-marked for the grammatical function of subject in the canonical position post-verb.
v. The context to a polar yes-no question, before the question is answered, has S uncertain as to whether the proposition is true, or false. Only one of (P | ¬P) holds.

The evidence is that the propositional content in a question-answer interaction is inferred from the context, specifically from the question with which the answer is paired.

7.3 The information question

The felicitous use of an information question typically presupposes an information gap on the part of the speaker S and a presumption of relevant knowledge on the part of the hearer H. However, we know that S, who may already possesses the relevant information, can felicitously pose the question to H, if there is some element of doubt about H's knowledge. The goal is still to gain information. The felicity conditions for the speech act are proposed in (26).

The information question is used to seek information on a specific point within the information gap, and this information point is signalled within the question. It has the syntactic cues of an information question interrogative, and it requires an answer, or some response, from H.

(26) Felicity conditions for the information question directive speech act
S questions H about proposition P *iff*
i. S does not know about P.
ii. S wants to know about P.
iii. S believes H knows about P.

In the information question, interrogative words introduce an question. These information questions are also known as WH-questions. Sometimes these question words are called Interrogative PARTICLES[7] but, more correctly and importantly, they are best considered as a PROFORM because they stand for a named entity of a particular kind, interrogated by S of H within the information question.

Proforms (PF) are divided into several categories, according to which part of speech they relate to (27).[8] The syntactic constructional schema of the information question is shown in (27). The information question word proform in a particular information question casts into focus a certain kind of knowledge gap (28). This information gap may relate to an entity of some kind, or a person, location, or time, or indeed, to an event. To pose one of these information questions in Irish, one of closed set of the interrogative question proforms is used.

(27)

a. A pronoun substitutes for a noun, or noun phrase, with or without a determiner.
b. A pro-adjective substitutes an adjective or a phrase that functions as an adjective.
c. A pro-adverb substitutes an adverb or a phrase that functions as an adverb.
d. A pro-verb substitutes a verb or a verb construct.

---

7 This is defined by https://glossary.sil.org/term/particle as: *a particle is a word that does not belong to one of the main classes of words, is invariable in form, and typically has grammatical or pragmatic meaning.*

8 Some data is taken from the websites: http://mylanguages.org/irish_questions.php and https://en.wikipedia.org/wiki/Irish_grammar#Interrogative_pronouns

(28)The information question constructional schema is: QPF REL V.TNS NP where QPF is a question proform that interrogates for the kind of knowledge gap.

(29)The information question proforms and associated information gaps

QUESTION WORD PROFORMS		TARGET
Cé	who	person
Cé leis	whose	person.owner
Cé aige	whose	person.possessor
Cád	what	event /thing
Céard	what	event / thing
Cén	which	thing
Cá	where	location
Cén áit / *Cén háit*	what place	location
Cathain	when	time
Cén uair	what time	time
Cá huair	what time	time
Cén t-am	what time	time
Cén fáth	why	reason / cause
Conas	how	state / method
Cad é mar	how	state / method
Cé mhéad	how many	quantity / scale / degree
Cá mhéad	how many	quantity / scale / degree

The information gap linked to the proform can map to the semantic logical structure of the event within the situation of the questioning utterance (Figure 7.1).

Syntactically, the question proform in Irish is always found at the beginning of the sentence.

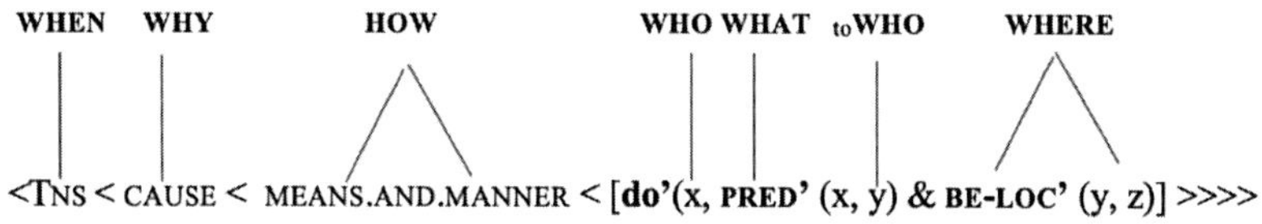

Figure 7.1 Mapping the proform gap to the logical structure of the situational event

7.3.1 Information focus in an Information question

Information questions require answers in which the kind of information specified by the interrogative word (wh-words like *who*, *what*, *where*, *when*, *why*, and *how* in English) is provided. In these, the set of possible answers is restricted lexically, by virtue of the meaning of the particular question pro-form (*who*, *what*, *where*, *when*, *why*, *how*, etc.) and its co-constituents in the sentence, and restricted pragmatically by the discourse context. Here, part of the meaning of the question is guided directly from its syntactic structure. We argue here that information focus is also important.

The answer to a question necessarily has focus on a constituent. There is an understanding of the word focus which is close to ordinary language usage, where focus in the sense of '*centre of attention*'. Intuitively, the centre of attention in a question is the question word. In the context of question-answer pairs, the new information in the answer is provided by that constituent which corresponds to the question word. Therefore, the questioned constituent (the question word) is the *centre of attention* in the question. Information question sentences using a copula and relative clauses are common in Irish to highlight one individual element over others involved in an event. These sentences single out one element of the clause. While a speaker of English would simply use stress to signal the emphasis, this is not done in Irish – instead, the copula construct with a relative clause is employed. We have already mentioned the copula of Irish. The nature of the copula of Irish is reported in Nolan (2012:192–215) to have the schematic structure shown in (30).

(30)Copula schematic structure, repeated from earlier (22)

a. Classification: COP Predicate Subject

b. Classification: COP $\text{Predicate}_{\text{part-1}}$ Subject $\text{Predicate}_{\text{part-2}}$

c. Identification: COP Predicate Subject

d. Ownership Identity: COP $[\text{Preposition } \textit{le} \text{ 'with'} + \text{NP}]_{\text{Predicate}}$ Subject

e. Emphasis: COP Predicate Subject_1

Where

$\text{Predicate}_{\text{part-2}}$ may contain a relative clause

Subject_1 may be either [RP] or [RP + a relative clause]

The copula of Modern Irish, as a marked focusing construction, brings particular terms into focus. These terms may be an NP, an adverb, an adjective, an adposition, or other constituent including the verb. In a copula of Modern Irish, the copula predicate contains the new focused information and the copula subject contains the given topic. The focalisation purpose of the predicate presents the new information, and this is in a contrastive focus in the 'emphasis' function. The copula, then, always marks focus in its predicate. The focus element has prominence as the predicate in the copula construction, typically in the structure in (31).

(31)

Copula [Focal element] **focus-predicate** [NP (or relative clause)] **subject-comment**

Definiteness is a major distinction between the classification and identification functions of the copula constructions. Definiteness is a distinguishing criterion for copula subject, which must be [DEF +]. The predicate of the classification copula construction must be [DEF -] while the subject must be [DEF +].

In identification copula constructions the predicate is usually [DEF +] and, as we mentioned, the subject must be [DEF +].

Within the copula construction of Irish, there is a distinct preference for first position to contain focus information. Consequently, fronting for focus is achieved typically by means of copula constructions.

In (31), we have an example of where the NP subject is the focus domain and in which we state the proposition, pose a focal question and in provide the relevant answer in which the focal element is indicated in focus position in a copula construction as the immediate post-copula constituent.

We underline the predicate for clarity of exposition, and the emphasised element is bolded. The 'x' variable in the assertion-comment gloss is instantiated in the syntax by a pronoun within the copula predicate that agrees in number and gender with its associated nominal within the predicate.

(32)NP: Subject is Focus Domain

a.

Ghlan *Aifric* *an* *cistin.* **:The Proposition**
Clean:V-PST Aifric DET kitchen
P=(AIFRIC CLEANED THE KITCHEN)

b.

Focal Q: **Cé** a ghlan an cistin?
QFP.who REL clean-PST DET kitchen
Who cleaned the kitchen?
Given: *Ghlan* [SOMEONE] *an cistin.* **:Presupposition**

c. New: *Is* í Aifric *a ghlan an cistin.* **:Focal element**

Is í Aifric a ghlan an cistin.
COP 3SG.F Aifric REL clean:V-PST DET kitchen
Lit: It is her Aifric that cleaned the kitchen.
It is (her) Aifric that cleaned the kitchen.

d. Sentence: Is í Aifric a ghlan an cistin.
Presupposition: 'Someone = x cleaned the kitchen'
Assertion-comment: 'x = Aifric'
Focus: 'Aifric'
Focus domain: NP

In RRG, the focal question would reside in a pre-core slot in the layered structure of the clause. Only the asserted part of the sentence can be negated (Van Valin & LaPolla 1997:219).

In (33), we have an example of where the NP object is the focus domain.

In (34), we have an example of where the verbal event focus domain is the clause nucleus.

In (35), we provide an example of predicate focus where the focus domain is the verb, plus its undergoer argument.

(33)NP: Object is Focus Domain

a.
Ghlan Aifric an cistin. **:The Proposition**
Clean:V-PST Aifric DET kitchen:N
P=(AIFRIC CLEANED THE KITCHEN)

b.
Focal Q: ***Cad*** *a ghlan Aifric?*
QPF.what REL clean:V-PST Aifric
Lit: What is it that Aifric cleaned?
What did Aifric clean?
Given: *Ghlan Aifric* [SOMETHING]. **:Presupposition**

c.
New: Is é an **cistin** a ghlan Aifric. **:Focal element**
Is é an cistin a ghlan Aifric.
COP 3SG.M.ACC DET kitchen REL clean Aifric
Lit: It is it the kitchen that Aifric cleaned.
It is the kitchen that Aifric cleaned.

d. Sentence: Is é an **cistin** a ghlan Aifric.
Presupposition: 'Aifric cleaned x'
Assertion-comment: 'x= the kitchen'
Focus: 'The kitchen'
Focus domain: NP

(34) V: Event – Focus domain is the clause nucleus

a.
Ghlan Aifric an cistin. **:The Proposition**
Clean:V-PST Aifric DET kitchen
P=(AIFRIC CLEANED THE KITCHEN)

b.
Focal Q: ***Cad*** *a rinne Aifric leis an cistin?*
QPF.what REL do:V-PST Aifric with:PREP DET kitchen
What did Aifric do with the kitchen?
Given: *Aifric* [DID SOMETHING] with the kitchen **:Presupposition**

c.
New: Ghlan sí é. **:Focal element**
Glan sí é.
Clean:V-PST 3SG.F.NOM 3SG.M.ACC
She cleaned it.

d. Sentence: ***Ghlan sí é.***
Presupposition: Aifric did something with the kitchen .
Assertion-comment: Something happened = event'
Focus: Situation
Focus domain: Nucleus

(35) Sentence: Focus domain is full situation with event and arguments

a.
Ghlan Aifric an cistin. **:The Proposition**
Clean:V-PST Aifric DET kitchen
P=(AIFRIC CLEANED THE KITCHEN)

b.

Focal Q:	**Cad**	a	tharla	leis	an cistin?
	QPF.what	REL	happened	with:PREP	DET kitchen

What happened with the kitchen?
Given: [SOMETHING HAPPENED] with the kitchen **:Presupposition**

c.

New: Ghlan Aifric é. **:Focal element**

Ghlan	*Aifric*	*é.*
Clean:V-PST	Aifric	3SG.M.ACC

Aifric cleaned it.

d. Sentence: ***Ghlan Aifric é.***

Presupposition:	Aifric did something with the kitchen.
Assertion-comment:	Something happened = ‘event’
Focus:	Situation
Focus domain:	Predicate focus of verb plus actor and undergoer arguments.

7.3.2 The information question as a syntactically complex clausal construction

The information question is a complex construction consisting of two constructs in a certain relationship, with certain syntactic consequences which we briefly discuss here. The construction is structured as two related constructs within the information question (36), with the constructs indicated via use of the subscripts $_A$ and $_B$ in (37). The first part, the construct with the subscript, indicated by the subscript $_A$, consists of the question word proform with a copula clause. In use, the copula itself is frequently elided such that the clause may consist only of the visible question proform.

This elided copula is nonetheless understood in context. On occasion it may be explicit in the syntax. The second part, the construct with the subscript $_B$, follows the first construct as a Direct or Indirect Relative clause and this relative clause is the subject of the preceding copula clause. The VSO word order of the relative clause is preserved.

(36) [**Q**PF Copula [Focal element] $_{\text{focus-predicate}}$] [REL (relative clause)] $_{\text{subject-comment}}$]

(37) The structure of the information question construction

Information question – Direct Relative clause

i. $_{A}$[**QPF** (COP) RP $_{\text{Focal element}}$] $_{B}$[REL [V NP (PPN)]] $_{\text{COPULA.SUBJECT}}$

Information question – Indirect Relative clause

ii. $_{A}$[**QPF** (COP) RP $_{\text{Focal element}}$] $_{B}$[REL [V NP NP (PPN)]] $_{\text{COPUA.SUBJECT}}$

where

RP stands for REFERRING PHRASE – it is not necessarily an NP, though it may be. The RP may be an appropriate embedded clause of some kind.

A relative clause gives supplementary information about somebody or something without starting another sentence. For example, relative clauses modify referring phrases (RP) to tell us more about the constituent they describe. The RP that the relative clause modifies comes first in word order, followed by the relative particle *a* and lenition on the verb.

In Irish, there are two types of relative clause: Direct Relative clauses and Indirect Relative clauses. The mutations caused by the relative particles are different in that the Direct Relative particle lenites its following verb, while the Indirect Relative particle nasalises it. In the literature, the difference between the two relative particles is frequently represented by writing the *a* of the Direct Relative as *aL* and the *a* of the Indirect Relative as *aN*.

The deployment of direct vs. indirect relative clause is summarised in (38) and (39).

(38) Characteristics of the Direct Relative

Syntax: The relativised constituent is the subject or direct object of its clause.

Morphology: The particle *aL* of the Direct Relative lenites its following verb.

(39) Characteristics of the Indirect Relative

Syntax:

a. The relativised constituent is not the subject or direct object of its clause.
b. The Indirect Relative uses a resumptive pronoun in its relativised clause.

c. The Indirect Relative type is used to manage ambiguity as to the grammatical relation of an argument as subject or direct object within the relativised clause.
d. When the relativised constituent is the object of a preposition or a possessive modifier of a NP then the use of the pronoun-retaining Indirect Relative is obligatory.

Morphology:

e. The particle *aN* of the indirect Relative nasalises (eclipsis) its following verb.

According to McCloskey (1979), the primary syntactic difference between the Direct Relative and the Indirect Relative is that the Indirect Relative involves *retention* of a resumptive pronoun at the site of the relativised constituent inside the relative clause, while the Direct Relative involves *removal* of the relativised constituent and is used when the site of the relativised constituent is 'subject' of its clause. McCloskey (1979) indicates that the choice between Direct and Indirect Relative types is free when the relativised constituent is the direct object of its clause. Additionally, when the relativised constituent is the object of a preposition, or a possessive modifier of an NP, then it is the case that the use of the pronoun-retaining Indirect Relative is obligatory. The Indirect Relative type is used only if use of the Direct Relative type would cause ambiguity as to whether the missing constituent is subject or direct object in its clause.

A Direct Relative clause is one in which the person or thing described in the clause is the subject or object of the verb. Some examples of these are shown in (40) and (41).

An Indirect Relative clause is one in which the person or thing described in the clause is not the subject or object of the verb. In particular, the Indirect Relative clause is used when the noun defined by a relative clause functions within that clause as the object of a preposition or possessor of another noun.

(40) The entity described is the subject

An múinteoir	*a*	*thiocfaidh*	*anseo*	*amarach.*
DET teacher	REL	come:V-FUT	here	tomorrow

The teacher who will come here tomorrow.

(41) The entity described is the object

An teach	*a*	*cheannaigh*	*mé.*
DET house	REL	buy:V-PST	1SG

The house which I bought.

A resumptive pronoun is employed in (42).

(42) Relates the resumptive pronoun to the object of the preposition
*Sin í an bhean a bhfanann siad **léi**.*
That **3SGF** DET woman REL stay:V-PST 3PL **with:PREP+3SG.F**
Lit: That is the woman that they stay with her.
That is the woman that they stay with.

We now examine the information questions of Irish along with their various question proforms (QFP) to see how these proforms map to the information gaps of S, the questioner.

The information question may target a person or event information gap. It can be used to code the locative meaning sense 'where from' and it can be used to interrogate the time dimension. The information question can be used to target the reason why some situation exists.

Additionally, the question proforms can target method, means, and manner, and state within the information question, and can also be used to interrogate quantity, scale, and degree.

7.3.2.1 Person

Specifically, here we see examples of information questions that are constructed as Direct Relative clauses which have the subject or object as the person information gap target.

(43) Target is subject / person
Question:
Cé a rinne é?
QPF.who REL do.make.V-PST 3SG.M.ACC
Who did it?

Answer:
Rinne Aifric é.
do.make.V-PST Aifric 3SG.M.ACC
Aifric did it.

Questions formulated with *cé* 'who' or *céard* 'what', and targeting the object of a preposition, place the prepositional pronoun at the beginning with the question word. Note that *ceard* is a conflation of *cé+an+rud* 'who'+DET+'thing', with the meaning sense of 'what'.

(44) Target is grammatical object

Question:

Céard *a* *fuair* *tú?*
QPF.what REL get.V-PST 2SG
What did you get?

Answer:

Fuair *mé* brioscaí seacláide.
get.V-PST 1SG biscuits chocolate
I got chocolate biscuits.

Questions asked about objects of prepositions and possessors are formed according to the rules of Indirect Relative clauses, i.e., eclipsis or dependent verb form *ar* for regular past verbs and a pronoun referring to the head as the object of a preposition or possessor.

(45) Target is object of preposition

Question:

Cén *chathaoir* *ar* *chuir* *tú* *an* *leabhar* ***uirthi****?*
QPF:which chair REL put:V-PST 2SG DET book on:PREP+**3SG.F**
Which chair did you put the book on?

(46) Target is possessor

Question:

Cén *bhean* *a* *bhfuil* *a* *mac* *tinn?*
QPF:which woman REL be:V-PST **POSS** son SICK
Which woman's son was sick?

The information question proform *cé* is used with a prepositional pronoun as a part of the copular clause in the form of as *cé leis* 'whose' for ownership and *cé aige* 'whose' for possession (47).

(47) Target is object of a preposition

Question:

Cé ***leis*** *a* *bhfanann* *tú?*
QPF:who with:PREP+3SG.M REL stay:V-PRS 2SG
Who do you stay with?

(48) Target is object of a preposition

Question:

Céard ***faoi*** *a raibh sibh ag caint?*
QPF:what under:PREP REL be:V-PST 2PL at:PREP talk:VN
What were you talking about?

(49) Target codes ownership (vs. possession)
Question:
Cé ***leis*** *é?*
QPF:who with:PREP 3SG.M.ACC
Who owns it?

Answer:
Is le Pól é.
Cop with:PREP Paul 3SG.M.ACC
Lit: It (ownership) is with Paul.
It is Paul who owns it.

(50) Target codes ownership (vs. possession)
Question:
Cér ***leis*** *é an carr?*
QPF:who with:PREP 3SG.M.ACC DET CAR
Who owns the car?

Answer:
Is leatsa an carr.
Cop with:PREP+2SG.EMP DET CAR
Lit: The car (ownership) is with you.
It is you who owns the car.

(51) Target codes possession (vs. ownership)
Question:
Cé ***aige*** *a bhfuil an arán?*
QPF:who at:PREP+3SG.M REL BE:AUX-PRS DET bread
Who has the bread?

Answer:
Tá Pól i seilbh é.
Be:AUX-PRS Paul in:PREP possession 3SG.M.ACC
It is Paul who possesses it.

7.3.2.2 Event

The information question proform *cé*, with the conflation of cé + *rud* → *céard* 'what (thing)', is used with a 3rd person prepositional pronoun and the indirect relative clause. This targets a situational event and its RP is typically verbal in nature, for example, to encode reported speech.

(52) Target is a verbal event

Question:
Céard *a* *dúirt* *tú?*
QPF:what REL say:V-PST 2SG
What did you say?

Answer:
Duirt *mé* *x.*
Say:V-PST 1SG x
I said x.

7.3.2.3 Thing

The information question proform *cad* 'what' targets the information gap of an NP entity (thing) as to its identity or type.

(53) Target is NP entity – 'thing'

Question:
Cad *é* *seo?*
QPF:what 3SG.M.ACC this
What is this?

7.3.2.4 Location

The information question proform *cad* can be used with the preposition *as* 'from' to code the locative meaning sense 'where from'.

(54) Target is some location

Question:
Cad *as* *é?*
QPF:what from:PREP 3SG.M.ACC
Where is he from?

7.3.2.5 Time

The information question proform *cathain* 'when' can be used with the direct relative clause. The information question proform *cé* 'what' can be used with the definite determiner *an* 'the' in the conflation of *cé+an* as *cén*. These information question proforms interrogate the time dimension (55)–(57).

(55) Target is time
Question:
Cá huair a tharla sé?
QPF.what hour REL do.make.V-PST 3SG.M
What time did it happen?

Answer:
Tharla sé ag x huair.
do.happen.V-PST 3SG.M at:PREP x time
It happened at x time.

(56) Target is time
Question:
***Cathain** a dhíolfaidh sibh bhur dteach?*
QPF.when REL sell.V-FUT 2PL your:POSS house
When will you sell your house?

Answer:
Dhíolfaidh muid ár teach amarach.
sell.V-FUT 1PL our:POSS house tomorrow
We will sell our house tomorrow.

(57) Target is time
Question:
***Cén** t-am é?*
QPF.what+DET time 3SG.M.ACC
Lit: What is it, the time?
What time is it?

7.3.2.6 Reason/cause

The information question proform *cé* 'what' can be used with the definite determiner *an* 'the' in the conflation of *cé+an* as *cén*. This conflated *cén* is used with *fáth* 'reason/cause' to target the reason why some situation exists (58).

(58) Target is reason

Question:

Cén	*fáth*	*a*	*bhfuil*	*brón*	*ort?*
QPF.**what**+DET	reason	REL	BE:AUX-PRS	sadness	on:PREP+2SG

Lit: What is the reason for sadness being on you?

What is the reason for your sadness?

7.3.2.7 Method, means and manner, state, and attribute

The question proforms can target method (59), means and manner (60), and state (61) within the information question. The information question proform *cá* 'how' can be used to target an attribute of an NP, coded with an adjective (62).

(59) Target is method

Question:

Cén	*chaoi*	*ar*	*mhaith leat*	íoc*?*
QPF.**what**+DET	method	REL	prefer	2SG	pay:VN

What way do you prefer to pay?

(60) Target is means/manner

Question:

Conas	*a*	*tharla*	*sé?*
QPF.**how**	REL	do.happen:V-PST	3SG.M

How did it happen?

(61) Target is state

Question:

Conas	*atá*	*tú?*
QPF.**how**	REL+BE:AUX.PRS	2SG

How are you?

(62) Target is adjective

Question:

Cá	***hard***	*é?*
QPF.**how**	high	3SG.M

how high is it?

7.3.2.8 Quantity, scale, and degree

The information question proform *cé* 'how (+many/much/often)' can be used to interrogate the quantity, scale and degree (64)–(66).

(63) Target is quantity and scale

Question:

Cé *mhéad* *mile* *a* *shiúil* *tú?*

QPF.how many miles REL walk.V-PST 2SG

How many miles did you walk?

Answer:

[~~*Shiúil mé*~~]$_{\text{elided}}$ *trí* *mile!*

[walk.V-PST 1SG]$_{\text{elided}}$ three miles

[I walked]$_{\text{elided}}$ three miles!

Answer:

Trí *mile!*

three miles

Three miles!

(64) Target is quantity and scale

Question:

Cén *méad* *ar* *seo?*

QPF.what+DET much on:PREP this

How much is this?

(65) Target is noun of degree

Question:

Cá *mhinice?*

QPF.what often

How often?

The information question proform *cé* along with the comparative form of an adjective can be used to query an attribute of the entity discussed. In this instance, the format of the question presents a choice from a list of alternatives to be chosen. These are similar to the alternative question of Irish in that it allows an answer to be formulated only from the closed set of entities (*x nó y*, '*Peader nó Seosamh*?, '*feoil nó iasc*') listed in the questions shown in (66)–(67).

(66) Target is comparative with NP

Question:

Cé	*acu*	*is*	*daoire,*	*feoil*	*nó*	*iasc?*
QPF.which	of:PREP+3PL	COP	expensive	meat	or	fish

Which of them is more expensive, meat or fish?

(67) Target is comparative with NP

Question:

Cé	*acu*	*an*	*garsún*	*is*	*cliste,*	*Peader*	*nó*	*Seosamh?*
QPF.which	of:PREP+3PL	DET	boy	COP	clever	Peter	or	Joseph

Lit: Which of them the boys is more clever, Peter or Joseph?

Which of the boys is cleverer, Peter or Joseph?

Answer:

is	*é*	*Peadar*	*an*	*té*	*is*	*cloiste*	*acu.*
Cop	3sg.M.ACC	Peter	DET	one	COP	clever	of:PREP+3PL

It is Peter that is the one who is more clever.

7.3.3 Information questions and ellipsis

We have seen that the Information questions of Irish contain an interrogative question proform (the question word: *who*, *what*, *how*, *where*, *why*, *with what*, *wherefore*), and argue that this proform forms part of a copula construct with an *elided* copula. The copula casts the information gap proform into focus.

The elements that are elided need to be in the common ground between S and H to facilitate a felicitous speech act. Syntactically, this question proform in Irish is always found at the beginning of the sentence. The information gap proform may relate to a thing or an event or some kind.

(68) Target is a grammatical subject

Question:

Cé	*a*	*rinne*	*é*	*sin?*
QPF.who	REL	do.make:V-PST	3SG.M.ACC	that

Lit: Who(-is-it), that did it that?

Who did that?

Answer:

Rinne	*sé*	*é*	*sin.*
do.make:V-PST	3SG.M	3SG.M.ACC	that

Lit: He did it that.
He did that.

(69) Target is a verbal event
Question:
Cad a rinne sé?
QPF.what REL do.make:V-PST 3SGM
Lit: What(-is-it), that he did?
What did he do?

Answer:
Rinne sé x.
do.make:V-PST 3SG.M x
He did x (… where x is some event or action).

(70) Target is instrument
Question:
Cad leis ar scríobh sé é?
QPF.what with:PREP+3SG.M REL write:V-PST 3SG.M 3SG.M.ACC
Lit: What with-it(-is-it), that wrote he it?
What did he write it with?

Answer:
Scríobh sé le peann é.
Write:V-PST 3SG.M with:PREP pen 3SG.M.ACC
He wrote it with a pen.

As well as an elided copula in the information question, ellipsis frequently plays a role in answers to information questions. The elided elements are retrieved from common ground between S and H.

(71) Elided elements – Target is a verbal event
Question:
Cad a rinne sé?
QPF.what REL do.make:V-PST 3SG.M
What did he do?

Answer:
(Is é)$_{\text{elided}}$ *sin a rinne sé.*
COP 3SG.M.ACC) that REL do.make:V-PST 3SG.M

Lit.: (is it) $_{elided}$ that, that did he.
He did that.

One may answer an information question with just one word (72)–(73).

(72) Elided elements – Target is person
Question:
Cén *t-ainm atá ar an mbean sin?*
QPF.what+DET name REL+BE.AUX-PRS on:PREP DET woman that
Lit: What (is) the name that is on that woman?
What is that woman's name?

Answer:
Aifric (an t-ainm atá ar an mbean sin) $_{elided}$.
Aifric (is the name of that woman) $_{elided}$.

(73) Elided elements – Target is person
Question:
Cé *a rinne sin?*
QPF.who REL do.make:V-PRS that
Who did it?

Answer:
(____________) *Pól* (~~*a rinne sin*~~) $_{elided\ elements}$.
(it was) $_{elided\ elements}$ Paul (REL do.make:V-PST that) $_{elided\ elements}$
(it was) Paul (that did it).

A complete articulated sentence can form the answer when a lack of knowledge (74)–(75) is professed by H – in this instances ellipsis is not employed.

(74) Target is some unknown location
Question:
Cá *bhfuil Donncha?*
QPF.where be.aux-PST Donncha
Where is Donncha?

Answer:
Níl a fhios agam ***cá*** *bhfuil Donncha.*
NEG POSS knowledge at:PREP+3SGM **QPF.where** BE.AUX-PST Donncha
I don't know where Donncha is.

(75) Target is unknown person
Question:
Cé *hé* *sin?*
QPF.who 3sg.M.ACC that
Lit: Who he that?
Who is that?

Answer:
Níl a fhios agam ***cé*** *hé sin.*
NEG POSS knowledge at:PREP+3SG.M **QPF.who** 3SG.M.ACC that
Lit: I don't possess the knowledge of who he that is
I don't know who that is.

7.4 Some comments on questions

Question-answer interactions facilitate the construction and maintenance of common ground. As we have seen in this chapter, Irish has clausal strategies for requesting different kinds of information through the use of questions. This includes the question types discussed here. The question forms of Irish have distinct morphosyntactic and clausal characteristics. In the act of asking questions, people interact with each other in an activity that is central to communication and understanding.

The maintenance of common ground is one of the central functions of information questions. In this, the context and situation of the speech act of requesting information, as a directive speech act, play an important role in the process of meaning construction while contributing to a successful question-answer interaction. The information gaps in a dialogue between S and H are fulfilled through the question-answer interaction. Contextual knowledge that is relevant enters common ground of S and H. The consequential unpacking of the meaning of the interrogative speech act depends on the associated situation in which the dialogue utterance occurs and the context concerning that situation. Context, through the situational frame, contributes to a felicitous speech act.

8 The commissive speech act

8.1 Introduction to the commissive speech act

The expression of the commissive speech act in Irish can take a variety of linguistic forms. In this chapter, we examine a) the form the commissive takes as a speech act, b) the felicity conditions under which these commissive speech acts can be successful, and c) the range of commissive speech acts of Irish and their distinguishing features. While a commitment can be made to oneself, typically, it is made to another person. In this instance, the role of H, then, is essential as, if the commitment is made by S to H, and H does not understand, hear, or accept the commitment made, then it is taken as invalid. In other words, one needs a cooperating discourse partner, H. Searle (1969:57ff) specifies a variety of conditions for the success of a commissive speech act. These conditions are necessary and rely on extra-linguistic knowledge, from both context and from common ground. Shared knowledge in the form of common ground has significance as an extra-linguistic source for the success of the speech act. The commissive speech act expresses the intention and belief of S that S's utterance obligates S to do something that may necessitate certain contextual conditions. The commissive speech acts, then, are acts of obligating oneself, or of proposing to obligate oneself, to do something specified in the propositional content, which may also specify conditions under which the deed is to be done or does not have to be done.

In committing oneself to do some action X, one expresses the intention to do X and the belief that one's utterance commits one to doing it, at least under the conditions specified or mutually believed to be relevant. These conditions may include H accepting the proposal of S or commitment to do X or at least H not rejecting it. The absence of an explicit rejection by H is typically taken as acceptance. In addition to expressing such intention and belief, S expresses the intention that H believe that S has this intention and belief. The perlocutionary intention is that H believe S has this intention and belief and that H believe that S is obligated to do X, once the required conditions are met (Bach & Harnish 1979:45).

The illocutionary force of the commissive is to oblige S to perform some action or to bring about some state of affairs, that is, to commit S to a future action. The commissive may, for example, take the form of promises, offers, threats and vows, and so on. Commissive illocutionary forces have the world-to-word direction of fit. It is a consequence of the illocutionary point of the commissive illocutions that they create reasons for S/H to change the world by acting in such a way as to bring about success in achieving the direction of fit (Searle & Vanderveken 1985:94). The commissive speech acts that we examine include: commit, promise, threaten, vow, pledge, swear, offer, bid, contract, bet.

8.2 The commissive utterances

8.2.1 Commit

A commitment is a relation between a speaker S, hearer H, and a proposition. This speech act causes S to become committed to H to act on a propositional content. The verb commit is used to name the commissive illocutionary force.

(1)

a.
Gabhaim orm féin an obair a chríochnú.
undertake:V-PST 1SG on:PREP SELF DET work REL finish:VN
I commit myself to finishing the work.

b. Constructional signature: [V.TNS NP to RP]

(2)

a.
Geallaim go gcríochnóidh mé an obair.
promise:V-PRS+1SG that finish V-FUT 1SG DET work
I promise (=commit) to finishing the work.

b. [**do'** (1SG, **commit'** (1SG, SELF) CAUSE BECOME **finish'**(1SG, work))]

c. Constructional schema: [V NP RP]

Example (3) explicitly mentions the obligation within the commitment.

(3)

a.
Cuireann sé de cheangal ar an dá thaobh fanacht.
Put:V-PRS 3SG.M to:PREP obligation on:PREP DET both side wait:VN
It commits both sides to wait.

b. [**do’** (3sg, **put’** (3sg, [**be-on**’ (obligation, both sides) CAUSE **wait’** (both sides)]))]
c. Constructional schema: [V NP RP]

8.2.2 Promise

Making a promise is a commissive speech act with the illocutionary force that S promises to do an action X in some future time, for the benefit of H, by expressing its proposition (e.g., a promise) to H (Searle 1969). In making a promise, S commits to doing this future action X and is under an obligation to do so.

As we will see, it is possible distinguish commissive promises and commissive offers. Specifically, a promise is an act of obligating oneself while an offer is simply a proposal to obligate oneself.

The commissive promise has several special features:

- A promise is always made to H to do something for the benefit of H.
- A promise involves an obligation on S to actually do the thing promised in some future course of action. This increases the degree of strength on the commitment by S to H.

(4) The commissive promise
With S uttering utt, S promises H to do X

Precondition	Illocutionary force	Commissive
	IFID	• In a direct promise use of verb *geall* ‘promise’ in present tense plus is identification of promised action X. • In an indirect promise, use of some verb in future tense, plus commitment made by S to do specified action X.

	Intention of S:	S to do X
	Intention of S:	H to believe S's UTT obligates S to do X
	Desire of S:	S wants to do X
	Belief of S:	S believes that S obliged to do X
	Desire of H:	H desires to benefit from the action X
	Degree of Strength:	+++ 3
	Mode of Achievement:	S must do X.
	Mode of Achievement:	X to occur in some future T > T.now
	Obligation:	Modal obligation on S to do X
	Ability:	S able to do X
	Core common ground established	S expresses the proposition P
Realisation	S obliged to do X S expresses the BELIEF that that S obliged to do X S intends to do X because of S's utterance Emergent common ground constructed	
Postcondition	S does X H benefits from X Common ground updated	

Searle (1969:57–61) states nine conditions that must be met in order for a promise to be successfully executed. The promise is correctly and sincerely uttered if and only if all conditions are held. These conditions are paraphrased below:

i. The S and H must understand the language and the commitment meant by the speech act to ensure that it not jokingly made but is serious in intent.
ii. S expresses the proposition P.
iii. The utterance of a promising speech act obliges S to do a specified future action X.
iv. Under the preparatory condition, H desires the promised future action X to be done for H's benefit.
v. Under the preparatory condition, it is not obvious that the future action X would have been done by S prior to S's act of promising.

vi. Under the sincerity condition of promising, S intends to do the future action X, and furthermore S believes that the action X is possible for S to achieve.
vii. S understands that the utterance of a promise imposes an obligation on S to commit the future promised action X under the essential condition.
viii. The utterance of a promise by S is a linguistic sign that transmits and expresses the intended promise, which is understood by H as such.
ix. Once all conditions are met, the promise is correctly and sincerely uttered as felicitous.

Searle distinguishes between two IFIDs for a promise, those of direct vs. indirect. The direct delivery of a promise (5) contains the formula *I promise that...*, whereas evasive, satirical, and conditional promises represent indirect deliveries of a promise. The indirect IFID (6)–(7) may be characterised by grammatical devices such as future tense or the conditional.

(5) Direct promise
a.
Geallaim cabhrú leat le do chuid obair bhaile.
Promise:V-PRS+1SG help with:PREP+2SG with your homework
I promise to help you with your homework.
b. [**do'** (1SG, **promise**(1SG, [**be-at**' (2SG, **help'** (1SG, your homework))]))]
c. Constructional schema: [V.PRS NP NP NP RP]

(6) Indirect promise
a.
Tiocfaidh mé go dtí an searmanas.
Come:V-FUT 1SG to:PREP DET ceremony
I will come to the ceremony.
b. < TNS: FUT <[**do'** (1SG, **come'** (1SG, [**be-at**' (1SG, ceremony)]))]>>
c. Constructional schema: [V.FUT NP PP-LOC]

(7) Indirect promise
a.
Cuirfidh mé glaoch ort uair éigin.
Put:V-FUT 1SG call ON:PREP+2SG hour sometime
Lit: I will put a call on you some time.
I will give you a phonecall sometime.

b. < TNS: FUT < **some.time’ [do’** (1SG, **put’** (1SG, **[be-on**’ (phonecall, 2SG)]))]>>
c. Constructional schema: [V.FUT NP NP PP (ADV)]

8.2.3 Threaten

A threat is a promise which has negative consequences for H or some other third party or entity.

There is no obligation involved in a threat. A threat need not be a speech act in that it can simply involve menacing gestures. In contrast, a threat, as a type of promise, must be a speech act. A threat is H directed and must involve a public performance where H is not the same person as S.

(8)
a.
Bagraím caingean dlí ort.
threat:V-PRS+1SG action legal ON:PREP+2SG
I threaten you with legal action.
b. Constructional signature: [V.TNS NP NP PP]

(9)
a.
Cuirim bagairt air.
put:V-PRS+1SG threat ON:PREP+3SG.M
I threatened him.
b. Constructional signature: [V.TNS NP NP]

(10)
a.
Tá triobláid ag bagairt leis an long úd.
Be.AUX-PRS trouble at threaten:VN with DET ship that
Trouble is threatening that ship
That ship is in trouble.
b. Constructional signature: [AUX.TNS NP at VN NP]

(11)
a.
Déanaim bagairt ar a theaghlach.
do.make:V-PRS+1SG threat on poss family
I make a threat on his family.

b. Constructional signature: [V.TNS NP NP PP]

8.2.3 Vow, pledge, and commissive swear

The idea of a vow, pledge, and (commissive) swear are very similar and are employed as a type of promise. While they have individual characteristics, they are used interchangeably and differ in their mode of achievement. Like commit, vow, swear, and pledge are oriented towards S. Vow and swear are typically more formal while pledge is less formal. We allocate an indicative degree of strength of 4 to vow, pledge, and swear. In reality, the illocutionary force and the degree of strength are informed by the nature of the context and the common ground of the discourse interlocutors.

Therefore, the degree of strength is considered to be indicative rather than absolute. A vow is a type of promise but a vow need not be directed to H. In vowing to do something, I undertake to do it, but not necessarily for the benefit or obligation to H. A vow has a more formal or solemn quality to it that is not found in making a promise or a threat and which contributes to its mode of achievement. Because of this solemnity, the degree of strength is greater than the degree of strength of a commitment. As regards the MoA, a vow need not be directed to H and it has a more formal or solemn quality to it.

(12)

a.

Geallaim *duit* *mo* *thír.*
promise:V-PRS+1SG to:PREP+2SG POSS country
I vow to you my country.

b. Constructional signature: [V.TNS PP NP]

(13)

a.

Geallaim *go* *mbeidh* *mé* *ann* *duit* *i gcónaí.*
promise:V-PRS+1SG that be:AUX.FUT 1SG there to:PREP+2SG always
I vow/promise that I will always be there for you.

b. Constructional signature: [V.TNS NP that RP]

(14)

'Deirimse agus móidím dar gach mionn is dual dom mhuintir nach bhfuil aighneas agam ná ag aon duine de mo chlann le Lúcás Ó Briain ná lena mhuintir agus nach ceart go mbeadh agus mar chomhartha air sin tugaim an claíomh gearr dó atá ar an urlár eadrainn agus iarraim air béile a chaitheamh in éineacht linn i gCathair na gCeapach anocht.'

> 'I say and I swear by all the oaths of my people that I and any of my family have no quarrel with Luke O'Brien or his family and that there should not be and as a sign of that I give him the short sword that is on the floor between us and I ask him to spend a meal with us in Cappagh City tonight.'

A pledge is like vow but is less solemn. A pledge involves an undertaking by S but need not involve H. Typically, one makes a pledge to an idea or institution, such as when one pledges allegiance to a country or a national flag. A pledge tends to have a quality of personal commitment to an idea. For the MoA: a pledge need not be directed to H and it has a less formal or solemn quality to it.

(15)

a.
Geallaim *di* *rúndacht.*
promise:V-PRS+1SG to:PREP+3SG.F secrecy
I pledge secrecy/confidentiality to her.

b. Constructional signature: [V.TNS NP PP NP]

(16)

a.
Geallaim *dílseacht* *d'*Éirinn.
promise:V-PRS+1SG allegiance to:PREP+Ireland
I pledge allegiance to Ireland.

b. Constructional signature: [V.TNS NP NP PP]

With the commissive swear, S commits, in a solemn way by invoking some formal institution or perhaps a religious object, to carry out some course of action X at a time T.future > T.now. In essence, S makes a public commitment to do the future action X. The commissive swear therefore has a stronger degree of strength than vow, and a distinctive mode of achievement by virtue of the public nature of the utterance, and the formal/religious dimension to the commitment. The MoA of a swear is directed to H in public and it has a distinct formal or solemn quality to it

(17)

a.
Móidím *go* *mbainfeadh* *mé* *díoltas* *amach.*
swear:V-PRS+1SG that take:V-FUT 1SG payment out

I swear that I will take out revenge.

b. Constructional signature: [V.TNS NP THAT RP]

(18)

a.

Mionnaím faoi rún í.

swear:V-PRS+1SG under secrecy 3SG.F.ACC

I swear her to secrecy.

b. Constructional signature: [V.TNS NP PP NP NP]

8.2.4 Offer vs. bid

An offer is a promise that is conditional on the acceptance by H. An offer becomes binding upon acceptance. After acceptance by H, an offer commits S to perform a certain action X. Offer and accept are therefore reciprocally related. Typically, this is formally reflected legally in contract law.

(19) Commissive offer

With S uttering UTT, S offers H to do X

Precondition	Illocutionary force	Commissive
	IFID	use of offer
	Intention of S:	S to do X on condition that H indicates desire for S to do X
	Intention of S:	H to believe S's UTT obligates S to do X
	Desire of S:	S wants to do X
	Belief of S:	S believes that S obliged to do X if the condition exists that H indicates desire for S to do X
	Desire of H:	H desires to benefit from the action X
	Degree of Strength:	+++ 3
	Mode of Achievement:	S must do X if a specified condition holds
	Mode of Achievement:	X to occur in some future T > T.now
	Obligation:	Obligation on S to do X
	Ability:	S able to do X
	Core common ground established	S expresses the proposition P

Realisation	S obliged to do X S expresses the BELIEF that that S obliged to do X S intends to do X because of S's utterance Emergent common ground constructed
Postcondition	S does X H benefits from X Common ground updated

(20)

a.

Tairgim dul ag canbhasáil suas i mbarr na mbailte.

Offer:V-PRS+1SG go:VN at canvas:VN up in top (OF) DET towns

I offer to go canvassing up in the tops of the towns.

b. Constructional signature: [V.TNS NP RP]

(21)

a.

Tairgim é a thiomáint.

Offer:V-PRS+1SG 3SG.M.ACC PRT drive:VN

I offer to drive him.

b. Constructional signature: [V.TNS NP NP PRT RP]

(22)

a.

Tairgim é a scaoileadh óna ghealltanas.

Offer:V-PRS+1SG 3SG.M.ACC PRT free:VN from+POSS commitment

Lit: I offer him the freeing from his commitments.

I offer to released him from his commitment.

b. Constructional signature: [V.TNS NP NP PRT RP]

(23)

a. Tairgim *dá dheoin féin é.*

Offer:V-PRS+1SG voluntarily SELF 3SG.M.ACC

I offer it voluntarily.

b. Constructional signature: [V.TNS NP ADV NP]

A bid is a specialised form of an offer. When one makes a bid, one offers to buy something at a certain price. Specifically, in a bid, S offers to give something (i.e. money to a certain value or amount) in exchange for something.

(24) Commissive bid

With S uttering UTT, S bids H to do X

Precondition	Illocutionary force	Commissive
	IFID	use of bid
	Intention of S:	S to do X on condition that indicates desire for S to do X
	Intention of S:	H to believe S's UTT obligates
	Desire of S:	S to do X
	Belief of S:	S wants to do X S believes that S obliged to do X if the condition exists that H indicates desire for S to do X
	Desire of H:	H desires S to do action X
	Degree of Strength:	+++ 3
	Mode of Achievement:	S to do X if a specified condition holds
	Mode of Achievement:	The condition must be accepted by H
	Mode of Achievement:	The condition is typically transactional
	Mode of Achievement:	X to occur in some future T > T.now
	Obligation:	Obligation on S to do X
	Ability:	S able to do X
	Core common ground established	S expresses the proposition P
Realisation	S obliged to do X S expresses the BELIEF that that S obliged to do X S intends to do X because of S's utterance Emergent common ground constructed	
Postcondition	S does X H benefits from X Common ground updated	

The verb *tairg* 'is used with the meanings of 'offer' and 'bid'. They are differentiated by context.

(25)

a.
Tairgim *deich bpunt dó.*
offer:V-PRS+1SG ten pounds for:PREP+3SG.M
I bid ten pounds for it / I offer ten pounds for it.

b. Constructional signature: [V.TNS NP NP NP]

(26)

a.
Tairgim *punt air.*
offer:V-PRS+1SG pound on:PREP+3SG.M
I bid a pound on it.

b. Constructional signature: [V.TNS NP NP NP]

The verb *cuir* 'put' is used in the context of an auction to bid an amount, whereas the verb *glaoch* 'call' is used in the context of a game to place a bid.

(27)

a.
Cuirim *deich bpunt é.*
put:V-PRS+1SG ten pounds 3SG.M.ACC
I bid ten pounds for it.

b. Constructional signature: [V.TNS NP NP NP]

(28)

a.
Glaoim *trí mhuileata.*
Call:V-PRS+1SG three diamonds
I bid three diamonds.

b. Constructional signature: [V.TNS NP NP]

8.2.5 Bet, contract, covenant

In a bet, S makes a wager with H. In a bet, S promises to do something (for example, pay a certain money amount) if a certain event occurs, on the condition that H promises to do a certain thing if a certain other event occur, or condition triggers, such as a win or lose in a game. Bets are joint conditional promises by S that requires an acceptance by H to come into effect.

The speech act of a BET can be considered to be framed with certain components (29) to which the various felicity conditions apply.

The speech act of a commissive bet in Irish has two forms which can be schematised (30). As is seen from these schemata, the bet can be verbalised as an action, as in schema (30a), or occur as a nominal object, as in schema (30b).

(29) Frame schema for bet commissive speech act

a. Participant 1: the bet initiating-participant appears as agent/subject
b. Participant 2: the bet accepting-participant appears as dative object
c. The bet itself appears as THEME and grammatical object
d. The nature of the bet, what it's about, appears in a subordinate clause
e. The possibilities resulting from the uptake of the bet
f. The reward from winning the bet (in a subordinate clause)

(30) The commissive frame schemas

a.
S_{ACTOR} (will) bet_v with interlocutor H [that *some event occurs*]
Syntactic pattern → [bet_v S_{ACTOR} interlocutor H bet.event]

b.
S_{ACTOR} places/puts a bet_N with interlocutor H [(on) *some event occurring*]
Syntactic pattern → [put_v S_{ACTOR} bet_n.THEME (interlocutor H) bet.event]

Within these schemata, the initiating-participant S_{ACTOR}, is in the grammatical relation of subject immediately after the verb as Irish is a VSO language, the bet is again the THEME nominal in the grammatical relation of object. In a ditransitive clause, the accepting-participant occurs as the object of a preposition, as a dative grammatical object. The accepting-participant, interlocutor H, may be a full nominal as [prep N] or as a prepositional-pronoun (PPN), a conflation of prepositions with pronouns that is found in Irish. The nature of the bet is identified in a subordinate clause. In these examples, according to schema.a and schema.b respectively, the nature of the various bets is underlined.

Schema a.	S_{ACTOR} (will) bet_v with interlocutor H [that *some event /result occurs*] Syntactic pattern → [bet_v S_{ACTOR} interlocutor H bet.event]

(31)

a.

Geallaim ***duit*** *go bhfágfaidh sé*

Bet:V-PRS+1SG to:PREP+2SG that leave:V-FUT 3SG.M

do chraiceann an-bhog go deo.

POSS skin very soft forever

I bet you that it will leave your skin very soft forever.

b. Constructional signature: [V. PRS NP NP THAT RP]

(32)

a.

Geallaim ***anois*** *go mbeidh 'iontas'*

Bet:V-PRS+1SG now that be:AUX-FUT surprise

ar an bhliain seo chugainn!

on:PREP DET year next

I bet now that next year will be a 'surprise'!

b. Constructional signature: [V. PRS NP THAT RP]

(33)

a.

Geallaim nach mbeidh maolú faobhair ann.

Bet:V-PRS+1SG not be:AUX-fut mitigation sharpen:VN there

I bet (that) there will be no sharpening mitigation.

b. Constructional signature: [V. PRS NP THAT RP]

(34)

a.

Geall ***liom*** *nach mbeidh an bua agat.*

Bet:V-PRS with:PREP+1SG not be:AUX-FUT DET success at:PREP+2SG

I bet that you won't win.

b. Constructional signature: [V. PRS NP THAT RP]

(35)

a.

Geall ***liom*** *nach raibh sí*

Bet:V-PRS with:PREP+1SG not be:AUX-PST 3SG.F

fágtha le cleite uirthi.

left:ADJ with feather on:PREP+3SG.F

Lit: Bet with me that she was not left with a feather on her.

I bet she was not left with a feather on her.

b. Constructional signature: [V. PRS NP THAT RP]

Schema b. S_{ACTOR} places/puts a bet_N with interlocutor H [(on) *some event occurring*]
Syntactic pattern → [put_v S_{ACTOR} bet_n.THEME (interlocutor H) bet.event]

In Irish, the actor puts/places the bet, so here the bet_N is the THEME and grammatical object. Also, the initiating of the putting of a bet involves a time projection into the future and this is marked on the 'put' verb with future tense. The accepting participant to the bet can be encoded with either the preposition *ar* 'on' or *le* 'with' (34), showing that mutuality is a core feature and, as such, is part of the common ground to a bet situation. In these examples, both prepositions are conflated with the respective pronouns into prepositional pronouns. These prepositional pronouns are forms typical of Irish.

When it is necessary to identify the accepting participant H within the bet a dative object is used and the BET speech act is explicitly encoded as having three participants. These are the initiating participant (the agent) encoded as grammatical subject, the bet (THEME) encoded as grammatical object, and the accepting participant H encoded as the object of a preposition in the form of a prepositional pronoun (PPN). The PPN conjugates for person, number, and gender so the appropriate morphosyntactic form of this will be realised within the clause.

(36)

a.
Cuirfidh mé geall ***leat*** *go dtosóidh mé inniu*
Put:V-FUT 1SG bet with+2SG to start-FUT 1SG today
ar mo shlí bheatha a bhaint amach dom féin agus go
on my way (of) life REL take-PST out to+1SG RFLX and to
*n-*éireoidh *liom maireachtáil ar mo thuarastal leathbhliana.*
rise with+1SG living-VN on my salary half-year
I will put a bet with you that I will start today to earn my living for myself and that I will succeed in living on my salary for half a year.

b. Constructional signature: [V.FUT NP NP THAT RP]

(37)

a.

Cuirfidh mé geall **ort** *gur fearr dhuit fanacht.*

Put:V-FUT 1SG bet on+2SG that prefer to+2SG remain

I will put a bet on you that you prefer to stay.

b. Constructional signature: [V. FUT NP NP THAT RP]

(38)

a.

Cuirfidh mé geall ar bith nár éirigh leat.

Put:V-FUT 1SG.NOM bet on any NEG rise with+2SG

I will put any bet that you won't win.

b. Constructional signature: [V. FUT NP *geall* NP THAT RP]

(39)

a.

Cuirfidh mé geall go gcuala tú é

Put:V-FUT 1SG bet to hear-PST 2SG 3SG.M.ACC

'cainnt ar Mhicheál Dhubh.

talking-VN on Michael Dubh

I will put a bet that you heard him talking about Michael Dubh.

b. Constructional signature: [V. FUT NP *geall* (NP) THAT RP]

(40)

a.

Cuirfidh mé do rogha geall go mbéidh tú 'briseadh

Put:V-FUT 1SG your choice (of) bet to AUX-FUT 2SG broken

na gcos 'na ndiaidh.

DET.PL foot in+POSS after

I will put your choice of bets that you will be 'broken of foot 'afterwards.

b. Constructional signature: [V. FUT NP *geall* (NP) THAT RP]

The conditional in (41) is used for describing events that may or may not happen.

(41)

a.

Chuirfinnse geall gur gunnaí iad sin.

Put:V-COND+1SG+EMP bet that guns 3PL.ACC there

I would put a bet that these are guns.

b. Constructional signature: [V. FUT NP *geall* (NP) THAT RP]

That a bet speech act has various important dimensions and components, as represented by the frame schema for bet commissive speech acts, indicated earlier in (30), can be shown by the (assertive) examples (42) that foreground these. One can therefore talk about features of the bet and its nature without identifying either the initiating or the accepting participant, and this construct may involve using the impersonal passive form of the auxiliary verb. A bet can be for some event to occur, or some event not to occur.

(42) Showing the dimensions of a bet

a. Showing that the bet is seriously placed

'Táim lándáiríre faoin ngeall seo.
BE-AUX-PRS+1SG serious under+DET bet this
'a dhearbhaigh Colm.
at announce.V-PST Colm
'I'm fully serious about this wager,' declared Colm.

b. Showing that agreement is needed for a bet to be placed

Ní chuirfidh mé geall leat.
NEG put:V-FUT 1SG bet with+2SG
I won't put a bet with you.

c. Showing the nature of the bet

Bíodh geall go mbéadh sí arais roimhe mhí.
BE-AUX-FUT.IMPERS-PASS bet to AUX.FUT 3SG.F returned before month
There will be a bet that she will be back before a month

d. Showing the nature of the bet

Bíodh geall air go n-abhraidh
BE-AUX-FUT.IMPERS-PASS bet at+3SG.M to say-IMPERATIVE
mise cupla focal leis.
1SG+EMP few words with+3SG.M
There will be a bet that I say a few words with him.

These various important dimensions and components of the commissive bet speech act are a part of the interlocutors common ground, and mutually understood as such in the realisation of a successful bet. In essence, S agrees with H to bet on action X happening, H agrees to accept the bet and commits to do action Y in return if X does not happen.

(43) Commissive bet (schema a and schema b)

With S uttering UTT, S bet H to do X under the agreed bet condition(s)

Precondition	Illocutionary force	Commissive
	IFID	use of verb *geall* 'bet' according to schema a: [V-PRS NP NP THAT RP] use of verb *cuir* 'put' according to schema b: [V-FUT NP *geall* (NP) THAT RP]
	Intention of S:	S to do X on condition that H indicates desire for S to do X and H accepts the P of S's UTT to do X under the agreed conditions
	Intention of S:	H to believe S's UTT obligates S to do X under the agreed conditions
	Intention of H:	H to do Y on condition that S indicates desire for H to do Y and S accepts the P of UTT to do Y under the agreed conditions
	Desire of S:	S wants P to be true
	Belief of S:	S believes that S obliged to do X if the condition exists and H agrees
	Desire of H:	H desires S to do action X
	Desire of H:	H accepts the bet
	Degree of Strength:	+++++ 5
	Mode of Achievement:	S to do X if a specified condition holds
	Mode of Achievement:	The bet condition must be accepted by H
	Mode of Achievement:	The condition is typically transactional
	Mode of Achievement:	X to occur in some future T > T.now
	Obligation:	Obligation on S to do X under the agreed conditions
	Ability:	S able to do X
	Core common ground established	S expresses the proposition P

Realisation S obliged to do X under the agreed conditions
S and H evaluate the condition to determine if it triggered
S expresses the BELIEF that that S obliged to do X <u>or</u> H expresses the BELIEF that H obliged to do Y
S intends to do X because of S's bet utterance <u>and</u> H intends to do Y because of H's (agreement) utterance according to the bet condition
Emergent common ground constructed
Dynamics of bet understood between S and H
Specific nature of the bet agreed by S and H
Conditions of bet trigger agreed
Consequential actions X or Y achieved

Postcondition S does X <u>or</u> H does Y, subject to bet event outcome
H benefits from X <u>or</u> S benefits from Y
Common ground updated
Conditions of bet trigger evaluated
Consequential actions X or Y achieved

A contract (44) is different to a bet or a promise. A contract is a mutually binding pair of commitments made by two contracting parties, whereby S promises to do action X for H in return for which H promises to do action Y for S. The two commitments are not independent. They are intrinsically related and one is directly made in return for the other. Therefore, in a contract, S and H make mutually conditional promises such that the fulfilment of each is conditional on the fulfilment of the other. A contract a binding agreement between two or more persons or parties, and one that is legally enforceable. Contracts are joint promises.

(44)

a.
Déanaim *conradh.*
Make:V-PRS+1SG contract
I make a contract.

b. Constructional signature: [V.TNS NP NP]

That a contract has a number of core features which need to be mutually shared and understood in the common ground of the interlocutors can be demonstrated by the (assertive) examples indicated in (45).

(45) The core features of a contract

a. Showing that mutual agreement is needed for a contract
D'aontaigh an fear agus bhí an conradh déanta.
Agreed:V-PST DET man and be:AUX-PST DET agreement made
The man agreed and the contract was made.

b. Showing the monetary value of a contract to a contract party
Anuraidh, b'fhiú €54 milliún an conradh seo
Last year was+worth €54 million DET agreement this
do na hoifigí poist.
to:prep DET offices post
Last year, this contract was worth € 54 million to the post offices.

c. Showing that a contract may be time limited
Mairfidh an conradh sin 2 bhliain eile.
Will_last DET agreement that 2 years another
That contract will run for a further 2 years.

d. Showing the mutual conditionality of a contract
Dá mbrisfidís an conradh sin an mbeadh orthu
If break+3PL DET agreement this would on:prep+3 PL
an t-airgead a thabhairt ar ais?
DET money REL give on back
If they broke that contract would they have to return the money?

In contrast to a contract, a covenant is a formal perhaps solemn, binding agreement, typically a written agreement (though it may be verbalised as an utterance) or promise, made under legal seal between two or more parties for the performance of some action (46).

(46)

a.
Déanaim cúnant.
Make:V-PRS+1SG covenant
I make a covenant.

b. Constructional signature: [V.TNS NP NP]

A covenant has a somewhat similar sense to a contract but a covenant is more archaic, being favoured in law and religion (47).

(47) A covenant is more archaic and formal

a.

Ach an cúnant a scríobh ina gcroí arís, ní hamháin go ngnóthóidh siad flaitheas Dé sa saol eile ach athshealbhóidh siad a bhflaitheas saolta abhus.

But to write the covenant again in their hearts, they will not only gain the sovereignty of God in the afterlife but will regain their heavenly realm.

b.

*Ar na príomh-mholtaí, tá: coinníollacha teanga trí chonradh scríofa idir an forbróir agus an t-*údarás *pleanála faoi réir alt 47 den Acht Pleanála sara gcuirtear tús leis an bhforbairt agus an t-aontú sin le bheith ina chuid de chonradh díolacháin na n-aonad cónaithe; cúnant pionóis bheith sa chomhaontú sin inaisghabhála mar fhiach conartha simplí; 60 faoin gcéad ar a laghad de na haonaid chónaithe le cur go leataobh dóibh sin leis an chaighdeán Gaeilge a theastaíonn chun deontas a fháil faoi Scéim Tithíochta na Gaeltachta.*

Key recommendations include: language conditions through a written contract between the developer and the planning authority subject to section 47 of the Planning Act prior to the commencement of the development and that agreement to form part of the sales contract-residential unit; that agreement contain a penalty covenant recoverable as a simple contract debt; At least 60 per cent of residential units to be set aside for those with the required standard of Irish to receive a grant under the Gaeltacht Housing Scheme.

8.3 Some comments on commissive speech acts

The syntactic patterns underpinning the commissive speech acts of Irish, their constructional schemas (48) are generalised to (49). In these, the tense is non-past as the commissive commitment, while delivered in real time, commits to a present or future action. The speaker S is the actor and the hearer H is the undergoer.

The illocutionary point of the commissive reflects its internal purpose. The degree of strength of the illocutionary point differentiates across stronger or weaker acts having the same point. The mode of achievement indicates how this illocutionary act is to be achieved in a certain way or under certain conditions. A set of propositional content conditions constrains the content of the act. A set of preparatory conditions reflect what is necessary for the successful and non-defective performance of the speech act.

(48)The syntactic patterns underpinning the commissive speech acts of Irish

Speech act	IFID/SA Verb	Constructional schema
Commissive	commit	[V.TNS NP to RP]
	commit	[V.TNS NP RP]
	Direct promise	[V.PRS NP NP NP RP]
	Indirect promise	[V.FUT NP PP-LOC]
	Indirect promise	[V.FUT NP NP PP (ADV)]
	threaten	[V.TNS NP NP PP]
	threaten	[V.TNS NP NP]
	threaten	[AUX.TNS NP at VN NP]
	threaten	[V.TNS NP NP PP]
	vow	[V.TNS PP NP]
	vow	[V.TNS NP that RP]
	pledge	[V.TNS NP PP NP]
	pledge	[V.TNS NP NP PP]
	pledge	[V.TNS NP THAT RP]
	swear	[V.TNS NP PP NP NP]
	swear	[V.TNS NP NP THAT RP]
	offer	[V.TNS NP RP]
	offer	[V.TNS NP NP PRT RP]
	offer	[V.TNS NP NP ADV]
	bid	[V.TNS NP NP]
	bid	[V.TNS NP NP NP]
	bet	[V.PRS NP NP THAT RP]
	bet	[V. FUT NP *geall* (NP) THAT RP]
	contract	[V.TNS NP NP]
	covenant	[V.TNS NP NP]

These syntactic patterns the commissive speech acts of Irish generalise to that found in (49).

(49)

[V.TNS:PRS|FUT [actor]NP ([undergoer]NP) (PP-loc) (at VN) (to) (RP) (ADV)]

A set of sincerity conditions specify the cognitive states that need to be expressed for the speech act to succeed. The degree of strength of the sincerity conditions indicates of the intensity of the state that should be expressed. The preparatory condition is that S be capable of carrying out the action is expressed by a belief of S. That is, S is believed to be capable of carrying out the action X if both S and H accept that S intends to carry out X at some point in the future.

The illocutionary force of a commissive has:

- a commissive point which consists in S committing to a future course of action X
- a mode of achievement
- a degree of strength
- the condition that the propositional content represents a future course of action X by S
- the preparatory condition that S is capable of doing that action X
- the sincerity condition that S intends to do the action X

The speech act of promise is always made by S to H, and has the special preparatory condition that the promised action is good for H. It involves the explicit undertaking of an obligation on S that may be implicit in other types of commissive speech acts, and this increases the degree of strength of the sincerity conditions. The speech act of threatening differs from promising in that the undertaking is to the detriment of H. Also, with a threat, S has no obligation to do X. The speech act of pledging is similar to vowing, but with reduced formality or solemnity. The pledge by S may be personal and need not involve H. Unlike the speech acts of promises and threats, vows need not be directed at H. In vowing to do something, one undertakes to do it but H may not be involved. The speech act of vowing typically has some element of formality or solemnity, and this is informed by context. The speech act of offer is a promise that is conditional based on the acceptance by H, and it becomes binding only on H's acceptance. It commits S to perform a certain course of future action once accepted by H.

We summarise the degrees of strength of the various commissive speech acts. It is important to remember that these are indicative, relative from one commissive speech act to another, rather than absolute, and serve to help determine the relatedness of one commissive to another in conjunction with other dimensions such as mode of achievement, obligation on S, formality of occasion, etc. Context provides this information, along with the common ground of the interlocutors S and H. The indicative degrees of strength of the various commissive speech acts discussed are: 5: bet; 4: vow, pledge, swear; 3: promise, offer, bid; 2: threaten; 1: commit. The mode of achievement reflects whether the act is oriented towards S alone (commit, vow, swear, pledge), or oriented towards S and H (threaten, promise, offer, bid, bet). The obligation can be on S alone (promise, commit, vow, swear), or be mutually conditional on S and H (offer, bid, bet).There is no obligation on S or H in the speech act of threatening. Some commissive speech acts are more formal while other are less so and are more informal, such that formal include: vow, swear, bid, bet, and less formal: commit, promise, threaten, offer.

In the next chapter we discuss the expressive speech act.

9 The expressive speech act

9.1 Introduction to the expressive speech act

In this chapter, we examine for Irish how expressive speech acts communicate S's feelings about themselves or the world. Our discussion in this chapter on expressive speech acts includes consideration of how various expressions of emotion are rendered and communicated in Irish. According to Searle (1976:12), expressive speech acts are those speech acts that express S's feelings about themselves or the world, and include thanking, apologising, congratulating, greeting, amongst other expressions of emotion. The use of expressive speech acts can be found with several types of speaker-hearer interactions. Norrick (1978:284–290) identifies a number of expressive categories and these are indicated in Table 9.1.

Searle & Vanderveken (1985:211) find that these expressive speech acts name expressive forces. They argue that expressive speech acts are typically hearer-centred. Expressive speech acts are public expressions of emotional states (Guiraud at al. 2011:1031) and outline the different emotions behind expressive speech acts, such that 'whenever there is a psychological state specified in the sincerity condition, the performance of an act counts as an expression of that psychological state' (Searle 1969, chapter 9). They report that emotional states are divided into basic emotions and complex emotions. Basic emotions derive from the beliefs and goals of an agent. When agents believe something to be true, they feel joy or sadness at it being true. For Guiraud at al. (2011:1035), if agents hold something to be an ideal state of affairs (or not), they feel either approval (or disapproval). They define joy as a situation where an agent's belief in a situation being true coincides with the same agent's desire for the situation to be true. Sadness is defined as an agent's desire for something to be true but believing that it is not. The basic emotions include joy, sadness, approval, and disapproval. Complex emotions (Guiraud et al. 2011:1035–1037) are based on an agent's beliefs that their own responsibilities lead to their goals or ideals becoming true or not. Complex emotions lead to the expressive acts of thanking, rejoicing, complimenting, regretting, deploring, apologising, expressing satisfaction or guilt, reproaching, accusing, and protesting. These emotions are categorised following in Table 9.2.

Table 9.1 The expressive speech acts

Expressive Speech Act	Comment
Thank	• H does a favour to S which causes S to employ the expressive speech act of thanking H. • S expresses positive feelings to H who has done a service for S.
Welcome/greet	• H approaches S causing the expressive speech act of greeting by S. • S expresses positive feelings towards the arrival of H. This has a conceptual similarity with thanking.
Apologise	• S expresses regret or sorrow towards H for some event which S instigated. • H is offended by something, for which S apologies via the expressive speech act of apologising.
Congratulate	• H achieves something of a positive nature, which leads to the speech act of S congratulating H. • S has observed that H has either benefitted from, or carried out, a positively valued event.
Condole	• S has observed that H has suffered some loss. • This resembles congratulating, except that the experienced event is construed as negative or unfortunate.
Deplore	• H is criticised for an event which had a negative impact on H or a third person.
Forgive	• H is forgiven for an event which had a negative impact on S or a third person This has a similar conceptual set-up as deploring, except for the fact that S does not resent H's action.
Lament	• S expresses and regrets their own misfortune, either at their own or somebody else's doing.

It is argued by Ortony, Clore, & Collins (1988:13) that the broad classes of emotions result from our focusing on salient aspects of the world-events and their consequences, agents and their actions, or objects, pure and simple, construed within some situation. Emotions can have different intensities. The capacity to construe a situation from different perspectives is central to the realisation that different people can experience different emotions in response to the same objective event. Emotions have many facets, and they involve cognitions and conceptualisations. Emotions arise as a result of certain kinds of cognitions. As we argued in Chapter 2, we take the situation to be the locus of the individual and cultural conceptualisations, where context and common ground enrich the underspecification of a speech act.

Table 9.2 Emotions expressed in expressive speech acts

Emotions	What is expressed by S?
Being delighted	S expresses JOY about reaching a goal to H.
Being saddened	S expresses SADNESS to H about an outcome of some action or event.
Approving	S expresses APPROVAL to H about a goal that has been reached.
Disapproving	S expresses DISAPPROVAL to H about something not considered ideal.
Being sorry	S expresses to H REGRET about something.
Sympathising	S expresses to H REGRET about an outcome of some unfortunate incident.
Thanking	S expresses GRATITUDE for having received something.
Greeting	S expresses PLEASURE at meeting or seeing someone.
Apologising	S expresses REGRET for having harmed or bothered the hearer.
Condoling	S expresses SYMPATHY for H's having suffered some misfortune (not S's doing).
Congratulating	S expresses GLADNESS for H's having done or received something notable.
Acknowledging	S expresses RECOGNITION to H of something in context and is mutually recognised by S and H.

Ortony, Clore, & Collins (1988:2–4), report that the structure of individual emotions are such that if an individual conceptualises a situation in a certain kind of way, then the potential for a particular type of emotion exists. According to Ortony, Clore, & Collins, emotion is one of the most central and omnipresent dimensions of human experience, and people experience a wide range of emotions, from joy to grief. Yet while emotions influence and enrich our human experience, they can also cause dramatic disruptions in an individual's judgment and functioning. If the underlying situation contains the eliciting conditions for a particular emotion, the experience of that emotion can be inferred. If the eliciting conditions of an emotion are to be effective, the experiencing individual must encode the relevant situation in a particular way. If an emotion such as distress is a reaction to some undesirable event, framed within the situation, the event itself must be construed as undesirable, and because construing the world is a cognitive process, the eliciting conditions of emotions embody the cognitive representations that result from such construals. To say that emotions arise from cognition is to say that they are determined by the structure, content, and organisation of knowledge representations and the processes that operate on them. These representations and processes might sometimes be available to consciousness, but there is no reason to suppose that they necessarily are so. Of course, the way we describe emotions is through language. The working characterisation by Ortony, Clore, & Collins (1988:13) view emotions as nuanced reactions to events, agents, or objects, with their particular nature being determined by the way in which the eliciting situation is construed.

The expressive speech act expresses S's feelings to H. These feelings and their expression are appropriate to different kinds of occasion. In addition, these feelings may be expressed in some routine manner, to address some social formality, or genuinely and warmly expressed. The context therefore informs the expressive speech act. Expressive illocutionary forces have the null or empty direction of fit.

Many of the words that name the expressive illocutionary acts (thank, congratulate, apologise) name illocutions which are expressions of psychological states which have no direction of fit. In each case, the states reflect a belief and a desire. The belief has a mind-to-world direction of fit while desire has a world-to-mind direction no fit. According to Searle & Vanderveken (1985:95), the point of the expressive speech act is not to express the belief and desire but rather to express the state of gratitude, pleasure, or sorrow. Expressive verbs name illocutionary forces whose point is to express the attitude(s) of S about the state of affairs presented by the propositional content. They indicate something good or bad about the state of affairs represented by the propositional content of the expressive. Most are directed towards some H.

9.2 The expressive utterances

In this section we begin our examination of the expressive speech acts of Irish. These can involve the expression of positive attitudes either towards a person or a proposition. It includes liking, as expressing a positive attitudes and sentiments towards a person or thing, and expressing positive agreement with a proposition (1)–(2). Of course, it is also possible to express negative sentiments towards a person, thing, or proposition. Through various non-directed exclamations, one can express emotionally charged utterances reflecting a variety of sentiments. They may include expletives and other emotionally charged utterances, including religious or non-religious expletives.

(1) Expressing surprise, shock, or confusion

a.
In ainm Dé!
in:PREP name God
In the name of God!

b. Constructional signature: [PP]

c.
Ó, a *Chríost*!
oh PRT Christ
Oh Christ!

d. Constructional signature: [NP]

e.
Damnú!
damn
Damn!

f. Constructional signature: [ADV]

g.
Gan chiall, náireach, uafásach!
Senseless disgusting awful
Senseless, shameless, awful!

h. Constructional signature: [ADV]

i.
Go. mbeire an diabhal leis é!
To:PREP take:V-SUBJ DET devil with:PREP 3SG.M.ACC
Lit: May the devil take him!
To hell with him!

j. Constructional signature: [PREP V.TNS NP NP]

(2) Expression of liking and positive sentiment

a.
Tá an mhaidin go deas bog.
BE.AUX.PRS DET morning to nice soft
The morning is nice and soft.

b. Constructional signature: [V.TNS NP PP]

c.
Is mór an pléisiúr dom an oiread seo daoine a fheiceáil, bailithe le chéile ag ceiliúradh ról ár *dteanga i mbunú* ár *stáit agus sa lá atá inniu ann.*
It is a great pleasure for me to see so many people, gathered together celebrating the role of our language in the founding of our state and today.
d. Constructional signature: [V.TNS NP NP RP]

e.
Is mór an pléisiúr dom mo gharinÍon a chur in aithne daoibh anocht
It is a great pleasure for me to introduce my granddaughter to you tonight.
f. Constructional signature: [V.TNS NP NP RP]

In the following subsections, we characterise thanking, greeting and welcoming, apologising, congratulating, condoling, deploring, forgiving, lamenting, and acknowledging, as uttered in Irish.

9.2.1 The expressive speech act of thanking

The expressive speech act of thanking is used to express gratitude or appreciation to someone and to indicate to them that you are pleased about, or grateful for, something that they have done. That is, the point of S thanking H is to express gratitude to H. The targets of the gratitude may include items and actions, or actors who are not direct participants in the discourse. The preparatory conditions are that some (previous) action X benefits or is, in some way, good for S and that H is responsible for its occurrence. There are many ways to express thanks or gratitude (3). The targets of the gratitude may or not be overtly expressed but are, in any event, known within the shared common ground to the discourse interlocutors.

(3) Thanking
a.
Go raibh maith agat.
to:PREP BE:AUX good at:PREP+2SG
Lit: Good be at you.
Thank you.
b. Constructional signature: [PREP AUX.TNS ADJ NP]

c.
Is mór agam do ghníomh.
COP big at:PREP+1SG your action
I have much appreciation for your action.
d. Constructional signature: [COP.TNS ADJ NP NP]

e.
Tá do ghníomh an-bhuíoch liom.
BE.AUX.PRS your action very-grateful to:PREP+2SG
Your action is very much appreciated by me.
f. Constructional signature: [AUX.TNS NP ADJ NP]

g.
Is mór an meas atá agam ar do ghníomh.
COP big DET appreciation that+BE:AUX.PRS at:PREP+1SG on your action
Your action is very much appreciated by me.
h. Constructional signature: [COP.TNS ADJ NP RP]

i.
Táim an-bhuíoch díot.
BE.AUX.PRS+1SG very-grateful to:PREP+2SG
I am very grateful to you.
j. Constructional signature: [AUX.TNS NP ADJ NP]

k.
Is mór an meas atá agam ar lucht eagraithe na féile seo a chuireann clár den scoth ar siúl gach bliain.
Is mór an meas atá agam
COP big DET appreciation that+be:AUX.PRS at:PREP+1SG
ar lucht eagraithe na féile seo a chuireann clár den scoth
on group organisers DET festival this that put:V-PRS programme excellent
ar siúl gach bliain.
on progress each year
I have great respect for the organisers of this festival who put on an excellent programme every year.
l. Constructional signature: [COP.TNS ADJ NP RP]

(4) The expressive speech act of thanking
With S uttering UTT, S greets to H for X

Precondition	Illocutionary force	Expressive
	IFID	use of *thank*
	Intention of S:	S shows gratitude to H for X
	Intention of S:	H believe that S is grateful to H for X
	Intention of S:	S show gratitude at having benefited
	Intention of S:	H take S's UTT as satisfying expectation
	Desire of S:	S wants to show gratitude to H for X
	Belief of S:	S believes that S benefited from X
	Degree of Strength:	++ 2
	Mode of Achievement:	S makes UTT to H
	Mode of Achievement:	X occurred in some past T < T.now
	Core common ground established	X in common ground
Realisation	S utters gratitude to H for X S (may) express the BELIEF that S benefited from X S intends to show gratitude to H for X because of H's prior action X Emergent common ground constructed	
Postcondition	S benefits from X S is grateful to H for X X may be unexpressed within UTT but understood from the common ground Common ground updated	

9.2.2 The expressive speech act of greeting, welcoming, and wishing

The expressive speech act of greeting is the act of giving a sign of welcome to someone, or their recognition. The expression of greeting can be said or written. An expressive speech act of greeting is an expression of good wishes towards someone, and is something friendly that you say or do when you meet someone. In this category of expressives, greetings occur when, typically, H approaches S and this causes S to utter an expressive speech act of greeting to H. It may take diverse forms such as (5).

(5) Greeting

a.

Maidin mhaith gach duine!
Morning good every person
Good morning, everyone!

b. Constructional signature: [NP NP]

c.

Is mór an pléisiúr é a Angela,
Cop big DET pleasure 3SG.M.ACC PRT Angela
bualadh leat arís.
meet:VN with:PRT+2SG again
It is a great pleasure, Angela, to meet you again.

d. Constructional signature: [COP.TNS ADJ NP NP RP]

The expressive speech act of welcoming is to behave in a polite or friendly way to a person, perhaps a guest or new arrival. In the expressive speech act of welcoming, one behaves in a way that is friendly to someone when they arrive somewhere so that they feel happy and accepted. The expressive speech act of welcoming occurs when, typically, S approaches or happens upon H and this causes S to utter an expressive speech act of welcoming H (6)–(7).

(6) Welcoming

a.

Tá fáilte romhat!
Be:aux.prs welcome before:PREP+2SG
Lit: A welcome is before you.
You are welcome!

b. Constructional signature: [AUX.TNS ADJ NP]

c.

Tá fáilte romhat cónaí i mo theach,
Be:aux.prs welcome before:PREP+2SG live in POSS house
más mian leat.
if wish with:PRT+2SG
You are welcome to live in my house, if you wish.

d. Constructional signature: [AUX.TNS ADJ NP RP]

(7) The expressive speech act of greeting
With S uttering utt, S greets H

Precondition	Illocutionary force	Expressive
	IFID	use of greet
	Intention of S:	S shows pleasure at seeing/ meeting H
	Intention of S:	H believe that S is pleased to see H
	Intention of S:	S to satisfy social expectation of showing pleasure at meeting H
	Desire of S:	H take S's utt as satisfying expectation
	Belief of S:	S wants pleasure at seeing/ meeting H S believes that S happy to see H
	Degree of Strength:	++ 2
	Sincerity condition	S makes UTT to H
	Mode of Achievement:	S seeing/meeting H occurs in time T.now
	Mode of Achievement:	Seeing/meeting event in common ground
	Core common ground established	
Realisation	S utters greeting to H S intends to show pleasure in seeing/meeting H Emergent common ground constructed	
Postcondition	S expresses pleasure at meeting H Common ground updated	

The expressive speech act of wishing is the act by S of making a wish and indicates a desire, hope, or longing for something or for something, typically good and positive, to happen to H. The expression of wishing occurs when, typically, S expresses positive sentiments towards H as befits the occasion (8).

(8) Wishing
a.
Oíche mhaith!
Night good

Good night!
b. Constructional signature: [NP]

c.
Oíche Shamhna faoi mhaise!
Night Halloween under prosperity
Happy Halloween!

d.
Go maire sibh an lá!
to:PREP best 2SG DET day
Lit: The best to you on the day
Happy Anniversary!

9.2.3 The expressive speech act of apologising

This category of expressive speech acts consists of expressions of being sorry (9) and of apologising (10). The point of apologising is to express sorrow or regret for some state of affairs that S is responsible for. The preparatory condition is that S must be responsible for the thing about which sorrow is expressed. Mostly, S apologises for S's own actions where S accepts responsibility for the actions. However, this need not always be the case. Another preparatory condition is that the P is true and the state of affairs represented by the propositional content is bad for H. The actions or thing for which the apology is made need not be overtly expressed but is understood from the common ground.

(9) Expressing sorrow
a.
Tá an-bhrón orm
BE.AUX.PRS much+sorrow on:PREP+1SG
gur chuir mé stró ort.
that put:V-PST 1SG stress on:PREP+2SG
I'm very sorry I bothered you.
b. Constructional signature: [AUX.TNS ADJ PP RP]

c.
Tá an-bhrón orm é sin
BE.AUX.PRS much+sorrow on:PREP+1SG 3SG.M that
a chloisteáil, a Naoise.
PRT hear:VN oh Naoise

I am very sorry to hear that, Naoise.
d. Constructional signature: [AUX.TNS ADJ PP RP]

e.
An locht orm féin nár leigh mé an treoirleabhar le breis dúthrachta.
An locht orm féin nár leigh mé
DET fault on:PREP+1SG SELF NEG read:V-PST 1SG
an treoirleabhar le breis dúthrachta.
DET guidebook with more diligence
It was my own fault that I did not read the guidebook with more diligence.
f. Constructional signature: [NP NP RP]

(10) Expressing an apology
a.
Gabh mo leithscéal le do thoil.
Take:V-PRS POSS apology with:PREP your will
Please accept my apologies.
b. Constructional signature: [V.TNS NP ADV]

c.
Gabh mo leithscéal ar mo Ghaeilge ach táim ag foghlaim Gaeilge arís.
Gabh mo leithscéal ar mo Ghaeilge
Take:V-PRS POSS excuse on my Irish
ach táim ag foghlaim Gaeilge arís.
but BE.AUX.PRS+1SG at learn:VN Irish again
Excuse me for my Irish but I'm learning Irish again.
d. Constructional signature: [V.TNS NP NP RP]

(11) The expressive speech act of apologising
With S uttering UTT, S apologies to H for X

Precondition	Illocutionary force	Expressive
	IFID	use of *apologise*
	Intention of S:	S shows regret to H for X
	Intention of S:	H believe that S is regretful to H for X
	Intention of S:	S show regret at having done X
	Intention of S:	H take S's UTT as satisfying expectation

Desire of S:	S wants to express regret to H for X
Belief of S:	S believes that S doing X upset H
Degree of Strength:	+++++ 5
Sincerity condition	S makes UTT to H
Mode of Achievement:	X occurred in some past T < T.now
Mode of Achievement:	X in common ground
Core common ground established	

Realisation	S utters regret to H for X S express the BELIEF that H is upset from S doing X S intends to show regret to H for X because of S's prior action X Emergent common ground constructed
Postcondition	S apologised to H for doing X S is regretful to H for X X may be unexpressed within UTT but understood from the common ground Common ground updated

9.2.4 The expressive speech act of congratulating

To offer congratulations in an expressive speech act is to give someone our good wishes when something special or pleasant has happened to them, or to praise them for an achievement. It is used to express pleasure to some person on their success or good fortune. Therefore, when S congratulates H, the mode of achievement is that the utterance is public. At a personal level, one can also feel pride or satisfaction in one's own abilities or achievement, and one congratulating oneself for a job well done. Here, S's utterance is private.

Under the expressive speech act of congratulating, S gives S's good wishes to H, and it is typically done when H has achieved some success or good fortune, done something special or pleasant. S praises H for their achievement and S feels pride, joy, or satisfaction in H's achievement. The achievement X of H need not be explicitly mentioned in the utterance, but is, in any event, in the discourse common ground.

(12) The expressive speech act of congratulating
With S uttering UTT, S congratulates H for X

Precondition	Illocutionary force	Expressive
	IFID	use of congratulate/compliment
	Intention of S:	S to express joy to H for H achieving X
	Intention of S:	H believe that S is pleased with H for X
	Intention of S:	H take S's UTT as satisfying expectation
	Desire of S:	S wants to express gladness to H for X
	Belief of S:	S believes that H achieving X worthy of compliment
	Degree of Strength:	+++++ 5
	Sincerity condition	S makes UTT to H
	Mode of Achievement:	X occurred in some past T < T.now
	Mode of Achievement:	X in common ground
	Core common ground established	
Realisation	S utters gladness to H for achieving X S expresses the BELIEF that H achieving X worthy of compliment S intends to show gladness to H for achieving prior action X Emergent common ground constructed	
Postcondition	S congratulates to H for doing X S is pleased that H achieved X X may be unexpressed within UTT but understood from the common ground Common ground updated	

To offer a compliment is to give a polite expression of praise or admiration, for something. The utterance of a compliment in an expressive speech act is therefore to give an expression of esteem, respect, affection, or admiration, containing some appropriate and admiring remark, or to give a formal and respectful recognition to someone for something. That is, S publicly utters a compliment to H for some X.

(13) Congratulating

a.
Déanaimid comhghairdeas ó chroí
make:V-PRS+1PL congratulate from:PREP heart
libh as bhur mbua.
with:PREP+2SG from:PREP your win
We heartily congratulate you on your win.

b. Constructional signature: [V.TNS NP NP PP PP PP]

c.
Tréaslaímid bhur mbua ó chroí libh.
Congratulate:V-PRS+1PL your win from:PREP heart with:PREP+2SG
We congratulate your victory from our heart.

d. Constructional signature: [V.TNS NP NP PP PP]

e.
Comhghairdeas libh agus guím
congratulations with:PREP+2SG and wish:V-PRS+1SG
gach rath oraibh.
every success on:PREP+2PL
Congratulations to you, and I wish you every success.

f. Constructional signature: [V.TNS NP PP]

(14) Expressing a compliment

a.
Molaim do chuid Fraincise.
Praise:V-PRS+1SG your part French
I compliment your French.

b. Constructional signature: [V.TNS NP NP]

c.
Molaim do chulaith nua.
Praise:V-PRS+1SG your suit new
I compliment your new suit.

d. Constructional signature: [V.TNS NP NP]

e.
Molaim do mhisneach, a bhuachaill.
Praise:V-PRS+1SG your courage PRT boy
I commend your courage, boy.

f. Constructional signature: [V.TNS NP NP]

9.2.5 The expressive speech act of condoling and commiserating

The illocutionary point of the expressive speech act is to express the psychological state specified in the sincerity condition about a state of affairs specified in the propositional content.

With the expression of condolences (15), the emotion that S expresses to H is sympathy over some event X that was not beneficial to H and is to be regretted. There is no direction of fit. In performing an expressive, the speaker is not trying to get the world to match the words or the words to match the world. The truth of the expressed proposition is presupposed.

(15) Expressing condolences

a.
Is mian liom mo chomhbhrón a chur in iúl leatsa féin agus le d'fhear céile.
Is mian liom mo chomhbhrón
COP desire with:PREP+1SG POSS condolences
a chur in iúl leatsa féin agus
PRT put:VN in knowledge with:PREP+2SG-EMP SELF and
le d'fhear céile.
with your+husband
I want to express my condolences to you and your husband.

b. Constructional signature: [COP.TNS ADJ NP NP RP]

c.
Mo chomhbhrón lena bhean, Máirín, agus a chlann, a aireoidh uathu é.
Mo chomhbhrón lena bhean, Máirín.
My condolences to+his wife Máirín
agus a chlann, a aireoidh uathu é.
and her family who miss:V-FUT from:PREP+3PL 3SG.M.ACC
My condolences to his wife, Máirín, and his family, who will miss him.

d. Constructional signature: [NP RP]

(16) The expressive speech act of condoling and commiserating

With S uttering UTT, S commiserates to H regarding X

Precondition	Illocutionary force	Expressive
	IFID	use of commiserate /condole
	Intention of S:	S shows sympathy to H for X
	Intention of S:	H believes S has sympathy with H for X
	Intention of S:	H take S's UTT as satisfying expectation

	Desire of S:	S wants to express compassion to H for X
	Belief of S:	S believes H worthy of sympathy for X
	Belief of S:	S believes X carries misfortune for H
	Degree of Strength:	+++++ 5
	Sincerity condition	S has significant discontent or sadness
	Mode of Achievement:	S makes UTT to H
	Mode of Achievement:	X occurred in some past T < T.now
	Core common ground established	X in common ground
Realisation	S utters sympathy to H for achieving X S expresses the BELIEF that H's misfortune with X worthy of sympathy S intends to show sympathy to H for misfortune with prior action X Emergent common ground constructed	
Postcondition	S commiserates with H for X S shows compassion to H X may be unexpressed within UTT but understood from the common ground Common ground updated	

9.2.6 The expressive speech act of deploring

In using the expressive speech act of deplore, one expresses a complaint with a high degree of strength and a preparatory condition that someone (not necessarily H) is responsible for something considered to be bad. The sincerity condition is indicative of a significant discontent, disgust, sorrow or sadness (17).

(17) Deploring

a.

Tá an-bhrón orm faoin mhéid

Be.AUX.PRS very-sad on:PREP+1SG under amount

a tharla an oíche sin.

that happened DET night that

I am very sorry about what happened that night.

b. Constructional signature: [AUX.TNS ADJ NP NP RP]

c.

Mar bhean Fhrancach, mar ealaíontóir, mar dhuine a oibríonn le hirisí agus, thar aon ní eile, mar bhall den chine daonna, chuir an t-ionsaí gránna ar oifigí Charlie Hebdo inné samhnas agus brón ar mo chroí.

As a French woman, as an artist, as someone who works with magazines and, above all, as a member of the human race, the heinous attack on Charlie Hebdo's offices yesterday made disgust and sadness on my heart.

d. Constructional signature: [RP NP PP]

(18) The expressive speech act of deploring

With S uttering UTT, S deplores to H regarding X

Precondition	Illocutionary force	Expressive
	IFID	use of deplore-like constructs in syntax
	Intention of S:	S shows discontent to H re X
	Intention of S:	H believes S has discontent re X
	Intention of S:	H take S's UTT as satisfying expectation
	Desire of S:	S wants to express discontent to H re X
	Belief of S:	S believes worthy of discontent
	Degree of Strength:	+++++ 5
	Sincerity condition	S has significant discontent or sadness
	Mode of Achievement:	S makes UTT to H
	Mode of Achievement:	X occurred in some past T < T.now
	Core common ground established	X in common ground
		X caused by someone, not (necessarily) H

Realisation	S utters discontent to H regarding X S expresses the BELIEF to H's that X worthy of discontent S intends to show discontent to H for prior action X Emergent common ground constructed
Postcondition	S deplores X to H S has significant discontent, disgust, or sadness H not necessarily responsible for H X may be unexpressed within UTT but understood from the common ground Common ground updated

9.2.7 The expressive speech act of forgiving

The expressive speech act of forgiving occurs when we express forgiveness to someone for something that they have done. The speech act of forgiving is typically public and uttered to H, though it may be privately made (19). We can define forgiveness as a conscious, deliberate choice by S to release feelings of emotion, such as anger or retribution, toward a person or group who has offended S in some way X. As a personal matter of release of emotion by S, forgiveness may occur regardless of whether the offenders actually deserve S's forgiveness or not. The speech act of forgiving is used when we express, typically to H, that we cease to feel resentment against an offender for doing X. The expressive speech act of forgiving is related to speech act of apologising. While in an apology, S expresses sorrow to H for something S have done to H, it is the case that, in forgiving, S give forgiveness to H typically after H has apologised to S for something H has done to S.

(19)Forgiving

a.
Maithim *duit.*
forgive:V-PRS+1SG to:PREP+2SG
I forgive you.

b. Constructional signature: [V.TNS NP NP]

c.
Maithim *duit* *ach ná* *déan* *arís* *é.*
forgive:V-PRS+1SG to:PREP+2SG but NEG do:V-PRS again 3SG.M
I forgive you but don't do it again.

d. Constructional signature: [V.TNS NP NP RP]

(20) The expressive speech act of forgiving

With S uttering UTT, S forgives H for doing X

Precondition	Illocutionary force	expressive
	IFID	use of forgive
	Intention of S:	S gives forgiveness to H re X
	Intention of H:	S believes H has regret for doing X to S
	Intention of H:	Exhibit regret to S for doing X to S
	Intention of H:	S take H's UTT as satisfying expectation
	Desire of S:	S wants to express forgiveness to H re X
	Belief of S:	S believes H regrets doing X to S
	Belief of S:	S believes H forgivable
	Degree of Strength:	++++ 4
	Sincerity condition	S feels significant clemency towards H
	Mode of Achievement:	S makes UTT to H
	Mode of Achievement:	H has previously apologised to S re X
	Mode of Achievement:	X occurred in some past T < T.now
	Core common ground established	X in common ground H caused X with negative result for S
Realisation	S utters forgiveness to H regarding X S expresses the belief to H's that X worthy of clemency S intends to show clemency to H for H's prior action X Emergent common ground constructed	
Postcondition	S forgives to H for doing X to S S is content that H regrets X X may be unexpressed within UTT but understood from common ground Common ground updated	

9.2.8 The expressive speech acts of lamenting and mourning

The expressive speech act of lamenting is used to express passionate regret or disappointment over the loss of something and this constitutes the propositional content condition (21). The use of lament by S denotes a strong public expression of sorrow, and this is the mode of achievement. No responsibility need be assigned to H as the responsibility for the object of the lament may reside elsewhere with some third party, or event that occurred.

Lament is closely related to mourning. The expressive speech act of mourning shows deep sorrow and grief for the death of someone, the constitutes the propositional content condition. Typically, mourning is reserved for the loss of a person, while one can lament just about anything that does not involve dearth of a person. One can mourn publicly or privately, and this is the mode of achievement.

(21) The expressing of lament

a.
Caoinim *easpa suime na ndaltaí sa stair.*
Lament:V-PRS+1SG lack interest DET students in:PREP+DET history
I *lament* the students' lack of interest in history.

b. Constructional signature: [V.TNS NP NP]

c.
Caoineann mé imeacht na ndaoine óga, fosta.
Lament:V-PRS 1SG depaerture (of) DET people young too
I lament the departure of the young, too.

d. Constructional signature: [V.TNS NP NP]

e.
Caoinim bean nach raibh aon leanaí uirthi.
Lament:V-PRS+1SG woman NEG be.AUX.PST any children on:PREP+3SG.F
I lament the woman who had no children.

f. Constructional signature: [V.TNS NP RP]

The verb *caoin* has the three senses of lament, mourn, and keen/cry. Its exact meaning determination depends on context. Specifically, this is informed by whether the object of the sorrow is over the death or loss a person, or not. We see this in examples (22) and (23). The sense reflecting cry is shown in (23).

(22) The expressing of mourning

a.
Caoinim i mo dhéfhiús,
Lament:V-PRS+1SG in my devotion
an fáil ar bhás atá ag gach a mairean.
DET availability on death BE.AUX-PRS at all that live
I mourn, in my devotion, the death of all who live.

b. Constructional signature: [V.TNS NP RP]

c.
Mé ag caoineadh slua na marbh.
1SG at:PREP mourn:VN crowd (of) DET dead
I mourn the crowd of the dead.

d. Constructional signature: [NP AT VN NP]

(23) The expressing of sorrow

a.
Tá mé ag caoineadh mar tá mo chroí briste.
Be.AUX-PRS 1SG at:PREP mourn:VN because BE.AUX-PRS POSS heart broken
I am crying because my heart is broken.

b. Constructional signature: [AUX.TNS NP AT VN RP]

(24) The expressive speech acts of lamenting

With S uttering UTT, S laments to H over X

Precondition	Illocutionary force	Expressive
	IFID	Use of lament
	Intention of S:	S express sorrow to H re X
	Intention of S:	S believes S has sorrow over loss re X
	Desire of S:	S wants to express sorrow to H re X
	Belief of S:	S believes H has empathy with S
	Degree of Strength:	++++ 4
	Sincerity condition	S has significant sorrow over loss re X
	Mode of Achievement:	S makes UTT to H
	Mode of Achievement:	S's UTT is expressed publicly
	Mode of Achievement:	X occurred in some past T < T.now

	Core common ground established	X in common ground X is a thing or event The loss of X has negative result for S
Realisation	S utters public lament to H regarding X S expresses the belief to H's that X causing deep sorrow to S S intends to show that X causing deep sorrow to S Emergent common ground constructed	
Postcondition	S expresses deep sorrow to H over X S is content that H has empathy with S re lament over X X may be unexpressed within UTT but understood from common ground Common ground updated	

(25) The expressive speech acts of mourning

With S uttering UTT, S mourns to H over X

Precondition	Illocutionary force	Expressive
	IFID	use of mourn
	Intention of S:	S express sorrow to H re X
	Intention of S:	S believes S has sorrow over loss re X
	Desire of S:	S wants to express sorrow to H re X
	Belief of S:	S believes H has empathy with S
	Degree of Strength:	++++ 4
	Sincerity condition	S has significant sorrow over loss re X
	Mode of Achievement:	S makes UTT to H
	Mode of Achievement:	S's UTT may be public or private
	Mode of Achievement:	X occurred in some past T < T.now
	Core common ground established	X in common ground X is a person, and not an event or thing The loss of X has negative result for S

Realisation	S utters (public) lament (to H) regarding X S expresses the belief (to H) that X causing deep sorrow to S S intends to show that X causing deep sorrow to S Emergent common ground constructed
Postcondition	S expresses deep sorrow (to H) over loss of X S is content that H has empathy with S over loss of X X may be unexpressed within UTT but understood from common ground Common ground updated

9.2.9 The expressive speech act of acknowledging

What does to acknowledge mean? When one acknowledges, one publicly accepts or admits the existence, or truth, of something, or we can recognise the importance or quality of something. One can acknowledge a mistake, or acknowledge that something has been received or noticed. One to recognise the rights or authority using an acknowledge, and one can acknowledge a gift or a good deed. The expressive speech act of acknowledging is concerned with these matters.

In the case where the acknowledging utterance is routine or formal, an acknowledgment expresses S's intention that the utterance satisfy some social expectation to express certain feelings along with S's belief that the utterance fulfils that expectation. Commonly, an occasion that is worthy of an acknowledgement is mutually recognised by S and H, and then it is appropriate and expected, by H, that S will issue the relevant acknowledgment (Bach & Harnish 1979:45). Because acknowledgments are expected on particular occasions and in a particular context, they are often issued to satisfy the social expectation that such a feeling be expressed, rather than to express a genuine feeling or emotion. In using the expressive speech act of acknowledging, S utters an acknowledgement to H, after some action X undertaken by H, for which S is appreciative.

(26)The expressive speech act of acknowledging
With S uttering UTT, S acknowledges to H for some action X

Precondition	Illocutionary force	Expressive
	IFID	use of acknowledge
	Intention of S:	S shows appreciation to H for X
	Intention of S:	H believe that S is appreciative of H for X
	Intention of S:	H take S’s UTT as satisfying expectation
	Desire of S:	S wants to shows appreciation to H for X
	Belief of S:	S believes H worthy of acknowledgement
	Degree of Strength:	+ 1
	Mode of Achievement:	S makes UTT to H
	Mode of Achievement:	X occurred in some past T < T.now
	Core common ground established	X in common ground
Realisation	S utters acknowledgement to H for X	
	S intends to show appreciation to H for X	
	Emergent common ground constructed	
Postcondition	S is appreciative to H for X	
	X may be unexpressed within UTT but understood from common ground	
	Common ground updated	

(27)

a.
Admhaím go bhfuil fadhb ann.
admit:V-PRS+1SG that be.AUX problem there
I acknowledge that there’s a problem.
b. Constructional signature: [V.TNS NP RP]

c.
Admhaím go raibh fiúntas leis.
admit:V-PRS+1SG that be.AUX.PST value with:PREP+3SG.M
I admit/acknowledge it was worth it .
d. Constructional signature: [V.TNS NP RP]

e.
Aithním *í* *mar an t-imreoir is fearr ar domhan.*
recognise:V-PRS+1SG 3SG.F.ACC as DET player COP best on world
I acknowledge her as the best player in the world.
f. Constructional signature: [V.TNS NP NP RP]

Within our society, obligatory or routine acknowledgments are generally regarded as acts of courtesy as they do not express genuine feelings. When the acknowledgment is prompted by something trivial, or when an occasion merits nothing more than a routine acknowledgment, for H to question S's sincerity would be an act of rudeness and discourtesy. In issuing an acknowledgment to H, S presumes the existence of the occasion to which the acknowledgment is appropriate, as residing in the shared common ground. For example, in S thanking H for something, S presumes that S has received something from H, and, in S apologising to H, S presumes that S has done something regrettable to H. That 'something' resides in common ground and is shared knowledge between S and H. The existence of the relevant occasion also resides in the discourse common ground. As such, it is presumed by S, and not asserted, and it is therefore unnecessary for S to mention the occasion explicitly. An acknowledgement may occur in response to some other speech act, and this might be construed as a perlocutionary effect if this is intended, for example, when greetings and farewells are exchanged, thanks are accepted ('You're welcome'), congratulations and condolences are accepted ('Thank you'), and apologies may be accepted or rejected (Bach & Harnish 1979:47).

9.3 Some comments on expressive speech acts

Expressive speech acts are utterances that convey S's emotions and feelings. Depending on the situation, different expressives can be used to communicate different feelings, as we have seen. Many of the psychological states of these expressive speech acts, the emotive states, carry the belief that the object of the state is good or bad, as in pleasure, joy, sorrow, or discontent. These expressive speech acts have as their illocutionary point to express S's attitudes about the state of affairs represented by the propositional content. The syntactic patterns found for the expressive speech act are quite varied, ranging from a simple [PP] to a full clause, based on the examples discussed in this chapter. We summarise these in (28).

In thanking, welcoming and greeting, S expresses positive feelings to H, as appropriate to the context and occasion. Congratulating and condoling have a similarity. In congratulating, something of a positive nature has happened to

H and is commented upon by S whereas in condoling, the experienced event is construed as by S and H negative or unfortunate. In deploring, S make a strong criticism on some event that has occurred which has negative consequences that are resented by S. Forgiving has a similar conceptual set-up as deploring, except that, in this speech act, S does not resent H's action.

(28)The syntactic patterns for the expressive speech act

Speech act	IFID/SA Verb	Constructional schema
Expressive	surprise expletives	[PP]
	expletives expletives	[NP]
	liking	[ADV]
	liking	[PREP V.TNS NP NP]
	thanking	[V.TNS NP PP]
	thanking	[V.TNS NP NP RP]
	thanking	[PREP AUX.TNS ADJ NP]
	thanking	[COP.TNS ADJ NP NP]
	thanking	[AUX.TNS NP ADJ NP]
	greeting	[COP.TNS ADJ NP RP]
	greeting	[AUX.TNS NP ADJ NP]
	Welcoming Welcoming	[NP NP]
	Wishing	[COP.TNS ADJ NP NP RP]
	sorrow	[AUX.TNS ADJ NP]
	sorrow	[AUX.TNS ADJ NP RP]
	apology	[NP]
	apology	[AUX.TNS ADJ PP RP]
	Congratulating	[NP NP RP]
	Congratulating	[V.TNS NP ADV]
	Congratulating	[V.TNS NP NP RP]
	Complimenting	[V.TNS NP NP PP PP PP]
	Condoling	[V.TNS NP NP PP PP]
	Condoling	[V.TNS NP PP]
	Deploring	[V.TNS NP NP]
	Deploring	[COP.TNS ADJ NP NP RP]
	Forgiving	[NP RP]
	Forgiving	[AUX.TNS ADJ NP NP RP]
	lamenting lamenting	[RP NP PP]
	mourning mourning	[V.TNS NP NP]
	mourning	[V.TNS NP NP RP]
	acknowledging	[V.TNS NP NP]
	acknowledging	[V.TNS NP RP]
		[V.TNS NP RP]
		[NP AT VN NP]
		[AUX.TNS NP AT VN RP]
		[V.TNS NP RP]
		[V.TNS NP NP RP]

Apologising is also related to forgiving in that S often forgives some action after an apology has been received. In an apology, S expresses regret or sorrow towards H for some event which S instigated. Lamenting and mourning are related in that both express sorrow and regret over some loss by S. In the case of lamenting, this loss relates to some event or thing while, in mourning, the loss is typically to do with the death of a person.

Expressive illocutionary forces have an empty direction of fit, as many of the words that name the expressive illocutionary acts (English: thank, congratulate, apologise) name illocutions which are expressions of states which have no direction of fit. Expressive verbs name illocutionary forces whose point is to express the attitude(s) of S about the state of affairs presented by the propositional content. The states contains a belief and a desire, and the belief has a mind-to-world direction of fit while desire has a world-to-mind direction no fit. The point of the expressive speech act is not to express the belief and desire but rather to express the emotional states of gratitude, pleasure, or sorrow, and so on, as we have discussed in our examples.

We have examined thirteen expressive speech acts of Irish, and, consequently, we argue towards the following indicative degrees of strength for these expressive speech acts, relative to each other, as: 5: deploring; 4: forgiving, lamenting, and mourning; 3: apologising, congratulating, condoling and commiserating; 2: thanking, greeting, welcoming, and wishing; 1: acknowledging. As some of these expressive speech acts can be uttered in a routine, or perfunctory manner, there is likely to be some disparity in the degree of strength across varying contexts. The degrees of strength specified for the respective speech acts are indicative rather that absolute.

With several of these expressive speech acts, the sincerity conditions are particularly important in reflecting the strength of emotion felt. With deplore, for example, S has significant discontent or sadness. With forgive, S feels significant clemency towards H. With both lament and mourn, S has significant sorrow over S's loss re X.

The mode of achievement for these expressive speech acts require that S makes UTT to H. There is some variation amongst these speech acts with regards to other mode of achievement factors. All the expressive speech acts discussed here, for example, with the exception of greeting, have the requirement that some relevant action X occurred in some past T < T.now. With greeting, the mode of achievement requirement that S seeing/meeting H occurs in T.now. With lamenting, S's UTT is publicly expressed, while, in mourning, S's UTT may be made in public or in private.

We argue that a situation is the cognitive frame employed in resolving individual and cultural conceptualisations, where context and common ground contribute and enrich underspecification within the construal of a speech act by an interlocutor. If an individual conceptualises a situation in a certain kind of way, then the potential for a particular type of emotion exists.

10 The declarative speech act

10.1 Introduction to the declarative speech act

In this chapter we examine a selection of the declarative speech acts of Irish, in particular declare/pronounce, adjourn, resign, approve, confirm, and name. Declaratives are special in many ways and the defining characteristic of declarative speech acts (Searle 1975b:359) is that their successful performance brings about a correspondence between the propositional content and reality. That is, the successful performance of declarative speech acts guarantees that their propositional content corresponds to the world. Declarative speech acts bring about a change in the status or condition of the entities referred to by virtue of the fact that the act has been successfully performed. As an illocutionary act, declaratives are a special kind of action where the expression of the intention to perform the action in an appropriate context is sufficient for the performance of that action (Vanderveken & Kubo 2001:8). The function of the declarative speech act is therefore to establish social facts during its performance and, as such, is a causing event in itself. A declarative is satisfied if its proposition becomes TRUE for the first time *at the moment that it is said*, and during the time that S is saying it, S INTENDS for *that particular* condition to occur and KNOWS how to make it occur. Context is shown to be particularly important for the felicitous realisation of the declarative speech act.

As regards their direction of fit, we have seen for assertives that it is words-to-world whereas in the case of directives and commissives it is world-to-words. For expressives there is no direction of fit. In contrast, the declarative speech act brings about a fit by virtue of its performance in context being successful. The declarative speech act has a double direction of fit. The declaratives reflect a single illocutionary point that has two directions of fit (Searle & Vanderveken 1985:94), consisting of word-to-world and world-to-word, simultaneously, because the point of a declaration is to bring about a change in the world by representing the world as so changed. That is, in this double direction of fit of the declarative speech act, the world is altered to fit the propositional content of the utterance.

The declarative speech acts require an extra linguistic institution as necessary context for their successful realisation. Consequently, the preparatory conditions are non-linguistic in nature and bound to the appropriate context. Declarative speech acts also require that S, and often H, have particular formal roles within that institution and context, and that S have the appropriate authority within the particular extra linguistic institution to make the declaration and its successful realisation. The mode of achievement will then involve the invocation of the S's powers as vested by the institution.

Conditions concerning ability, authority, know-how of S are necessary to ensure that, at each moment, S is able to guarantee the completion of the declarative and ensure the occurrence of the appropriate condition. This eliminates instances where S has the intention, but is not in the right social or conventional position of authority, or not in the appropriate context, to make the declarative succeed. Accordingly, an appropriate and proper context is essential for the felicitous use of the declarative speech act, for example, with the English examples in (1).

(1)

a.	'I now PRONOUNCE you to be married'	: formal legal marriage context
b.	'I hereby SENTENCE you to X'	: formal court of law context
c.	'You are under ARREST'	: formal legal context
d.	'I now DECLARE this ship launched'	: formal naming ceremony

A general sincerity condition on declaratives has a similar function to the Gricean cooperative maxim of quality, where one endeavours to be truthful, and not give information that is false or that is not supported by evidence.

It is crucial that the context of the successful declarative speech act must be both correct, appropriate, and in place. The declarative speech acts are fundamentally culturally informed, they cause an event in themselves, in context, as in a court of law context or formal wedding ceremony. Such performatives have the effect they do because societies endow them with a certain power. While the context is of critical importance with the declarative speech act, as it turns out, common ground does not have the same importance here as it did with the assertive speech act discussed earlier.

10.2 The declarative utterances

10.2.1 Declare

The English word declare names the declarative illocutionary force. An example of a formal declaration is that given at a wedding of two people. For a valid wedding ceremony to occur in its proper formal legal context, that appropriate context, identified in (2), must be in place at the time of utterance.

(2) Required context for wedding ceremony DECLARATIVE
   a. The SETTING is a strict part of the context and must be formally correct.
   b. All of the PARTICIPANTS play important and necessary ROLES in the event.
   c. The officiating registrar, solemniser, priest, or minister, S, is vested with AUTHORITY by the state to perform the wedding as a legal event.
   d. The people getting married are WILLING PARTICIPANTS who both give free consent.
   e. The people getting married are of a LEGAL AGE to marry.

Example (3) gives two different versions of this declaration for a Christian religious ceremony using Irish as the official language. The setting is a strict part of the context and the participants play important, necessary, and designated roles in the event. As these two examples are of a religious ceremony (as a proxy for its formal legal context), the officiating priest or minister, S, as actor, is necessarily vested with authority by the state to perform the wedding as a formal legal event. The people getting married are willing participants that give consent, and legally free to marry each other, being of a legal age to marry. These participants getting married are denoted as H1.NAME and H2.NAME respectively in each. In example (3), the utterance UTT_1 contains the EXPRESSION_1 in the formalised representation (4).

(3) Two examples of religious declarations of marriage
   a.
   AN DEARBHÚ: *Labhraíonn an sagart leis an phobal. I bhfianaise Dé agus os comhair an phobail seo thug* H1.NAME *agus* H2.*name a gcead agus a móideanna pósta dá chéile. D'fhógair siad a bpósadh trí shnaidhmeadh lámh, agus trí fháinne a thabhairt agus a ghlacadh. Mar sin de, in ainm Dé, fógraím gur lánúin phósta iad.*

THE DECLARATION: In the presence of God, and before this congregation, H1.NAME and H2.NAME have given their consent and made their marriage vows to each other. They have declared their marriage by the joining of hands and by the giving and receiving of a ring. Therefore, in the name of God, I pronounce that they are husband and wife.

b. Constructional signature: [V.TNS NP THAT RP]

c.

AN DEARBHÚ: De bhrí gur aontaigh H1.NAME *agus* H2.NAME *le chéile i bpósadh naofa, agus gur thugadar Dia agus an comhluadar seo i bhfianaise air sin; agus gur thugadar a ngealltanas dá chéile faoi, agus gur dhearbhaíodar é trí fáinne a thabhairt agus a ghlacadh, agus trí shnaidhmeadh lámh. Fógraím ina lánúin phósta iad, in Ainm an Athar, agus an Mhic, agus an Spioraid Naoimh.* Áiméan.

THE DECLARATION: Whereas H1.NAME and H2.NAME were united in a holy marriage, and testified to God and this fellowship; and that they gave their vows to each other about it, and confirmed it by giving and receiving a ring, and by holding a hand; I proclaim them as a married couple, in the Name of the Father, and of the Son, and of the Holy Spirit. Amen.

d. Constructional signature: [V.TNS NP THAT RP]

The formalised representation of the declarative for the wedding situation (4) illustrates the important contribution of context to its successful realisation. We reflect this as part of the initial context which contains the preconditions/preparatory conditions.

(4) Formalisation of DECLARATIVE speech act (context: formal marriage ceremony)

Situation	*this-wedding*.SIT
Initial context	ONTOLOGY: *wedding* IS_A event PROCESS ACTOR of the speech act has appropriate AUTHORITY to marry people UNDERGOER(S) (Person_1 & Person_2) are willing participants LOCATION of speech act event is an appropriate location and setting TIME of speech act is appropriate to the wedding event
Speaker	S

Hearer	H1 AND H2 (i.e., Person_1 and Person_2, respectively)
Speech act	UTT$_1$: [**do'** (s, **say'** (s, EXPRESSION$_1$)) & CAUSE (**hear'** (H1 and H1, SA))]
PROP	Person_1 and Person_2 **WANT** to marry each other
Common ground	Common ground for S, H1 and H2 established
Preconditions/ Preparatory Conditions	The conditions are related to the formal institutional context: The SETTING is a strict part of the context and must be formally correct All of the PARTICIPANTS play important and necessary ROLES in the event The officiating registrar, solemniser, priest or minister, S, is vested with AUTHORITY by the state to perform the wedding as a legal event; The people getting married are WILLING PARTICIPANTS who both give free consent. **NOT** (**be'** (PERSON_1, MARRIED) : Person_1 is NOT ALREADY MARRIED **NOT** (**be'** (PERSON_2, MARRIED) : Person_2 is NOT ALREADY MARRIED **WANT'** (**marry'** (Person_1, Person_2)): The people WANT TO MARRY EACH OTHER
ILLOCFORCE (IF)	DECLARATIVE
IFID	*Fógair* 'declare' (used in the context of a formal marriage ceremony)
illocutionary point (IP)	S presents PROP as representing the new state of affairs of the world
Mode of achievement	S invokes S's authority within the institutional context in language to H1 and H2
position of authority	Authority of S must be correct and appropriate
position of power	Power of S must be appropriate to the contextual situation

Sincerity Conditions	The speech act is performed by S in accordance all beliefs, desires, and intentions (BDI) and informed by shared common ground, in the correct context.
BELIEF	H1 is free to marry H2 H2 is free to marry H1
DESIRE	H1 wants to marry H2 H2 wants to marry H1
INTENTION	S intends to change status of H1 and H2 through marrying them H1 intends to marry H2 H2 intends to marry H1
Realisation	S formally declares H1 and H1 to be married S expresses the BELIEF that P of UTT (H1 AND H2 WANT TO MARRY) S's invoking authority is sufficient for H1 and H2 to achieve X Emergent common ground constructed
Postconditions/ updated context	H1 and H2 are now married to each other S is interested in the successful outcome Common ground updated Context updated

An example of the declarative from a legal context is shown in (5), with the formalisation of this declarative speech act in (6). In the example, the utterance UTT$_1$ contains the EXPRESSION$_1$ '*Fógraím go bhfuil an cosantóir ciontach*'. These indicate how differences in context are important to the success of the speech act. The legal context as it occurs in the declaration (5) is represented in (6). Again, the formalised representation of the declarative for the legal situation demonstrates that context makes a crucial contribution of context to the speech act realisation. The initial context, contains the pre-conditions / preparatory conditions, is reflected as part of this formalisation.

(5)

a.

Fógraím	*go bhfuil*	*an*	*cosantóir*	*ciontach.*
Announce:V-PRS+1SG	that be.AUX.PRS	DET	defendant	guilty

I <u>declare</u> that the defendant is guilty.

b. Constructional signature: [V.TNS NP that RP]

(6) Formalisation of DECLARATIVE speech act (context: formal court room setting)

Situation	*this-legal-trial*.SIT
Initial context	ONTOLOGY: *Legal-trial* IS_A courtroom-based event PROCESS ACTOR of the speech act, the judge, has appropriate AUTHORITY to sentence people UNDERGOER (defendant) is to be sentenced UNDERGOER is charged with committing a crime LOCATION of speech act event is a formal court of law TIME of speech act is appropriate to the legal trial event
Speaker	S, the judge
Hearer	H, the defendant
Speech act	UTT$_1$: **[do'** (S, **say'**(S, EXPRESSION$_1$)) & CAUSE (**hear'** (H, SA))]
PROP	Defendant is guilty by verdict of the law court
Common ground	Common ground for S, H established
Preconditions/ Preparatory Conditions	The conditions are related to the formal institutional context: The SETTING is a strict part of the context and must be formally correct All of the PARTICIPANTS, JUDGE and DEFENDANT play specific ROLES in this legal event The JUDGE S, is vested with AUTHORITY by the state to perform the sentencing as a legal event The DEFENDANT is a PARTICIPANT in the legal court case. **NOT** (**be'** (defendant, SENTENCED) : Person_1 is NOT ALREADY SENTENCED ON THIS CHARGE **be'** (**accused'**(defendant, committing-crime)): The defendant is accused of a crime
ILLOCFORCE (IF)	DECLARATIVE
IFID	*Fógair* 'declare' (used in formal legal context)
illocutionary point (IP)	S presents PROP as representing the new legal state of affairs

Mode of achievement	S invokes S's authority as a judge within the institutional context in language to H to declare H guilty
position of authority	Authority of S must be formally correct and appropriate to the court of law
position of power	Power of S must be appropriate to the contextual situation
Sincerity Conditions	The speech act is performed by S in accordance all beliefs, desires, and intentions (BDI) and informed by shared common ground, in the correct context.
BELIEF	S is BELIEVES H guilty
DESIRE	S INTENDS to sentence H
INTENTION	S INTENDS to change the status of H through finding the defendant H guilty as a verdict
Realisation	S formally declares H to be guilty of the crime S expresses the BELIEF that P of UTT (Defendant is guilty by verdict of the court) S's invoking authority is sufficient for S to declare X Emergent common ground constructed
Postconditions/ updated context	S is interested in the successful outcome H is now found guilty of the crime by the verdict of court Common ground updated Context updated

Other declarative examples (7) reflect different situations and contexts. Here, we indicate a declaration of an official opening of a hotel for business, and also that of a formal book launch.

(7)

a.
Fógraím Óstán *Ros Geal ar oscailt go hoifigiúil.*
Announce:V-PRS+1SG hotel Ros Geal on open to official
I officially declare the Ros Geal Hotel is open.

b. Constructional signature: [V.TNS NP NP PP ADV]

c.

Fógraím go bhfuil an dá leabhar, leagan Sheáin Uí Shé de *Buile Shuibhne agus Cuimhní Pinn Cuimhní Cinn, ... fógraím go bhfuil an dá leabhar* áille *seo seolta agus ar fáil le ceannach ar chostas níos lú ná fiche euro.*

I declare that both books, Seán Ó Sé's version of Buile Shuibhne and Cuimhní Pinn Cuimhní Cinn, … I declare that these two beautiful books have been launched and are available for purchase at a cost of less than twenty euro.

d. Constructional signature: [V.TNS NP NP RP]

10.2.2 Resign

The declarative speech act resign (8) is an utterance used by S with the purpose of changing their situation in some way once the speech act has been uttered. To resign is to quit or retire from a position through declaring formally you are leaving some position, role, or job permanently.

(8)

a.

Éirím as an bpost agus mé bréan den scéal.

Rise:V-PRS+1SG from DET post and 1SG fed-up with+DET story

Lit: I resign from the position and I'm fed up with the situation/story.

I resign from the position in disgust.

b. Constructional signature: [V.TNS NP FROM RP]

(9)

a.

Leis seo éirím *as mar chathaoirleach.*

with this rise:V-PRS+1SG from as chairperson

Hereupon, I resign as chairman.

b. Constructional signature: [(ADV) V.TNS NP AS NP]

This declaration brings about a specific change in the world. To resign is therefore to perform a declaration to the effect that S terminates some formal position, role, or job, within some context. The declarative speech act resign has the preparatory condition that S actually has that role at the time of utterance, and is empowered to renounce it, and accordingly, to give it up.

(10) The declarative speech act of resign

With S uttering UTT, S declarative: resigns from X to all H

Precondition	Illocutionary force	Declarative
	IFID	Use of **éirigh** 'rise, with the sense of resign'
	Intention of S:	Change status of S in doing X
	Desire of S:	S wants to change status of S
	Authority of S:	S has authority to resign
	Power of S:	S has no power over H
	Mode of Achievement:	Permanent over time: T.now … T>now
	Mode of Achievement:	S utters resignation to all H.
	Mode of Achievement:	Refusal is allowed by H
	Obligation:	No obligation on H accept X
	Core common ground established	
Realisation	S formally resigns to H from X	
	S expresses the BELIEF that P of UTT (S WANT TO RESIGN FROM X)	
	S's invoking authority is sufficient to all H to achieve X	
	Emergent common ground constructed	
Postcondition	S is interested in the successful outcome	
	S has resigned from X	
	S no longer in X	
	Common ground updated	
	Context updated	

10.2.3 Adjourn

To adjourn, as a declarative speech act, is to make a formal declaration that some meeting or event X is terminated, probably for a specified time period, where X is a meeting or some kind of formal event such as a court case (12). The preparatory condition, for declarative speech act of adjourn, requires that the appropriate context is in place and that the speaker has the appropriate authority, in that context, to adjourn the meeting or event X. Examples of this are provided in (12)–(13).

(11) The declarative speech act of adjourn

With S uttering UTT, S declarative: resigns from X to all H

Precondition	Illocutionary force	Declarative
	IFID	Use of *cuir* 'put with the sense of adjourn'
	Intention of S:	Change status of X
	Desire of S:	S wants to change status of X
	Authority of S:	S has authority to adjourn
	Power of S:	S has no power over H
	Mode of Achievement:	effective from time: T.now till T>now
	Mode of Achievement:	S utters adjournment to all H.
	Core common ground established	
Realisation	S formally adjourns X to H S expresses the BELIEF that P of UTT (S WANT TO ADJOURN X) S's invoking authority is sufficient to all H to do X Emergent common ground constructed	
Postcondition	S is interested in the successful outcome S has adjourned X Common ground updated Context updated	

(12)

a.

Cuirim an cás ar athló ar feadh coicíse.

put:V-PRS+1SG DET case on postpone on duration fortnight.

I adjourn the case for a fortnight.

b. Constructional signature: [V.TNS NP NP FOR NP]

(13)

a.

Cuirim ár gcruinniú siar go dtí

put:V-PRS+1SG OUR meeting across to until

an chéad lá eile atá ar fail.

DET first day next BE.AUX-PRS available

I adjourn our meeting until the next available day.

b. Constructional signature: [V.TNS NP PP UNTIL RP]

10.2.4 Approve

The declarative speech act approve is used to declare that something is appropriately good, suitable, apt, useable, or valid according to the particular context, at time T.now. S has the appropriate authority to approve X. The declarative speech act of approve can be usefully contrasted with confirm, discussed next, where a higher level of approval authority may come into play.

(14) The declarative speech act of approve
With S uttering UTT, S declarative: approves X to H

Precondition	Illocutionary force	Declarative
	IFID	use of *mol* 'approve'
	Intention of S:	validate the status of X as good/positive
	Desire of S:	S wants to validate the status of X
	Authority of S:	S has authority to approve X
	Power of S:	S has no power over H
	Mode of Achievement:	Approval is effective from time T.now
	Mode of Achievement:	S utters approval to H.
	Core common ground established	
Realisation	S formally approves X to H	
	S expresses the BELIEF that P of UTT (S WANT TO APPROVE X)	
	S's invoking authority is sufficient to do X	
	Emergent common ground constructed	
Postcondition	S is interested in the successful outcome	
	S has approved X	
	Common ground updated	
	Context updated	

(15)

a.
Molaim do rogha.
Praise:V-PRS+1SG your choice
I approve/praise your choice.

b. Constructional signature: [V.TNS NP NP]

(16)

a.

Is maith liom go ndearna tú é.

Cop good with+1sg to do.make:v-pst 2sg 3sg.M.acc

Lit: I like that you did it.

I approve that you did it.

b. Constructional signature: [v.tns NP that RP]

10.2.5 Confirm

The declarative speech act confirm (17)–(19) alters the status of some entity through making it good or valid by virtue of use of this declarative. Confirm is a validation of some previous speech act, perhaps an assertive or an information question.

It may be the case that to confirm has the preparatory condition that some declaration has previously been made, with the same proposition, by someone else in the same formal institute but a with lesser or inappropriate authority than S.

(17)

a.

Deimhním d'áirithint.

Confirm:v-prs+1sg poss+booking

I confirm your booking.

b. Constructional signature: [v.tns NP NP]

(18)

a.

Deimhním do choinne leis an dochtúir.

Confirm:v-prs+1sg poss appointment with det doctor

I confirm your appointment with the doctor.

b. Constructional signature: [v.tns NP NP PP]

(19)

a.

Cinntím duit **é**.

ensure:v-prs+1sg to:prep+2sg 3sg.m.acc

I confirm it for you.

b. Constructional signature: [v.tns NP NP PP]

(20) The declarative speech act of confirm

With S uttering UTT, S declarative: confirms X to H

Precondition	Illocutionary force	Declarative
	IFID	Use of deimhnigh / cinntigh 'confirm'
	Intention of S:	Validate the status of X as good/positive
	Desire of S:	S wants to validate the status of X
	Authority of S:	S has authority to approve X
	Power of S:	S may have power over H
	Mode of Achievement:	Approval is effective from time T.now
	Mode of Achievement:	S confirms approval to H.
	Core common ground established	
Realisation	S formally confirms X to H	
	S expresses the BELIEF that P of UTT (S WANTS TO CONFIRM X)	
	S's invoking authority is sufficient to do X	
	Emergent common ground constructed	
Postcondition	S is interested in the successful outcome	
	S has confirmed approved for X	
	Common ground updated	
	Context updated	

10.2.6 Name

Naming is the process of giving names to things. The declarative speech act of naming (21) is an act of announcing the name of a person, organisation, or other entity, and may involve a special context such as a ritual or ceremony in which the name is given and applied. That is, the (new) name is confirmed and implicitly validated. S must have the appropriate authority in context to assign the name.

(21)

a.

Ainmním an long seo an Lusitania.

Name:V-PRS+1SG DET ship this DET Lusitania

I name this ship the Lusitania.

b. Constructional signature: [V.TNS NP NP NP]

(22) The declarative speech act of name

With S uttering UTT, S **declarative: names** X to H

Precondition	Illocutionary force	Declarative
	IFID	use of *ainmnigh* 'name'
	Intention of S:	Change the name of some entity E to X
	Desire of S:	S wants to name an entity as X
	Authority of S:	S has authority to name the entity E as X
	Mode of Achievement:	The name is effective from time T.now
	Mode of Achievement:	S confirms name X to H.
	Core common ground established	
Realisation	S formally names X to H	
	S expresses the BELIEF that P of UTT (S WANT TO NAME X)	
	S's invoking authority is sufficient to name X	
	Emergent common ground constructed	
Postcondition	S is interested in the successful outcome	
	S has names the entity as X	
	Common ground updated	
	Context updated	

In naming some specific thing/entity E as X, that thing/entity is now known as X instead of (the previous entity name of) E by virtue of the declaration in context. That thing/entity now has the name X, which is valid from time T.now. The new name is confirmed with this declarative act. S has authority to name X, and the felicitous declarative speech act brings about a change in reality. The clause must be constructed with the normal grammatical rules of Irish and contain the verb that names the illocutionary point of the utterance. In this instance, the verb is *ainmním* 'I name'. As well, the verb must be in the present tense. This is because the illocutionary act is defined in the moment of utterance.

10.3 Some comments on declarative speech acts

We have examined in this chapter a representative number of declarative speech acts of Irish and seen that a correct and appropriate context is crucial for their successful realisation. The syntactic patterns of the declarative speech acts, their constructional schemas, as seen from the examples in this chapter, have a consistency that does not exhibit any considerable variation. These constructional schemas can be generalised as indicated in (23).

(23)
[(ADV) V.TNS:PRS actorNP (undergoerNP) (PP) (THAT | FROM | AS | UNTIL | FOR) (NP | RP)]

The speaker S is the actor and the undergoer is the hearer H. Tense is always the present as the declarative happens and is effective in the real-time of the speaker and hearer, and context is immediately updated.

(24)The syntactic patterns of the declarative speech act

Speech act	IFID/SA Verb	Constructional schema
Declarative	declare	[V.TNS NP THAT RP]
	declare	[V.TNS NP NP PP ADV]
	declare	[V.TNS NP NP RP]
	resign	[V.TNS NP FROM RP]
	resign	[(ADV) V.TNS NP AS NP]
	adjourn	[V.TNS NP NP FOR NP]
	adjourn	[V.TNS NP PP UNTIL RP]
	approve	[V.TNS NP NP]
	approve	[V.TNS NP THAT RP]
	confirm	[V.TNS NP NP]
	confirm	[V.TNS NP NP PP]
	name	[V.TNS NP NP NP]

We have pointed out the preparatory preconditions needed for the various declarative speech acts, as well as the postconditions that holds in the updated context, after the speech has been successfully realised. We have seen that the special nature of the declarative speech act is that a large number of institutional facts or formal facts in the world are brought into existence just by saying one is doing it, or creating it, provided one has the appropriate authority in the appropriate situation, and the context is correct. As we have seen, we can adjourn a meeting by saying ‘I adjourn the meeting’. With the appropriate authority and context, we can declare war by saying ‘We declare war’, or pronounce somebody husband and wife by saying ‘I pronounce you husband and wife’, thereby creating a new institutional reality.

> If we look at our social life, it is a remarkable fact that there is a class of entities that have a very important role in our lives, but they only are what they are, because we believe that that is what they are.
>
> ...
>
> It looks as if in the case of these institutional phenomena, language doesn't just describe a pre-existing reality, but is partly constitutive of the reality that it describes.
>
> Searle (2007:16)

Language has a clear and specific role in the creation and maintenance of our social entities. These are created by the a successfully realised declarative speech act, a linguistic operation that results in the institutional fact. For a declarative speech act, the beliefs, desires, and intentions are important for a number of reasons. The intentional state represents the conditions of satisfaction, including truth conditions in the case of belief, carrying out conditions for intentions, and fulfilment conditions for desires. When we engage in a conversation, we are engaging in cooperative behaviour, with collective intentionality.

11 Indirect speech acts

11.1 The characteristics of the indirect speech act utterance

Indirect speech acts (ISA) as they occur in Irish are considered in this chapter. Indirect speech acts are tricky, and two questions arise here when we consider them: a) What exactly are indirect speech acts and b) how do they work? As regards the first question, we can, somewhat easily, say that an indirect speech act is an utterance that contains the illocutionary force indicators for one kind of illocutionary act but which is uttered to execute another type of illocutionary act (Smith 1991:19). Explaining the second question of how ISAs work is rather more difficult. An ISA may arise because of the authority status of one of the interlocutors, because of a mismatch between pragmatic maxims, or due to politeness considerations across a discourse. We propose a solution to the second question based on traversing a conceptual graph model of the situation, along with criteria such as salience and relevance. We consider here a (non-exhaustive) selection of ISAs: a) A question on H's ability to do something which yields a request for action X by S to H; b) A yes-no question which yields a directive request for action X by H; c) An assertion with a proposal which yields a directive yes-no question; and d) An assertion which yields a request for information of H.

Asher & Lascarides (2001) argue that the relationship between the surface form of an indirect speech act (ISA) utterance and its underlying purpose is not always straightforward. The ISAs present a puzzle of 'two speech acts in one'. However, we must remember that these ISAs arise from general principles of collaboration in discourse where, quite reasonably, we assume the interlocutors are rational and willingly cooperate with each other in a dialogue. Searle (1975a:59) points out that S's utterance meaning and the sentence meaning frequently vary, and this occurs frequently with instances of irony, metaphorical use, and insinuation.

With indirect speech acts, utterances that have illocutionary force indicators for one kind of illocutionary act can be used to perform another kind of illocutionary act. According to Collavin (2011:385–386), a way to treat utterances whose force differs from what their force indicators (IFID) suggest is to assume that they have a *literal* force, which is associated by rule, and an *indirect* force, which is inferred by virtue of information available to the interlocutor H.

In the next section, we examine the following ISAs:

a. Question on ability → yielding a request for action X
b. Yes-no question → yielding a directive request for action X
c. Assertion with proposal → yielding a directive yes-no question
d. Assertion → yielding a request for information

How do ISAs work and what are the prerequisites for a model of indirect speech act processing? Searle (1975a) argues that an ISA carries two illocutionary forces, the meaning that S intends to convey in performing the illocutionary act, and that one illocutionary act is performed indirectly by means of performing another. According to Asher & Lascarides (2001), speech acts must be understood relationally, because performing them successfully is logically dependent on the content of an antecedent utterance. The dual communicative role of an ISA is conventionalised within a language. Other ISAs get interpreted 'on the fly' rather than by convention, as a result of pragmatic reasoning and the demands of discourse interpretation. The linguistic characteristics of the utterance need to be considered (Landragin 2005:115–122). Is the utterance an assertive, commissive, directive, expressive, or a declarative? What is the category of the verb within the utterance? The dialogue history from common ground contains previous utterances and their interpretations represented with logical forms. The dialogue history is important as is the interpretative response by H, based on the nature of S's utterance as well as on the current state of the dialogue. The notions of common ground, sets of questions, and (list of) action(s)-to-do play a central role. The utterance of S's is represented by H with a logical structure into common ground, according to its illocutionary force and which corresponds to the result of H's interpretative analysis. This constitutes a part of the dialogue history. When H is determining the intended meaning of the speech act, the best premise is the one that has the most important contextual effects to the mental states, as per (Sperber & Wilson, 1995). Criteria such as salience and relevance may be exploited during this process. Identifying the intention behind S's ISA utterance appears to be the primary parameter for determining an adequate interpretation, by H, to this utterance. Also, when interpreting an indirect speech act. H needs to make some hypothesis on the mental states of S (beliefs, desires, intentions).

11.2 Unpacking the indirect speech act utterance

We now examine a selection of indirect speech acts as found in Irish. Searle (1975a:71) proposes an explanation, for the case of directives, that is based on felicity conditions (1). When we consider the utterance in (2), given S, H, and an action X (i.e., Can you pass the salt? → pass the salt) the felicity conditions for the illocutionary act are:

(1) Felicity conditions for the [question yielding a request for action] illocutionary act (Searle 1975a:71)

Preparatory condition:	H is ABLE to perform X
Sincerity condition:	S WANTS H to do X
Propositional content condition:	S predicates a future act X of H
Essential condition:	Counts as an attempt by S to get H to do X

The sentence in (2a) expresses a question. As we have seen in Chapter 7, we know that the speaker's goal in asking a question is to get an answer. Literally, this is a question on the *ability* of H to do the named action (can you pass the salt?). Specifically, (2a) is a directive request for information, a question, whereas in reality it is a directive request for action about the named object.

It is, however, quite reasonable to accept that this utterance in (2a) has a different purpose as it is actually masks a request for action, indicated in (2b), where the speaker has a different goal than asking a question, and politely signalled by use of *le do thoil* 'please'.

This is an indirect speech act (ISA), an utterance in which one speech act is performed indirectly by performing another. This request is considered an indirect speech act because, at face value, S seeks to ascertain if the interlocutor H is capable of performing the action ('can you …') on the named object while in fact S is actually requesting H to do the action X on that named object ('give me the salt'). The ability of H to perform the action X is a preparatory condition for requesting to do the action X.

(2) **Question → yielding a request for action on the named entity**

a.

Interlocutor S utters the question:

An	*féidir leat*	*an*	*salann a*	*thabhairt dom*?
QPRT	able with:PREP+2SG	DET	salt PRT	give to:PREP+1SG

Can you give me the salt?

b. **Underlying request for action**
Tabhair an salann dom le do thoil!
Give:V-PRS DET salt to:PREP+1SG please
Please give me the salt!

Collavin (2011:385–386) notes that this does not explain why it is the case that only certain requests are successfully made by asking if the interlocutor H can perform the wanted action. As a preparatory condition for any request, S must hold the belief that the interlocutor H can carry out the request. Why then is the speech act formulated as a question of ability by S of H (while actually requesting H to do the action X)? While the motivations to use an indirect act may be due to the diverse customs of social interaction within a society and its various social politeness constraints, this does not explain how one actually unpacks or retrieves the request for action from, in this instance, the uttered question. These dimensions of social interaction and politeness constraints are not assimilated in the notion of illocutionary force.

To understand how ISAs work, we propose a view of the ISA resolution process based on the construction of a situation that activates a mental model which can be represented by a conceptual graph. The graph is traversed by H in search of a relevant meaning. Example (2), as we have seen, is a directive request for information in relation to a named object that yields a request for action on the named object. In order to understand what happened with this utterance, we can assume a scenario such as this. *Scenario: There is a room with a table. On the table is a salt cellar. Participants A and B are sitting at the table. The salt cellar is located closer to B while out of reach of A.*

The conceptual graph is a visualisation of the cognitive model of the situation that is activated through the unpacking of an utterance speech act. The nodes in the conceptual graph exhibit a spreading activation according to the operations of salience, prominence, attention, and relevance. When interlocuter A, the speaker, utters the speech act indicated in (2a), interlocutor B, the hearer, maps the utterance to a situational frame and proceeds to unpack the speech act. Then B interprets the directive question on ability as trivial, non sensical, and not relevant in the context. B therefore begins the process of navigating the conceptual graph mental model to find a relevant meaning. At a certain point, Occam's Razor is applied and (2b) is deduced as the likely relevant intended meaning with respect to the named object. The named object is then moved by B to a new location close to A.

In relation to (2a), there are certain aspects that the uttered question and the underlying indirect speech act, the request for action on the named entity, have in common.

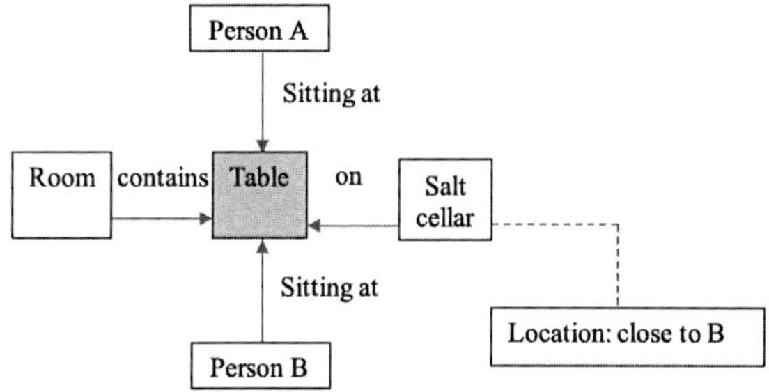

Figure 11.1 Conceptual graph modelling the scenario in (2)

Specifically, in the preconditions, the uttered question indirect speech act in (2) has the following in common with the underlying request for action:

Intention of S:	Get H to do X
Desire of S:	S wants H to do X
Mode of Achievement:	S is polite
Mode of Achievement:	H may or may not do X
Mode of Achievement:	Refusal is allowed by H
Obligation:	No obligation on H to do X
Ability:	H presumed to have ability to fulfil request
Core common ground established	

In turn, certain aspects of the uttered question (indirect speech act) in (2) differ with respect to the intended request for action speech act:

Authority of S:	S has no authority over H
Power of S:	S has no power over H
Degree of Strength:	++ 2

The directive request for action differs from the uttered question (indirect speech act) in (2) as follows:

Authority of S:	S may or may not have power over H
Power of S:	S may or may not have authority over H
Degree of Strength:	+++ 3
Ability:	H may not have the ability to fulfil the request

Earlier, we have seen that a request expresses the desire of S for H to do something. Moreover, along with S's desire, a request expresses S's intention that H take this expressed desire as reason to act. A request is a directive illocution (3) that has a polite mode of achievement in its illocutionary point and which allows for the possibility of a grant or refusal by H.

(3) The directive speech act of request (repeated from earlier)

With S uttering UTT, S requests H do X

Precondition	Illocutionary force	Directive
	IFID	use of request
	Intention of S:	Get H to do X
	Desire of S:	S wants H to do X
	Authority of S:	S has no authority over H
	Power of S:	S has no power over H
	Degree of Strength:	+++ 3
	Mode of Achievement:	S is polite
	Mode of Achievement:	H may or may not do X.
	Mode of Achievement:	Refusal is allowed by H
	Obligation:	No obligation on H to do X
	Ability:	H may not have the ability to fulfil the request
	Core common ground established	
Realisation	S requests H to do X	
	S expresses the BELIEF that P of UTT	
	S expresses the DESIRE that H do X	
	S INTENDS that H do X because of S's DESIRE	
	Emergent common ground constructed	
Postcondition	H may or may do X	
	S is interested in the outcome and that H do X	
	Common ground updated	

In a manner similar to example (2), the utterance in (4) lends itself to two interpretations. We can interpret this sentence in (4a) as one in which the speaker may utter and literally mean what was said. Taken literally, this is a question addressed to H seeking a yes-no answer ('Hasn't the mail arrived by now?'). However, it can also something quite different. Specifically, it can yield another illocution with a different propositional content, that of making the request to H to actually do the named action (get the post).

As an ISA, the example in (4) is a directive request for information, a question formulated in such a way as to require a yes-no answer, with respect to a named object. This yields a directive request for action on the named object. Again, the cognitive operations of salience, prominence, attention,

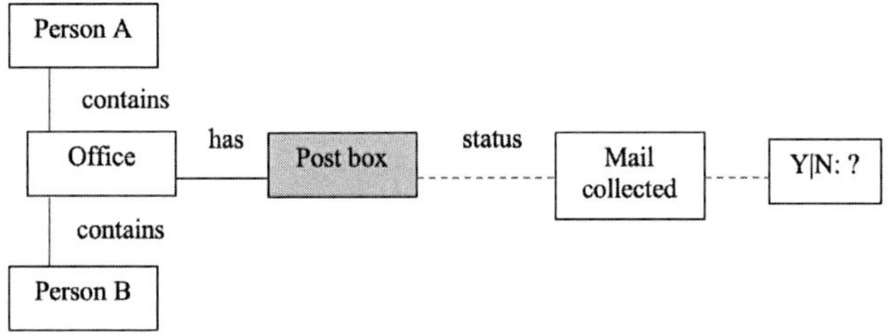

Figure 11.2 Conceptual graph modelling (4)

and relevance apply to the interpretative process. The directive request for action is 'Get the post!'

(4) **Question → yielding a directive request for action**

a.

Interlocutor A utters the question:

Nach bhfuil an post tagtha faoi láthair?

QPRT.NEG be:AUX DET post arrived:VA yet

Hasn't the mail arrived by now?

b. **Underlying directive for action**

Faigh an post le do thoil!

get:V-PRS DET post please

Please get the post!

Examples (5) and (6) both show an assertive utterance by S that masks an underlying question to H. These examples are of a speech act of assertion which states a proposition on a named event (meeting at the weekend, or meeting somewhere more private). It yields a directive request for information, specifically a confirmation. A typical response to (5a), containing the appropriate information by H, is given in (5b). The confirmation with respect to (5) and (6) can, of course, be a simple yes or no. In the instance of (5a), the response in (5b) is a question regarding the suitability of a suggested day to meet, which is implicitly a positive response.

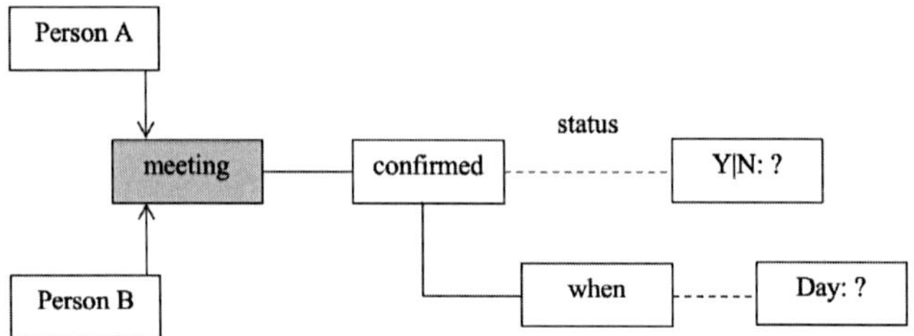

Figure 11.3 Conceptual graph of (5)

(5) **Assertion → yielding a question**

a.

Interlocutor A utters the assertion:

Buailfimid le chéile an deireadh seachtaine seo chugainn.

Meet:V-FUT+1PL with together DET weekend this coming

Lit: We will meet together this coming weekend. (= Let's meet this weekend.)

Underlying Q: Will we meet this weekend?

b.

Interlocutor B responds:

Cad faoi thráthnóna Dé hAoine?

QPRT about afternoon Friday

How about Friday afternoon?

(6) **Assertion → yielding a question**

Buailfimid linn chuig áit éigin eile níos príobháidí.

Meet:V-FUT+1PL with:prep+1pl to place some other more private

Let's meet somewhere else more private.

Example (7) shows an assertive utterance by S to H that masks an underlying request for information. Specifically, the example is an assertion about a named object that yields a directive request for information with respect to that named entity. This is an indirect speech act of assertion which, when unpacked, states a proposition on a named event ('I have no petrol!') but it yields a directive request for information on where one might get petrol.

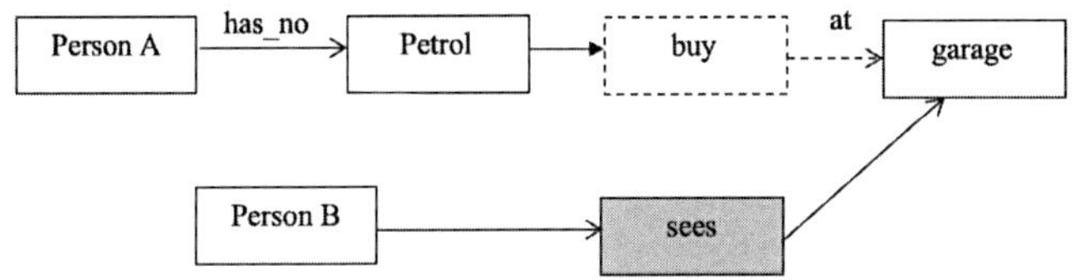

Figure 11.4 Conceptual graph of (7)

(7) **Assertion → yielding a request for information**

a.

Interlocutor A utters the assertion:

Níl aon pheitreal agam.

NEG any petrol at:PREP+1SG

Lit: I have no petrol.

I'm out of petrol.

Underlying Q: Where can I buy petrol?

b.

Interlocutor B responds:

Is féidir leat peitreal a

COP able with:PREP+2SG petrol PRT

cheannach ag an gharáiste ar an gcuinne!

buy at DET garage on the corner

You can buy petrol at the garage on the corner!

In this example, the context is that A utters the assertion regarding the named object (petrol). B does not have the named object. B applies a search for relevance over the conceptual graph behind the situation of the speech act of A (Where can A get the named object?). B realises that there is a garage close by, located at the corner of the road junction. B formulates a response and utters this to A. The response contains the required information, as to where A can get the named object.

11.3 Some comments on unpacking indirect speech acts

As we have indicated, a situation is complex, multidimensional, and dynamic, and encompasses the relation between the message and its encoding, the relation between interlocutors, and the relation between S and H and the larger social group(s) they belong to. All other things being equal, elements of a situation that are made salient by means of overt or covert cues incline the speech act utterance towards a certain interpretation. When H hears an uttered (indirect) speech act, a situation is construed and categorised in some way, as an assertion, a directive and so forth. The construal of the situation involves determining matters relating to structure and contents, and is guided by salience, prominence, attention.

As we have indicated, the cognitive model underpinning the situation of the uttered ISA is a dynamically maintained representation (here, in this discussion, modelled as a conceptual graph), within H's episodic memory, whereby some parts of the representation are more active than others during processing. When H navigates over the conceptual graph within the model of the situation in search of a meaning. Relevance is an important factor, along with salience, prominence, attention, and expectation.

Salience helps to advance the construction and maintenance of common ground, and information flow. It is a cognitive property of mental entities that are referred to within a discourse, and a high degree of salience is associated with the focus of attention. Salience describes a state of prominence, whereby certain 'things' or 'events' are in the foreground of our attention. Salience relates to the attentional state assigned to a discourse entity. One of the functions of utterances is the signalling of salience and attentional states, and the occurrence of salience foregrounds entities of various kinds as candidates for inclusion into common ground. Jaszczolt and Allan (2011:3) understand salience as: a) triggered by the recognition of the primary intended meaning, b) caused by the frequent occurrence of a lexical item, or c) a probable construal for the particular context. Especially in the case of the ISAs, recognition of the primary intended meaning and the consequential construal of the situation, yield the underlying intended speech act, for the particular context, and applies when the conceptual graph is traversed.

Salience represents a cognitive real-time evaluation of discourse information, and refers to the relative prominence of an element of some kind, such that the more important it is, the more accessible it is. Interlocutors activate the most salient information in their field of attention in the construction of utterances (by S) and their subsequent comprehension (by H). Prominence and attention play an role in motivating a potential meaning that may emerge as the most likely possible meaning. A prominence cue is a key mechanism in the-allocation of attention that contributes to the perception and production of salience in the ISA. Prominence is linked to a relation between an foregrounded element in a situation and the context of its occurrence.

Along with salience, prominence, attention, and expectation, relevance is also an important factor with the appropriate traversal of the conceptual graph of the situation. Sperber and Wilson (1995:260) observe that human cognition inclines to the maximisation of relevance. Utterances raise expectations of their relevance, and relevance may be assessed in terms of cognitive effects and processing effort, where the greater the processing effort required, the less relevant the input will be to the individual at that time. Relevance theory places emphasis on the role that context and contextual information play in contributing to the understanding of utterances. It therefore focuses on access to the context of the utterance, such that the immediate context affects the relevance of an utterance by decreasing its processing load. When a greater amount of positive cognitive effects are achieved by processing an input, then the greater the relevance of the input to H. In relevance theory, therefore, all enrichment is driven by context and the interpretation of an utterance by H is realised via principles of effectiveness and economy. Enrichment is the process whereby the content conveyed by an utterance include elements that are contextually implied but which are not part of the literal meaning of the utterance. Many utterances, whose meaning varies according to context, have one meaning and may be enriched at the pragmatic level by context-dependent assumptions, that is, via conversational implicatures.

Information is relevant to the extent that it incurs contextual effects at a reasonably small cost. Relevant information cost-effectively modifies H's cognitive environment. Sperber and Wilson particularly emphasise the role that relevance has in language comprehension, where participants' utterances are constrained by relevance in the communicative context. Relevance, then, is defined in terms of cognitive effects and processing effort: a) The greater the cognitive effects, the greater the relevance; and b) The smaller the effort needed to achieve those effects, the greater the relevance. Cognitive effects are achieved when new information interacts with existing contextual assumptions in one of three ways: a) Strengthening an existing assumption; b) Contradicting and eliminating an existing assumption; and c) Combining with an existing assumption to yield contextual implications. Processing effort is affected by the form in which the information is presented, the accessibility of the context, and the expectations of H. According to relevance theory, the linguistically encoded meaning is a starting point for inferring the speaker's meaning. Through processing and reasoning over the model represented by conceptual graph of the situation, H can identify the intended interpretation of an utterance. When the most probable meaning is activated, context helps to determine whether that is the relevant meaning or not. Linguistic decoding, a bottom-up process, requires the selection of appropriate contextual information, a top-down process, to support inferential processes.

We should incidentally note that relevance and salience are not the same, although often it is the case that what is salient can also be relevant. Reference is assigned to the most salient accessible candidate. However, if the resulting interpretation is pragmatically unacceptable, the set of saliencies are reordered, until an acceptable interpretation is found. Salience explains the ranking relating to objects or information, that arises from direct awareness of the world, context, or knowledge in the common ground of S and H. Salience then is a cognitive attribute of the mental model, represented here with the conceptual graph of the utterance, such that parts of the model are ranked according to their salience status. Several referents can be salient but with varying degrees of activation, or attention allocation, in memory. The situational context has a decisive role to play a role in guiding and determining the interpretation of an ISA utterance, along with search for relevance over the conceptual graph of the utterance.

12 Concluding comments on the speech acts of Irish

In this study we have provided a characterisation of the speech acts of Irish and analysed examples of assertive, directive, commissive, expressive, and declarative speech acts while noting their formal pragmatic characteristics within a model of a situation that included context, common ground, pre and post conditions. We also examined a number of indirect speech acts. As part of that characterisation, we developed a schematic representation of a speech act using the notion of a situation as a cognitive frame. The situation was argued to consist of what the speaker believes, desires, intends, and knows, in real time when the speaker makes a particular speech act utterance. The situation also incorporates what the speech act is intended to achieve, what is communicated to the hearer, and the IFID mechanism of signalling the illocutionary force of the utterance. In the model, we illustrated the role and contribution of common ground and context in the situation of the speech act during its successful and felicitous realisation.

We have seen that with the assertive, the syntactic patterns that act as a schema for these speech acts was identified. The clausal structure of these assertive exhibited a robust consistency in the syntactic pattern, showing just some small variations on (1) where the leftmost NP is the actor/speaker of the utterance. This functions as the IFID for the assertive speech act.

(1)
[V.TNS:PRS ACTORNP (NP|PP) (NP|PP) (THAT) (OBLIGATION) RP]

We have seen that the assertive commits S to a proposition being true such that, in uttering the assertive, S asserts that proposition if S expresses a) the belief that the proposition P holds, and b) the intention that H believes that P. With an assertive, it is the intention of S that H forms the belief that P. An assertive is satisfied simply if its P is *true* at the moment the utterance is made. In this analysis, we proposed the following relative degrees of strength of the assertives: 5: argue, rebut, insist; 4: testify, boast, lament, inform/notify; 3: assert, claim, recommend, predict, state; 2: affirm/confirm, remind, report, assure; and 1: suggest.

The various assertives differ in the belief(s) expressed and in the expressed intention. When one asserts something, the belief and intention that one expresses are very strong. In contrast, when one alleges or submits that something is the case, the belief and intention expressed are weaker. The evidential, as a form of assertive speech act, provides a mechanism whereby S can provide evidence or indicate variation over the level of commitment to the veracity of the assertation. This can involve epistemic judgements. We uncovered important facts on how evidentiality is expressed in Irish as a type of assertive speech act. This facts are that the evidential strategy of Irish has pragmatic dimensions. Irish employs uses a variety of means to code evidentiality including lexical, syntactic, and adverbial. Evidentiality is to do with signalling the source of information that is delivered in the information in the evidence channel. The clause complement type reflects a meaning difference between direct evidential strategy and marking of hearsay. With visual and aural modes, the verb in the first clause identifies the information channel, while the verb in the second clause identifies the event or information reported on. With the sense and cognitive modes, the clause organisation differs from that found in the visual and aural modes. Here, there is only one clause and the second argument encodes an RP encapsulating the sense of perceived information. An evidential hierarchy plays a role in the evidential strategy with one pole (see, hear) coding more credibility, with (smell, taste) towards in the centre of the continuum, followed by the verbs (aware, know), then followed by adverbials towards the other pole and coding less believable information. One of the evidential hierarchy poles, that with less believable information, overlaps with an epistemic stance on the knowledge, reflecting the speaker's commitment on the uttered statement. In a clause, the 'reported' term may have a connotation of 'unreliable' information. The evidential may strategically indicate surprise at unexpected admissions or new information. The expression of evidentiality as having epistemic connotations has been reported as something found in European languages.

The directive speech act is delivered in real time by S to H. The directive speech acts are seen to typically reflect the following degrees of strength: 5: require, command, order, forbit/prohibit ; 4: insist; 3: request; 2: direct, recommend, beg, ask; and 1:permit/allow, advise. The directives have unique syntactic patterns, their various constructional schemas. These can be generalised to (2), and which function as part of the IFID for the directive speech act.

(2)

[V.TNS:PRS ^{actor}NP NP|RP (TO NP | AT VN | FOR NP | PRT VN | THAT RP]

As an instance of a directive type, a question is a form of a request, whereby H is requested to provide S with certain information. We provided a deeper analysis of question forms, and their answers. The reason for this is that there are different types of questions, each with their own syntactic forms and distinct morphosyntactic and clausal characteristics. Question-answer exchanges facilitate both the construction and maintenance of common ground, and Irish was shown to have several clausal strategies for requesting different kinds of information through the formulation and use of different types of questions (3).

(3) Types of questions

Alternative questions	The answer must be based on one of the *options* presented within the question.
Polar yes-no questions	The answer can only contain an *affirmation or negative.*
Information questions (WH-questions)	The answer is guided by the question particle (QPRT) used which serves to target a *specific information gap*, allowing an open set of possible but relevant replies.

With the information question, contextual knowledge that is relevant enters the common ground of S and H, and the information gaps in a dialogue between S and H are fulfilled through the question-answer interaction. The consequential unpacking of the meaning of the interrogative speech act can be seen to depend on the situation in which the dialogue utterance occurs and the context concerning that situation. Context, through the situational frame, contributes to the felicitous speech act. The questioning directive types in (3) use one of the following constructional schemas in (4). These function as part of the IFID for the speech act.

(4) The questioning directive constructional schemas

- Use of the constructional schema:

QPRT:*an* V-PRS NP NP (*nó* 'or' NP) → indicates an alternative question.

- Use of the constructional schema:

QPRT:*nach* V-PRS NP NP or QPRT:*nar* V-PST NP NP → indicates a polar yes-no question.

- Use of the constructional schema:

QPF REL V.TNS NP → indicates an information question
where

> QPF is a question proform that interrogates for some kind of knowledge gap in which the proforms are: *Cé, Cé leis, Cé aige, Cád, Céard, Cén, Cá, Cén* áit / *Cén háit, Cathain, Cén uair, Cá huair, Cén t-am, Cén fáth, Conas, Cad é mar, Cé mhéad, Cá mhéad.*

In the act of asking questions, people interact with each other in an activity that is fundamental to communication and understanding. Here, the maintenance of common ground is one of the functions of information questions. In this, the context and situation of the speech act of requesting information, as a directive speech act, plays an important role in the process of meaning construction while contributing to a successful question-answer interaction. Through the question-answer interaction, contextual knowledge that is relevant enters the common ground of S and H, and the information gaps in a dialogue between S and H are fulfilled. The consequential unpacking of the meaning of the interrogative speech act can be seen to depend on the situation in which the dialogue utterance occurs and the context concerning that situation. Context, through the situational frame, along with common ground, contributes to the realisation of a felicitous speech act.

The illocutionary point of the commissive reflects its internal purpose. The illocutionary force of a commissive has a commissive point which consists in S committing to a future course of action X, a mode of achievement, a degree of strength, the condition that the propositional content represents a future course of action X by S, the preparatory condition that S is capable of doing that action X, the sincerity condition that S intends to do the action X. The syntactic patterns underpinning the commissive speech acts of Irish, their constructional schemas, are generalised to (5). The commissive commitment, delivered in real time, commits S to a present or future action. This functions as part of the IFID for the speech act.

(5)

[V.TNS:PRS|FUT actorNP (undergoerNP) (PP-LOC) (AT VN) (TO) (RP) (ADV)]

The degree of strength of the illocutionary point differentiates across stronger or weaker acts having the same point. The mode of achievement indicates how this illocutionary act is to be achieved in a certain way or under certain conditions. This set of propositional content conditions constrains the commissive, and a set of preparatory conditions reflect what is necessary for the successful and non-defective performance of the commissive speech act.

We have seen by way of example that the speech act of promise is always made by S to H, and has the special preparatory condition that the promised action is good for H. It involves the explicit undertaking of an obligation on S that may be implicit in other types of commissive speech acts, and this increases the degree of strength of the sincerity conditions. The speech act of threatening differs from promising in that the undertaking is to the detriment of H. Also, with a threat, S has no obligation to do X. The speech act of pledging is similar to vowing, but with reduced formality or solemnity. The pledge by S may be personal and need not involve H. Unlike the speech act of promises and threats, vows need not be directed at H. In vowing to do something, one undertakes to do it but H may not be involved. The speech act of vowing typically has some element of formality or solemnity, and this is informed by context. The speech act of offer is a promise that is conditional based on the acceptance by H, and it becomes binding only on H's acceptance. It commits S to perform a certain course of future action once accepted by H. The degrees of strength of the various commissive speech acts are summarised as follows: 5: bet; 4: vow, pledge, swear; 3: promise, offer, bid; 2: threaten; and 1: commit. The mode of achievement of the commissive reflects whether the act is oriented towards S alone (commit, vow, swear, pledge), or towards S and H (threaten, promise, offer, bid, bet). The obligation within the commissive can be on solely on S (promise, commit, vow, swear), or be mutually conditional S and H (offer, bid, bet). Some commissive speech acts are more formal (vow, swear, bid, bet) while other are less so and are more informal (commit, promise, threaten, offer).

Expressive speech acts convey the disparate emotions and feelings of S through some utterance, and can be used to communicate different feelings. Many of the psychological states of these expressive speech acts, the emotive states, carry the belief that the object of the state is good or bad, as in pleasure, joy, sorrow, or discontent. These expressive speech acts have as their illocutionary point to express the attitudes held by S on some state of affairs represented by the propositional content. The syntactic patterns found with the expressive speech acts of Irish are really quite varied, and range from a simple [PP] to a full clause. We have seen that the expressive illocutionary force has an empty direction of fit, as many of the words that name the expressive illocutionary acts name illocutions which are expressions of states. The point of the expressive speech act is not to express any belief and desire but simply to express the emotional states of gratitude, pleasure, or sorrow, and so on. As some of these expressive speech acts can be uttered in a routine, or perfunctory manner, there is likely to be some disparity in the degree of strength across varying contexts. Therefore, the degrees of strength specified for the respective speech acts are indicative rather that absolute. Having examined thirteen expressive speech acts of Irish, we propose the following indicative degrees of strength for these expressive speech acts, relative to each other, as: 5: deploring; 4: forgiving, lamenting, and mourning; 3: apologising , congratulating, condoling, and commiserating; 2: thanking, greeting, welcoming, and wishing; 1: acknowledging. With several of these expressive speech acts, the sincerity conditions are particularly important in reflecting the strength of emotion felt. For example, with deplore, S feels discontent or sadness. With forgive, S feels significant clemency towards H. With both lament and mourn, S has significant sorrow over S's loss regarding some event or action X. The mode of achievement for these expressive speech acts require that S makes an utterance directed towards H. There is some variation amongst these speech acts with regards to other mode of achievement factors. All the expressive speech acts discussed, with the exception of greeting, have the requirement that some relevant action X occurred in some past T < T.now. With greeting, the mode of achievement requirement that S seeing or meeting H occurs in time T.now. With lamenting, S's utterance is publicly expressed, while, in mourning, S's utterance may be made either in public or in private.

In our examination of examples of the declarative speech acts of Irish we have seen that a correct and fitting context is essential for their successful and felicitous realisation. The syntactic patterns of the declarative speech acts, their constructional schemas, have a consistency that does not exhibit any considerable variation. These constructional schemas, which act as part an illocutionary force indicating device, can be generalised as indicated in (6). These function as part of the IFID for the speech act. The tense of the declarative is always the present as the declarative happens and is effective in the real-time of the speaker and hearer, and context is updated immediately.

(6)

[(ADV) V.TNS:PRS ${}^{\text{actor}}$NP (${}^{\text{undergoer}}$NP) (PP) (THAT | FROM | AS | UNTIL | FOR) (NP | RP)]

For the various declarative speech acts, particular preparatory preconditions are necessary initial context. The postconditions of declarative speech acts are reflected in the updated context, after the speech has been successfully realised. An interesting point about the declarative speech act is that, due to the special nature of the declarative speech act, a large number of institutional or formal facts in the world are brought into existence just by saying one is doing it, or creating it, or provided one has the authority in the situation of the utterance, and the context is correct. This indicates that, via the declarative speech act in the correct context, language has a role in the creation and maintenance of our social entities. These social entities are created by the successfully realised declarative speech act, a linguistic operation that results in the institutional fact. For a declarative speech act, the beliefs, desires, and intentions are important for a number of reasons. The intentional state represents the conditions of satisfaction, including truth conditions in the case of belief, conditions constraining our intentions, and fulfilment conditions for desires.

The generalised syntactic forms, the constructional schemas, for each of the speech acts are therefore:

(7)

Assertive:	[V.TNS:PRS ACTORNP (NP|PP) (NP|PP) (THAT) (OBLIGATION) RP]
Directive:	[V.TNS:PRS actorNP NP|RP (TO NP | AT VN | FOR NP | PRT VN | THAT RP]
Commissive:	[V.TNS:PRS|FUT actorNP (undergoerNP) (PP-LOC) (AT VN) (TO) (RP) (ADV)]
Declarative:	[(ADV) V.TNS:PRS actorNP (undergoerNP) (PP) (THAT | FROM | AS | UNTIL| OR) (NP|RP)]
Expressive:	The syntactic patterns found for the expressive speech act are very diverse, ranging from a simple [PP] to a full clause, as summarised in Chapter 9.

The character of indirect speech acts are different to the direct speech acts in many respects. Indirect speech acts exhibit the behaviour that the syntactic form carries an IFID for a certain speech act yet the interpretation yields a different speech act altogether. They are productive in everyday use and their character is rather conventionalised as normal use of language. Indirect speech acts may be motivated by factors such as politeness. In our account of indirect speech acts, we made use of the notion of a mental model of a situation, represented as a conceptual graph, over which H traverses in search of a relevant meaning once the initial literal meaning of the utterance has been evaluated and found wanting in the context. Along with relevance, the cognitive operations of salience, prominence, attention, and expectation, all play an important role in guiding the traversal of the conceptual graph of the situation. The situational context has a decisive role to play a role in determining the interpretation of an ISA utterance, along with the search for relevance with respect to the utterance. When an meaning is arrived at, common ground and context are appropriately updated.

We will conclude with some apt observations from Vanderveken (1990:220), that are pertinent to Irish. Whenever an utterance is successful, the speaker respects certain logical rules determined by the logical form of language. These rules deal with features of language that are universal such as meaning, and understanding, speech acts, illocutionary forces, propositions, conditions of success, direction of fit with respect to the world and mind, and so on. The literal meaning of a sentence is systematically related to its use in the context of the utterance, where linguistic competence is inseparable from performance. The analysis of speech acts is therefore part of the study of the structure of language, contrary to the distinction between *langue* and *parole*. Natural languages, such as Irish, offer a vast vocabulary of nouns, verbs, and sentence types for specifying the illocutionary force of utterances, and these linguistic items enable people to express themselves and communicate with other.

References

Aikhenvald, Alexandra Y. 2003. Evidentiality in typological perspective. In Alexandra Y. Aikhenvald, & Robert M.W. Dixon (eds.). *Studies in Evidentiality* [Typological Studies in Language 54]. Amsterdam/ Philadelphia: Benjamins. 1–31.

Aikhenvald, Alexandra Y. 2010. *Imperatives and Commands*. Oxford: Oxford University Press.

Aikhenvald, Alexandra Y. 2018. Evidentiality: The framework. In Alexandra Y. Aikhenvald. (ed.). *The Oxford Handbook of Evidentiality*. Oxford University Press. 1–46.

Alston, William P. 2000. *Illocutionary Acts and Sentence Meaning*. Ithaca: Cornell University Press.

An caighdeán oifigiúil. 2017. *Gramadach na Gaeilge: An caighdeán oifigiúil, an dara cló*. Dublin: Seirbhís Thithe an Oireachtais. Available (September 2023) from: https://data.oireachtas.ie/ie/oireachtas/caighdeanOifigiul/2017/2017-08-03_an-caighdean-oifigiuil-2017_en.pdf.

Asher, Nicholas & Lascarides, Alex. 2001. Indirect speech acts. *Synthese* 128(1/2): 183–228.

Austin John. L. 1962. *How to Do Things with Words*. Oxford: Oxford University Press.

Bach, Kent H. & Harnish, Robert M. 1979. *Linguistic Communication and Speech Acts*. Cambridge, MA: MIT Press.

Bennett, Ryan, Elfner, Emily, & McCloskey, James. 2015. *Prosody, Focus and Ellipsis in Irish*. MS. Available (September 2023) from: www.linguisticsociety.org/sites/default/files/04_95.1Bennett.pdf.

Christian Brothers, The. 1997. *New Irish Grammar*. Dublin: C.J. Fallon, Mount Salus Press.

[*Collins*]. 2011. *Collins Irish Grammar*. Glasgow, UK: Harper Collins Publishers.

Coulthard, Malcolm (ed.). 1992. *Advances in Spoken Discourse Analysis*. London: Routledge.

Collavin, Elena. 2011. Speech acts. In Wolfram Bublitz & Neal R. Norrick (eds.). *Foundations of Pragmatics. HoPs 1*. Berlin/Boston: Walter de Gruyter GmbH & Co. KG. 373–376.

Dayal, Venetta. 2018. *Questions*. Oxford: Oxford University Press.

de Bhaldraithe, Tomas. [1959]1987. *English–Irish Dictionary* (With Terminological Additions and Corrections). Dublin: An Gúm.

Diewald, Gabriele & Smirnova, Elena. 2010. Evidentiality in European languages: the lexical-grammatical distinction. In Gabriele Diewald & Elena Smirnova (eds.). *Linguistic Realization of Evidentiality in European Languages*. Berlin/New York: De Gruyter Mouton. 1–14.

De Haan, Ferdinand. 1999. Evidentiality and epistemic modality: setting boundaries. *Southwest Journal of Linguistics*, 18, 83–102.

Doherty, Cathal. 1996. Clausal Structure and the Modern Irish Copula. *Natural Language & Linguistic Theory.* 14(1): 1–46.

Doyle, Aidan. 2001. *Irish*. Languages of the World/Materials Series. Muenchen: LINCOM Europa.

Dryer, Matthew. S. 2005. Polar questions. In Martin Haspelmath, Matthew. S. Dryer, David Gill, & Bernard Comrie. *The World Atlas of Language Structures*. Oxford: Oxford University Press. 470–473.

Givón, Talmy. 1990. *Syntax. A Functional–Typological Introduction*, volume 2. Amsterdam: John Benjamins.

Grice, H. Paul. 1957. Meaning. *Philosophical Review* 66: 377–388. Reprinted in P.F. Strawson (ed.). *Philosophical Logic*. London, 1967.

Grice, H. Paul. 1969. Utterer's meaning and intentions. *Philosophical Review* 78: 147–77. Reprinted in Grice, H. Paul. 1975. Logic and conversation. *Syntax and Semantics 3: Speech Acts*, ed. by Peter Cole and Jerry L. Morgan. 41–58. New York: Academic Press.

Grice, H. Paul. 1975. Logic and conversation. In Peter Cole and Jerry L. Morgan (eds.). *Speech Acts*. Syntax and Semantics 3. New York: Academic Press. 41–58 (also in Grice 1989. *Studies in the Way of Words*. Cambridge, MA: Harvard University Press).

Guiraud, Nadine, Dominique Longin, Emiliano Lorini, Sylvie Pesty & Jérémy Rivière. 2011. The face of emotions: A logical formalization of expressive speech acts. In Kagan Tumer, Pinar Yolum, Liz Sonenberg & Peter Stone (eds.). *Proceedings of the 10th International Conference on Autonomous Agents and Multiagent Systems (AAMAS 2011)*, May, 2–6, 2011, Taipei, Taiwan, Richland, SC: International Foundation for Autonomous Agents and Multiagent Systems. 1031–1038.

Hamblin, Charles Leonard. 1973. Questions in Montague English. *Language* 10(1): 41–53.

Haspelmath, Martin. 2001. Word classes/parts of speech. In Neil Smelser & Paul Baltes (eds.). *Encyclopedia of the Social and Behavioral Sciences*. 16538–16545. Oxford: Pergamon.

Holmberg, Anders. 2015. *The Syntax of Yes and No*. Oxford: Oxford University Press.

Huddleston, Rodney & Pullum, Geoffrey K. 2002. *The Cambridge Grammar of the English Language*. Cambridge: Cambridge University Press.

Jary, Mark, and Kissine, Mikhail. 2014. *Imperatives* [Key Topics in Semantics and Pragmatics]. Cambridge: Cambridge University Press.

Jary, Mark & Kissine, Mikhail. 2016. When terminology matters: The imperative as a comparative concept. *Linguistics* 54(1): 119–148.

Jaszczolt, Kasia M. & Allan, Keith. 2011. *The Cambridge Handbook of Pragmatics*. Cambridge: Cambridge University Press.

Kecskes, Istvan & Zhang, Fenghui. 2009. Activating, seeking, and creating common ground: A socio-cognitive approach. *Pragmatics & Cognition* 17(2): 331–355.

Kissine, Mikhail. 2013. *From Utterances to Speech Acts*. Cambridge: Cambridge University Press.

Landragin, Frédéric. 2005. *Indirect Speech Acts and Collaborativeness in Human-Machine Dialogue Systems*. halshs-00137698. Available (September 2023) from: https://halshs.archives-ouvertes.fr/halshs-00137698. 115–122.

Marín Arrese, Juana, Isabel, Haßler, Gerda, & Carretero, Marta (eds.). 2017. *Evidentiality Revisited: Cognitive Grammar, Functional and Discourse-Pragmatic Perspectives*. Amsterdam/Philadelphia: John Benjamins Publishing Company.

Mauri, Caterina & Sansò, Andrea. 2011. How directive constructions emerge: Grammaticalization, constructionalization, cooptation. *Journal of Pragmatics* 43: 3489–3521.

McCloskey, James. 1979. The syntax of relative clauses. In James McCloskey, *Transformational Syntax and Model Theoretic Semantics*. Synthese Language Library, vol 9. Springer, Dordrecht. 5–50.

McCloskey, James. 1991. Clause structure, ellipsis and proper government in Irish. *Lingua* 85: 259–302.

McGonagle, Noel. 1991. *Irish Grammar: A Basic Handbook*. Indreabhan, Conamara, Galway: Cló Iar-Chonnachta.

Monaghan, J. 1979. *The Neo-Firthian Tradition and its Contribution to General Linguistics*. Tubingen: Max Niemeyer Verlag.

Nolan Brian. 2008. Modality in RRG: Towards a characterisation using Irish data. In Robert D. Van Valin (ed.). *Investigations of the Syntax-Semantics-Pragmatics Interface*. Amsterdam: John Benjamins Publishing Company. 147–160.

Nolan, Brian. 2012. *The Structure of Modern Irish: A Functional Account*. Sheffield: Equinox Publishing Company.

Nolan, Brian. 2013. Constructions as grammatical objects: A case study of the prepositional ditransitive construction in Modern Irish. In Brian Nolan & Elke Diedrichsen (eds.). *Linking Constructions into Functional Linguistics* [Studies in Language Companion Series 145]. Amsterdam/Philadelphia: John Benjamins Publishing Company. 143–178.

Nolan, Brian. 2017. The syntactic realisation of complex events and complex predicates in situations of Irish. In Brian Nolan & Elke Diedrichsen (eds.). *Argument Realisation in Complex Predicates and Complex Events* [Studies in Language Companion Series 180]. Amsterdam/Philadelphia: John Benjamins Publishing Company. 13–41.

Nolan, Brian. 2022. *Language, Culture, and Knowledge in Context: A Functional-Cognitive Approach*. Sheffield: Equinox Publishing Company.

Norrick, Neal R. 1978. Expressive illocutionary acts. *Journal of Pragmatics* 2(3): 277–291.

Ó Baoill, Dónall P. 2010. Mood in Irish. In Björn Rothstein & Rolf Thieroff (eds.). *Mood in the Languages of Europe* [Studies in Language Companion Series]. Amsterdam/Philadelphia: John Benjamins Publishing Company. 273–291.

Ó Dónaill, Niall. 1981. *Gearrfhochlóir Gaeilge-Béarla*. Dublin: An Roinn Oideachais, Oifig an tSoláthair.

Ó Mianáin, Pádraig. 2020. *Concise English–Irish Dictionary (An Foclóir Nua Béarla–Gaeilge)*. Baile Átha Cliath: An Gúm, Foras na Gaeilge.

Ortony, Andrew, Clore Gerald L., & Collins, Allan. 1988. *The Cognitive Structure of Emotions*. Cambridge: Cambridge University Press.

Ó Sé, Diarmuid. 1990. Tense and Mood in Irish Copula Sentences. *Ériu* 41: 61–75. Royal Irish Academy. Available (September 2023) from: https://www.jstor.org/stable/30006287.

Ó Siadhail, Michael. [1989]1991. *Modern Irish: Grammatical Structure and Dialectal Variation*. Cambridge MA: Cambridge University Press.

Pittner, Karin, Elsner, Daniela, & Barteld, Fabian (eds.). 2015. *Adverbs: Functional and Diachronic Aspects.* Amsterdam/Philadelphia: John Benjamins Publishing Company.

Schachter, Paul & Shopen, Timothy. 2007. Parts-of-speech systems. In Timothy Shopen (ed.). *Language Typology and Syntactic Description* Volume 1, Clause Structure. Cambridge: Cambridge University Press.

Schenner, Mathias. 2010. Embedded evidentials in German. In Gabriele Diewald & Elena Smirnova (eds.). *Linguistic Realization of Evidentiality in European Languages*. Berlin/New York: De Gruyter Mouton. 157–186.

Searle, John R. 1969. *Speech Acts: An Essay in the Philosophy of Language*. Cambridge: Cambridge University Press.

Searle, John R. 1975a. Indirect speech acts. In Peter Cole & Jerry L. Morgan (eds.). *Speech Acts* [Syntax and Semantics 3]. New York: Academic Press. 59–82 (also in Searle, 1979:30–57).

Searle, John R. 1975b. *A Taxonomy of Illocutionary Acts*. Minneapolis: University of Minnesota Press. Retrieved from the University of Minnesota Digital Conservancy. Available (September 2023) from: https://hdl.handle.net/11299/185220.

Searle, John R. 1976. A classification of illocutionary acts. *Language in Society* 5(1): 1–23.

Searle, John R. 1979. *Expression and Meaning: Studies in the Theory of Speech Acts*. Cambridge: Cambridge University Press.

Searle, John R., & Vanderveken, Daniel. 1985. *Foundations of Illocutionary Logic*. Cambridge: Cambridge University Press.

Smith, Peter W.H. 1991. *Speech Act Theory, Discourse Structure and Indirect Speech Acts*. PhD thesis. The University of Leeds UK, Department of Philosophy.

Sperber, Dan and Wilson, Deirdre. 1995. *Relevance: Communication and Cognition*. 2nd Edition, Oxford: Blackwell.

Stalnaker, Robert. 1978. Assertion. In Peter Cole (ed.). *Syntax and Semantics 9: Pragmatics*. New York: Academic Press. 315–332.

van der Auwera, Johan. 1998. Introduction. In Johan van der Auwera (ed.). *Adverbial Constructions in the Languages of Europe*. Berlin: De Gruyter. 1–24.

van der Auwera, Johan. 2006. Imperatives. In Keith Brown (ed.). *Encyclopedia of Language and Linguistics*. Amsterdam: Elsevier. 565–567.

Van Olmen, Daniel & Heinold, Simone 2017. Imperatives and directive strategies from a functional-typological perspective: An introduction. In Daniel Van Olmen & Simone Heinold (eds.). *Imperatives and Directive Strategies*. 184 [Studies in Language Companion Series]. Amsterdam/Philadelphia: John Benjamins Publishing Company. Available (September 2023) from: https://www.researchgate.net/publication/308417365.

Van Valin, Robert D. 2005. *Exploring the Syntax–Semantics Interface*. Cambridge: Cambridge University Press.

Van Valin, Robert D. & LaPolla, Randy J. 1997. *Syntax: Structure, Meaning, and Function*. Cambridge: Cambridge University Press.

Vanderveken, Daniel. 1990. *Meaning and Speech Acts. Volume 1. Principles of Language Use*. Cambridge: Cambridge University Press.

Vanderveken, Daniel, & Kubo, Susumu. 2001. Introduction. In Daniel Vanderveken & Susumu Kubo (eds.). *Essays in Speech Act Theory*. Amsterdam/Philadelphia: Benjamins Publishing Company. 1–23.

Verschueren, Jef. 1980. On Speech Act Verbs. *Pragmatics and Beyond, Volume I-4: On Speech Act Verbs*. Amsterdam/Philadelphia: Benjamins Publishing Company.

Ward, Alan. 1974. *The Grammatical Structure of Munster Irish.* Ph.D. Thesis no. 78. Trinity College Dublin.

Wierzbicka Anna. 1987. *English Speech Act Verbs: A Semantic Dictionary*. Sydney: Academic Press.

Wiemer, Björn. 2010. Hearsay in European languages: toward an integrative account of grammatical and lexical marking. In Gabriele Diewald & Elena Smirnova (eds.). *Linguistic Realization of Evidentiality in European Languages*. Berlin: De Gruyter Mouton. 59–130.

Wittgenstein, Ludwig. 1953/1958. *Philosophical Investigations*, G.E. Anscombe and R. Rhees (eds). (English translation of *Philosophische Untersuchungen* [1953] by G.E.M. Anscombe). Oxford: Basil Blackwell.

Wittgenstein, Ludwig. 1961. *Tractatus Logico-Philosophicus*, D.F. Pears & B.F. McGuiness (English translation of *Logisch-Philosophische Abhandlung* [1918]; first published in *Annalendet Naturphilosophie* 14: 185–262 [1921]). London: Routledge and Kegan Paul.

Index